The First Session
with African Americans

Janis Sanchez-Hucles

The First Session with African Americans

A Step-by-Step Guide

Jossey-Bass Publishers
San Francisco

Jossey-Bass books and products are available through most bookstores. To contact Jossey-Bass directly, call (888) 378-2537, fax to (800) 605-2665, or visit our website at www.josseybass.com.

Substantial discounts on bulk quantities of Jossey-Bass books are available to corporations, professional associations, and other organizations. For details and discount information, contact the special sales department at Jossey-Bass.

 Manufactured in the United States of America on Lyons Falls Turin Book. This paper is acid-free and 100 percent totally chlorine-free.

Library of Congress Cataloging-in-Publication Data

Sanchez-Hucles, Janis.
  The first session with African Americans : a step-by-step guide /
Janis Sanchez-Hucles. — 1st ed.
    p. cm.
  Includes bibliographical references and index.
  ISBN 0-7879-4768-7 (alk. paper)
    1. Afro-Americans—Mental health. 2. Afro-Americans—Counseling of.
3. Psychotherapy. I. Title.
RC451.5.N4 S26 2000
616.89'0089'96073—dc21   99-6815

HB Printing 10 9 8 7 6 5 4 3 2 1   FIRST EDITION

Contents

Foreword

Much has changed over the thirty years that I have been a clinician, supervisor, teacher, and student of psychotherapy. Therapy is briefer, more people have access to help, psychotropic medications are more effective, and the stigma associated with psychological help has decreased.

One issue, however, remains constant: therapists have always known that the first session is crucial for both emergency intervention and beginning the process of change. Current mental health practice, moreover, renders the first session even more preeminent, since managed care and insurance benefits are limited and the nature of treatment has focused more on problem solving and short-term goals. In fact, 40 percent of all psychotherapy clients today attend only a single session, and the rest typically have four or five meetings.[1]

As therapists we know that we must use the first session to[2]

- Establish a relationship and working alliance

- Assess the need for crisis intervention

   Evaluate presenting problems and establish a diagnosis

   Explore emotions

   Focus the problem(s)

   Reach mutual agreement on what needs to be done

- Explore options for solution (one of the alternatives
  may be to continue therapy)

Consequently, the First-Session Series has been launched with full appreciation for the magnitude of accomplishing these goals in a single session. Likewise, this series is also intended to demonstrate sensitivity and respect for the diversity of background, culture, and experience of clients we hope to serve.

Much can be said for the generic skills necessary for a successful first session, but most therapists are aware of the necessity of customizing our interventions to the specific needs of our clients. What we need to know for a successful first session with a teenager may be very different from what we need to know for a septuagenarian. Consequently, this series provides students, educators, and practitioners with essential knowledge of how to enrich existing therapeutic skill with specific information fine-tuned to meet the demands of diverse populations.

Because Black clients are underserved, overpathologized, and frequently misunderstood, we were delighted that Dr. Sanchez-Hucles agreed to write this book on first sessions with African American clients. Her knowledge, warmth, and compassion guide readers into the understanding necessary to initiate culturally competent services for Black clients.

Because Dr. Sanchez-Hucles is both a clinician with years of experience working with clients from majority and minority cultures and also an educator skilled in making the mysteries of counseling accessible, she was the ideal choice to write this book. Readers from all backgrounds will find this volume informative, touching, and, most important, useful. Our blind spots are revealed and ways to handle racial issues are explored, as Dr. Sanchez-Hucles provides us with the necessary tools to assist Black clients to get the culturally relevant mental health services they deserve.

Discovering how their basic therapeutic skills must be adapted to meet the needs of African American clients is likely to inspire therapists to learn more about enhancing the effectiveness of their first sessions with other populations they serve. Upcoming titles in this series will provide the culturally competent direction necessary to facilitate first sessions with other groups that also require special sensitivity, including adolescents and substance abusers. With each new book in this series, we hope to instill not only greater understanding of your clients as a special group but also more compassion for the unique qualities of each individual.

Finally, we hope that the wisdom, experience, techniques, and strategies our authors present will enhance the overall effectiveness of each first session.

September 1999   Jeanne Albronda Heaton
Athens, Ohio

This book is dedicated to my parents, Lucy and Phillip Sanchez;
to my siblings, Penny, Sandy, Peter, Paul, and David;
and to my husband, Michael, my daughter, Angela, and my son,
Phillip. Thank you for all of your love and support.

Acknowledgments

I first want to acknowledge the grace of God that enabled all the right people and circumstances to enter my life and make this book a reality. Thank you, Nancy Boyd-Franklin. You recommended me for this book. You and your husband, A. J. Franklin, have been incredible friends and mentors, and I can't tell you enough what a profound impact you both have had in my development as a clinician.

I want to say thank you to all the faculty, colleagues, students, and clients who have trained me and shared their lives with me while I was at Swarthmore College, Purdue University, the University of North Carolina at Chapel Hill, Eastern Virginia Medical School, and in the Hampton Roads area of Virginia, where I now reside. I am also deeply appreciative of all the wonderful collegial and administrative support I have enjoyed at Old Dominion University over the last twenty years. Special thanks to all my friends in the Coalition of Black Faculty and Administrators and the Women's Caucus. Jenny Caja and Jacquline Winston have lent their ears, services, and hearts on innumerable occasions. Thank you, Jackie, Jenny, Peggy, Woody, and Mary also for all you do for me on a day-to-day basis.

This book was made possible by the prayers and help of my support systems, my churches, my meditation groups, and my African American women's book club. To all who helped in any way, thank you. I especially want to thank all my colleagues in the American

Psychological Association (APA) and the Association of Black Psychologists. Because of my mentors who are APA staff or members, I had the confidence to accept the challenge of writing this book. My colleagues in the Psychology of Women and Study of Ethnic Minorities divisions have been wonderful mentors. My immediate family—Michael, Angela, and Phillip—always gave me plenty of direction when I was on the verge of losing touch with what is really important in life: love, family, and service. Thanks for all you give me.

The staff at Jossey-Bass has been wonderful. Thank you, Katie Crouch and Danielle McNeary; thanks to Sophia Ho and to my copy editor, Michele Jones, for all your positive energy and expertise. Thank you, Alan Rinzler, for this project and for designating Jeanne Heaton as my editor. Jeanne, as you know, editing a book on African Americans with a Black author when you are White leads to some interesting discussions and challenges. Thank you for being willing to listen to me, validate my opinions, and gently and firmly keep me on course. You were a wonderful coach, you had great insights, and you stuck with me right up to the end. Thank you for your confidence, your generosity with your time, your speed, and your suggestions. You made invaluable contributions to this project.

September 1999   Janis Sanchez-Hucles
Norfolk, Virginia

Introduction

I am an African American woman of Cuban ancestry who has been doing therapy for more than twenty years. I have always been committed to making sure that counseling and psychotherapy are used in inclusive and relevant ways for all people, not just middle-class Caucasians. Counseling and psychotherapy can't work for all people, however, unless we can initially provide consumers with a successful first session.

PURPOSE OF THIS BOOK

I was excited by the challenge of writing this book. It allowed me to do two things I am passionate about: first, talk about the types of services and interventions that African American clients need and deserve but don't always receive when they seek mental health services and, second, reach and train service providers and thereby increase the number of therapists who can provide culturally competent care to African American clients.

I wrote this book to provide therapists, students, researchers, and educators with specific skills, techniques, and background information to facilitate their interactions with Black clients in a first session. Some of the material comes from research; other suggestions are based on my clinical, supervisory, and training experiences. In some situations I give very clear-cut directions, whereas in other cases I point out the factors that you should consider before you can make an informed decision. These factors relate to issues of race, gender, culture, and all the mediators that make each client unique.

I wanted to write this book on the first session with African American clients because there are issues that are unique to African American clients and special dynamics that African Americans bring to a first session of therapy.

Many colleagues and students from both majority and minority groups ask me questions about working with African American clients:

> What should I do so that I don't scare clients away in a first session?
>
> Can I talk about racial issues without being viewed as prejudiced?
>
> Should I just give up on working with clients who are different from me?
>
> How can I tell if I am connecting when I work with clients from backgrounds and perspectives that are different from my own?
>
> Is it possible for me to detect blind spots in my own work?
>
> How do I talk about our differences? It's so hard for me.

It's my conviction that all therapists, regardless of their backgrounds, can be more culturally competent. This book addresses issues that are helpful to White therapists as well as therapists of color. In this book I'll tell you what I've learned professionally and personally to ensure effective first sessions with African American clients.

The decision to seek help for a mental health problem is never easy. Unfortunately, too many African American clients encounter what is for them a "disconnect" during the first session. This disconnect can have multiple causes, but it typically relates to a failure on the therapist's part to understand, relate to, and appreciate the complexity of the client's problems. This shortcoming is compounded by therapists' refusal to confront and discuss their different values, perspectives, and ways of viewing the world.

Research tells us that 40 percent of all clients discontinue services after the first session.[1] We also know that this number is higher for populations that do not belong to the majority culture.[2] It is critical that we give African American clients a first session that works and that helps them make decisions about their next steps. For there to be an effective first session, we as therapists must create a climate that will allow all clients to explore their problems enough to resolve them or to feel comfortable and confident about their options, which include deciding that additional therapy is not indicated, seeking more sessions, or accepting an appropriate referral.

An effective first session means that clients feel connected to us and believe that the therapy can help them resolve their problems. After a first session, we want our clients to decide about continuing therapy based on their need for services rather than being turned off by insensitive therapists who are lacking in cultural competence. We know that therapy can help, but we also know that it won't work without a culturally competent therapist.

OVERVIEW OF THE CONTENTS

Each chapter in this book discusses issues critical to achieving success with African American clients during their first session. Chapter One is a description of the population, and it sets the context for working with African American clients. First of all, African Americans are a diverse group. We're individuals and want to be treated as such. But there is no escaping the fact that we share a history of encountering barriers to appropriate services. This history includes African Americans being overlooked, overmedicated, offered group rather than individual treatment, and pathologized based on racial, gender, and class considerations. Because of these historical and ongoing experiences, African Americans have good reasons for expecting negative experiences when interacting with societal institutions and authority figures.

Chapter Two sensitizes you to the broad array of presenting problems that African Americans face and how racial dynamics interface with mental health problems. This chapter highlights the background issues, psychosocial stressors, risk factors, and symptom pictures for some of the most common presenting problems for African American clients.

Chapter Three discusses establishing rapport and forming an alliance with the client, teaching you to identify the critical steps necessary for building a solid foundation right from the beginning. We'll explore how to support the client's decision to seek therapy, how to be alert to and manage potential areas of sensitivity and barriers to rapport, how to assess the strength of the working alliance, and how to repair ruptures when they occur. All therapists can work effectively with African American clients, but only if we are able to develop therapeutic trust and rapport during the very first session.

Chapter Four covers assessment and evaluation; it will review key issues that have made these processes intimidating and dangerous for African American clients. My goal is to increase your skills and confidence in establishing a climate of trust, honesty, and clear communication so that accurate assessment and evaluation are possible. We'll look at strategies for understanding our clients' psychosocial histories, review how to conduct mental status examinations, and discuss how to be accurate and efficient in the processes of making a diagnosis, planning treatment, and exploring options for referral or additional evaluation.

Chapter Five is a nuts-and-bolts chapter designed to facilitate all therapists' ability to create a successful and engaging structure for therapy. In this chapter I'll spell out how to have effective discussions about presenting problems. We'll also talk about some of the protective devices and communication styles that Black clients use in a first session and about how we can overcome clients' discomfort and reluctance. This chapter also includes a section on handling typical issues that arise during the first session, such as involuntary and resistant clients, and understanding client expectations and encouraging their involvement in therapy. We'll investigate the special significance these issues have for African American clients. By exploring these critical first-session issues, this chapter will help you orient clients to a first session as well as to the overall process of therapy.

Many first sessions involve a crisis situation. Chapter Six describes questions and options therapists must explore when African American clients present with a need for emergency services. We know that Black clients frequently refrain from seeking mental health services until they are in an emergency situation. This chapter focuses on how important it is for us to use the client's first contact with the mental health system as a vehicle to fully understand and meet the needs of the client and thus build a sturdy bridge that connects him or her with appropriate follow-up and support services.

Chapter Seven explores the complexity of how cultural background stimulates countertransference issues. This chapter gives you information on how to understand your biases, blind spots, prejudices, and stereotypes. The goal of this chapter is to help you learn how to function objectively and sensitively regardless of the similarities or differences between you and your African American clients. We identify specific signs of countertransference and discuss steps to using these complex feelings to help rather than hinder the first session.

Chapter Eight focuses on how you can increase your cultural competence by being attentive to yourself in all interactions with your clients. We'll explore issues of racial identity, privilege, power, status, and use of self. We'll talk about positive ways to have difficult dialogues with African American clients on sensitive subjects.

Throughout this book, I'll tell you about cases that illustrate appropriate and inappropriate interventions with African American clients. I will also give examples that illustrate the complexity of the issues involved in working with these clients. Most of Chapter Nine is devoted to a lengthy clinical example that illustrates the components of a successful first session with African American clients.

AUDIENCE FOR THE BOOK

Graduate and undergraduate students, supervisors, and course instructors, as well as beginning and seasoned therapists, will find this text to be a wonderful resource. It can augment previous training, and because it gives you many new insights and strategies for approaching first sessions, it will enable you to broaden your repertoire of skills with African American clients.

My hope is that this book will be useful to therapists and allied health professionals across the dimensions of gender, race, culture, class, sexual orientation, religion, age, ability status, and geographic locality. Throughout the book, I will explore the complexity of difference as it manifests in the first session, but I'll also examine the challenges associated with demographic similarity, such as the issues associated with an African American therapist or other therapists of color working with an African American client.

As the United States becomes more diverse, all of us must challenge ourselves to learn how to practice with the highest standards of cultural competence in every therapeutic encounter we have. My belief is that this book will enhance your opportunities to provide the kind of therapeutic assistance African American clients need in a first session.

1

Description of the Population
and Mental Health Experiences

Effective first sessions with African American clients require well-prepared therapists. This chapter outlines important demographic, philosophical, and cultural characteristics of African American clients. We'll explore the challenge of balancing information about African Americans as a group with the necessity of always focusing on the uniqueness of each individual client.

This chapter will help you appreciate important areas of diversity and similarity among Black clients. Naming and self-identity issues are critical variables to understand. We as therapists need to know how clients understand their racial, ethnic, and cultural heritage, as well as how they want others to view them. The term *naming* refers to the word or words used to describe a group, for example, *Black* or *African American*. The term *self-identity* refers to the terms individuals use to refer to who they feel they are, how they want to be identified, and with whom they feel affiliated. In this chapter, we'll explore some of the factors that lead individuals to prefer one term over another. Out of respect for the varied ways that this population of individuals self-identify, I'll deliberately use both the terms *African American* and *Black*.

RACIAL AND ETHNIC IDENTIFICATION

There are approximately thirty million African Americans in the United States; 47 percent are male, and 53 percent are female.

7

Black Americans currently compose about 12 percent of the population.[1] Of the total African American population, 60 percent reside in urban areas, and a trend toward moving north and east has reversed so that more and more Blacks reside in southern states.[2]

The population of African Americans is united by historical ties to the west coast of Africa, slavery, indentured servitude, discrimination, and ongoing traditions of resiliency. But at the same time, African Americans are also heterogeneous with respect to appearance, ethnic identity, religious affiliation, socioeconomic status, cultural expression, family composition, and geographical origin and residence.[3]

African Americans have diverse geographic backgrounds due to slave trade routes and because their ancestors may have settled in the Caribbean Islands, Central America, South America, the United States, and Canada. As a result of this geographic diversity, Blacks may speak Standard and nonstandard English, Spanish, French, Portuguese, and other languages and dialects.

African Americans vary on many demographic and cultural dimensions. Out of respect for the diversity of this population, we must try to understand how each individual client self-identifies. In the United States, traditional laws dictated that any individual with a drop of Black blood was considered Black. Today there are growing numbers of multiracial individuals, some of whom identify as Black; but there is a significant trend for many of these individuals to identify themselves as multiracial. Some Black individuals grow up in homes where the primary language is Spanish, French, or Portuguese, not English. Our society tends to force these individuals to ignore their multicultural heritage in favor of identifying themselves simply on the basis of their visible skin color.

What's in a Name?

It used to be that when a White person was comfortable with a Black person, the most typical question was, "I know this is personal, but can colored people get sunburned?" Over the last twenty years or so, the question most of us field from White individuals is, "Why do you people keep changing your name? First you were 'colored,' then 'Negro,' then 'Black,' then 'Afro-American,' and now 'African American.' How can we figure out what to call you when you can't find a name and stick with it?"

Majority group members' confusion about racial naming is understandable, but there are good reasons why racial names have changed over the years. Names matter. It is a positive development that more individuals are sensitive to these issues. African Americans have a history of being disrespected by the names they've been called. The terms *colored* and *Negro* were designations assigned by the majority culture. For years these terms were associated with second-class citizenship, segregation, and other symbols of repression. Whites have often forgotten that it was only one generation ago that many Black individuals were legally restricted to "Coloreds Only" entrances, bathrooms, water fountains, schools, and services that were consistently inferior to the resources available to White Americans.

In the 1970s the progress of the civil rights movement led to the rise of the sentiment "Black is beautiful." This was a remarkable development, because Black people chose to call themselves Black as a sign of pride. (In contrast, in American culture the connotations of the word *black* are usually negative.) The racial pride inherent in the use of the term *Black* led to a greater feeling of kinship with other people of African descent, and so the next popular term of self-identity was *Afro-American*. Most recently, the term *African American* is the preferred term for many Black individuals in the United States. Just as people use the terms *Italian American* and *Irish American*, Blacks have chosen to use the name *African American* because it gives recognition to the continent of their ancestors and to their cultural and citizenship ties to the United States.

Just to make this issue more interesting, not all Black Americans are able to make the switch to calling themselves Black or African American. Many older individuals who spent their lifetimes hearing negative and inaccurate information and stereotyping of Blacks and Africans still feel uncomfortable or ambivalent about these newer terms. We as therapists can't help but make assumptions about what a client prefers to be called based on the client's age, appearance, or background, but we'd all be wiser if we checked out these suppositions with each client. We will talk more about how to do this later.

Blacks from Outside the United States

Typically, the term *African American* is reserved for Black individuals born in the United States. Other individuals from Africa, the Caribbean, Central or South America, and Canada usually refer to themselves by their country of origin or as Black. Individuals who immigrate to the United States from other countries in Africa and elsewhere don't consider themselves to be African American. These individuals may in fact be very insulted if they're mistaken for a Black person whose heritage is from the United States. Individuals who come to the United States from other countries note that their experiences are different from those of Blacks in the United States with respect to the legacy of slavery, discrimination, and minority status. Although many of these Black individuals had ancestors who were slaves, their cultures are tied to Native American and European countries in ways that are different from those of Blacks born in the United States.

Blacks from outside the United States note that the nature of the discrimination and oppression they have faced is different from that of African Americans, especially in cases where Blacks were a numerical majority in their country of origin. Where Blacks are a numerical majority, there is often a greater sense of strength and solidarity, and more frequent placement in visible positions in society. This can contribute to a more positive self-concept and a greater sense of self-efficacy.

As therapists, we need to understand the diversity of background that the terms *Black* and *African American* represent. Table 1.1 illustrates the heterogeneity of individuals who self-identify as either

Black or African American. Census data also indicate that fewer than 1 percent of Black individuals in the United States are immigrants from countries in Africa.

Immigrant Versus Nonimmigrant Status

On many occasions I've been asked, "Why do immigrants achieve such success in their new country when African Americans continue to have such significant problems?" Those Blacks who are immigrants are often characterized by a strong desire to succeed in the United States, and by the belief that hard work can overcome all obstacles and that extreme sacrifices can pay off in the long run with high levels of accomplishment. Many of these individuals immigrate with a marketable trade, some meager financial reserves, and, most significant, with a strong psychological belief that they can be successful.

These Black immigrants are different from African Americans in many ways. African Americans born in this country have parents and grandparents who faced slavery, the Jim Crow era, and

Table 1.1. Heterogeneity of Blacks and African Americans.

Nationality	Total
Cuban	860,000
Dominican	506,000
Hispanic	1,113,000
Mexican	11,587,000
Puerto Rican	1,955,000
Salvadoran	499,000
Spanish	2,024,000
West Indian	435,000
French Canadian	2,167,000
Canadian	550,000
African American	23,777,000

Source: Statistical Abstract of the United States: 1998. Washington, D.C.: U.S. Bureau of the Census.

legalized segregation, as well as many generations of oppression, unemployment, and poor results from educational strivings. As a result of this history, many African Americans do not believe that it is possible to "pull themselves up by their own bootstraps." Many Blacks have found the forces of institutionalized oppression too overwhelming and consequently believe that success is only possible operating outside the mainstream culture.

Some African Americans have developed feelings of learned helplessness. These individuals know that education, skill, and experience do not open the same doors of opportunity for them as they have traditionally for those of European descent. Many families have endured generations of trying to pull themselves out of poverty, poor housing, jobs that do not pay enough to support a family, unsafe neighborhoods, and inadequate educational resources. These individuals have decided that it is better not to try than to continue to try without any hope of achieving success.

When these individuals turn to public assistance, they face the additional humiliation of being blamed for their own suffering. Those with learned helplessness are missing the activating forces that motivate many immigrants. Therapists must use sensitivity in gradually challenging clients' sense of impotence in order to overcome their long history of demoralization.

The Importance of Understanding Self-Identity

Race is a crucial variable that we can't overlook when understanding how clients view themselves. We therapists make assumptions, even when we know we shouldn't. As clients explain their ethnic backgrounds, we need to be aware of our own biases, prejudices, and assumptions. Problems can occur whether a therapist is White or a person of color.

One example of misunderstanding of backgrounds arose when I was supervising a Latina therapist at a university counseling center. The therapist, Lettie, had an intake session with an African American client named Tim, who sought assistance from the counseling center because of depression and anxiety related to his poor performance in one of his classes. Tim was initially pleased to have Lettie as his therapist. He told her that he thought it would be easier to open up and work with her because he felt that as a minority female she could understand how hard it could be for a minority student at a predominantly White university.

During the first session, Lettie focused on Tim's background. She learned that he came from a working-class background in an urban area and that he was the eldest in a family of four children. He was raised by his mother and had only a distant relationship with his father.

Lettie, now in her third year of a doctoral program, was pleased that she could diagnose Tim's problem by the end of the first session. She told him that "from what I've read in the newspaper, I know that most African Americans in the good universities are here because of affirmative action programs." She went on to explain her conclusion that he came from a culturally disadvantaged background and was unprepared for college work and that he should be referred to the special services office for tutorial and remedial work. She said to Tim, "I'm sure you're motivated enough to overcome your background and be successful in college."

Tim was insulted. In no uncertain terms, Tim told Lettie, "I graduated at the top of my class with excellent college board scores." He left that first session convinced that he would have to find some other way to cope with his problems, as it was clear that Lettie couldn't help him. What went wrong?

In this case, both the therapist and the client made some erroneous assumptions about each other. Tim thought that because Lettie was from a minority group she would understand how difficult it was to ask for help. He expected her to know how much pressure he felt to defy stereotypes and to be a top student academically.

Tim did not know that Lettie had immigrated to the United States in her senior year of high school and belonged to a very wealthy South

American family. Lettie did not feel any kinship with Tim or any under-standing of Tim's circumstances because her background bore no resemblance to Tim's. In fact, Lettie didn't self-identify as a minority at all. Because of her family's wealth, status, and Caucasian appear-ance, Lettie and her family members were treated with all the privilege and status typically accorded to White Americans. Lettie and her fam-ily had very conservative values and were opposed to programs that they felt were handouts to people capable of working hard and improving their circumstances. Lettie's only real identifiable tie to a minority group was having a Hispanic name. Tim and Lettie had very little in common, and Lettie was not a culturally competent therapist.

In subsequent chapters, we'll talk about how to raise the issue of race and self-identity. For now it's important to understand that clients make their own decisions about their cultural heritage, color, and iden-tity, and that all these variables most assuredly affect how they see themselves. It is therefore important for us to sensitively assess the guid-ing philosophies of individual African Americans. Similarity of color can obscure major differences in background, values, and behavior.

GUIDING VIEWS AND PHILOSOPHIES

In the past, a hot topic of discussion was whether Black people in the Western Hemisphere were more "American" or more "African." Historians, anthropologists, and other researchers now believe that Black culture was shaped by the integration of African traditions with the experiences in the Western Hemisphere.[4] It's important for us to understand this integration of values and traditions if we are to understand our African American clients.

Family Ties

There is a strong consensus supported by research that Black indi-viduals grow up in families that adhere to the African traditions of being communal and collectivistic.[5] In this tradition, interactions are valued that focus on the good of the whole family and group and not just on the needs of an individual.

Partially for survival reasons and partially due to African traditions, Blacks deeply value the strengths of the extended family. Grandmothers, grandfathers, aunts, uncles, and even so-called fictive kin all play a major role in raising children and providing support to parents. The term *fictive kin* refers to those people who are treated like blood relatives although they're really only close family friends. Members of African American families are taught to share their resources with other family members. Likewise they are taught that when they are in need, they can ask "family" for help. In general, it is not OK to ask for help outside the family.

Another tradition is to hold a deep respect for the elderly. In fact, a stigma is often attached to placing relatives in nursing homes. Family members may feel that they are letting down long-held family and cultural traditions if they do not provide high levels of support and care for their elderly or infirm relatives. African American clients may experience guilt and anxiety if they receive the typical counseling adage "take care of yourself" while they are trying to be true to their family and cultural values that advise them that "family must come first."

Historically, social science literature has portrayed the African American family as inferior, disadvantaged, and different from White families. African American scholars countered these distortions by identifying the strengths of Black families. Pioneering and current research cites the strengths of African American families: the central role of extended families: a strong work ethic, high valuation of educational achievement, flexible gender roles, and high commitment to religious and spiritual themes.[6]

Many African Americans are unique in their ability to perform both instrumental and expressive functions without undue attention to gender roles. Although there are definite pressures to subscribe to the majority culture standards as to what constitutes "male work" and "female work," historical pressures have led to some flexibility in gender roles for Blacks. Specifically, Black women, as a group, have almost always had to work outside the home as well as inside the home due to racism and economic necessity. Because females had to work outside the home, men and children have historically assisted in what the majority culture has considered the "female" work of cooking, cleaning, and caring for children.

There are other characteristics of African traditions that we would be wise to consider. James Jones believes that what unites African descendants are the values of time, rhythm, improvisation, oral traditions, and spirituality (what Jones refers to as TRIOS).[7]

Time

It's imperative to be aware that some African Americans experience time as flexible. They don't believe that time commitments should bind activities. For example, if an African American client asks a question at the end of the therapy hour, he or she might expect that answering the question and building a relationship would be more important than delaying the end of the session for a few minutes.

Many African Americans are taught that valuing people and their feelings is more important than being "anal" about time. As a result, many Black people joke about C.P.T.—colored people's time. This phrase refers to the idea that sometimes scheduled events in the Black community may start a little after the advertised time. It can actually be considered in poor taste to show up exactly on time for a party or social gathering, as the expectation is for guests to arrive at least a half hour later than the announced time.

This issue of time can be confusing because some African Americans take pride in showing that they endorse more Eurocentric values of time and like to be early, prompt, or highly structured in their use of time. I frequently hear my White colleagues complain that when they attend an event in the African American community, they have to ask if the start time is based on colored people's time or Caucasian time.

Rhythm

Many African Americans rely on rhythm or "vibes" as a basic tool to process both verbal and nonverbal cues.[8] Many African American clients demonstrate this quality when they evaluate their therapist based on how "in sync" they feel: they notice whether the therapist's actions and verbalizations match; they have sharp antennae about any negative or masked feelings of the therapist; and they are highly aware of the degree of ease in the give and take of their conversation with the therapist.

When clients intuit that they are not establishing an effective rhythm with their therapists, they do not develop rapport. Likewise, a client's sense that the therapist is in sync can facilitate a strong working alliance.

Improvisation

Many African Americans value improvisation, which involves a desire to be unique and distinctive and to demonstrate flair or verve. People demonstrate this quality in their style of dress or in a colorful way of speaking. Richard Majors has commented specifically on the need of young Black males to adopt a "cool pose."[9] This posturing refers to a style of dress and speech that expresses bravado and hypermasculinity. "Cool pose" behaviors provide a positive sense of identity and validation for young men who are not likely to find societal reinforcement in academic and vocational pursuits.

I'm reminded of the first session I had with "Little Bit" and his family. Little Bit was a slightly built fourteen-year-old male who was referred to me for therapy because of his poor school achievement and fighting with peers. For our initial appointment, he wore an electric-green T-shirt and purple pants that hung so low on his hips that his boxer trunks were visible. He spoke using a lot of "gangsta rap" slang. He wore a baseball hat that was placed backwards on his head and always kept on whether he was inside or outside. His attire and speech pattern might have identified him as a hard-core gang member. But it quickly became clear to me that Little Bit was trying desperately in his poor grades, his fighting, and his dress to fit in with the dominant Black peer culture in his school and neighborhood so as not be "dissed"—as in disrespected.

It was important for me not to get hung up on his attire or to lecture him about how dressing less flamboyantly might help teachers and administrators be more accepting of him. Instead, I needed to use this first session as an opportunity to get the whole family involved in understanding Little Bit's feelings and behaviors with the goal of helping him feel affirmed and supported by his family.

It was clear to me that Little Bit had been coerced by his parents and school to attend therapy. When I first saw them in the waiting room, Little Bit was slouched in a chair as far away from his parents as he could be while still in the same room. He had on headphones and was nodding to the music. In contrast, his parents, Mr. and Mrs. London, were dressed neatly and conservatively in what looked like their church clothes. After I introduced myself and invited them into my office, Little Bit very slowly joined us.

After we settled into my office, I tried to break into Little Bit's passivity and distance by asking him why he was brought to see me. He shrugged and said, "I don't know. My parents are always on my case to do things their way—not my way. I don't want to be here. Just talk to them." I explained to Little Bit that although I didn't know all the circumstances around his visit to my office, he definitely had a major role to play in our session. I told him I needed to hear from him every bit as much as I needed to hear from his parents.

Finally, giving me some brief eye contact, Little Bit said, "Look, I'm almost a man, but my mom and dad want to treat me like I'm a little kid." At this point, I asked his parents if what Little Bit said was accurate. His father jumped in with a scowl at his wife and said,

"Actually, he's right. My wife, Lois here, doesn't know what it's like to grow up as a Black man today. He's got to learn to be a man by being tough and by knowing how to defend himself. I'm not telling him to go out there and start some foolishness with someone, but if someone starts something with him, he'd better know how to finish it in order to protect himself."

Mrs. London spoke very softly when I asked her what her thoughts were. I realized that her voice was shaky and that she was near tears. She said, "In our extended family, we've already had one of Little Bit's cousins shot, and we have another nephew in a detention center. If Little Bit gets out in the street and tries to prove something, he risks being put into jail or getting hurt. I don't want that. I want him to stay in school, get good grades, and have nice friends so he can make something of himself and get himself a job that pays better than the jobs my husband and I have."

We talked about how important it was for Little Bit to feel masculine and accepted. From his father, he was getting a message to "be a man and defend yourself," and from his mother it was "don't get into trouble and ruin your future."

I knew we had a lot to accomplish in this first session, and it wouldn't be easy to reconcile the different perspectives of this family. I started out slowly by saying, "I hear very clearly that all three of you are looking at what is happening from different angles. It's going to take some time for us to fully hear and appreciate the different views you all have. But I'm impressed that we're united in the goals of Little Bit's being safe, not winding up in jail, and being able to succeed at school and in life. There might be different interpretations of how we can accomplish these goals, but at least we have a starting point."

The first issue we addressed was how his mother and father needed to unite in sending a clear signal to him about expectations. Little Bit was finally able to hear that neither of his parents wanted to see him get hurt or be involved in activities that hurt his success in life. His parents started to understand how important it was for Little Bit to deal successfully with the peer pressure he faced.

We explored the idea of Little Bit participating in a basketball recreation league at the community center, spending more time with his father doing some part-time painting jobs to earn money, and bringing his friends to his home when one of his parents was present. Little Bit was slowly responding to the idea that he could make progress in school, receive praise from his family, and still feel accepted by a peer group. We strategized on how Little Bit could wean himself away from his peer group without losing their respect. The family agreed to return for additional sessions to try to implement and consolidate the plans we developed in that first session.

Oral Traditions

African Americans enjoy a long-standing cultural tradition of valuing oral expression. Black families encourage even very young children to memorize songs and dialogues from movies, television, and books. This oral tradition began in slavery when African Americans were prohibited from reading and writing. Blacks learned to pass on family history, issue warnings, and share stories, songs, jokes, parables, and biblical passages via the spoken word. Blacks used this oral tradition to learn how to problem solve and think quickly on their feet in case they were challenged by Whites or by other Blacks. African Americans have learned to be experts in oral activities like trading insults (as in "playing the dozens") and developing rap music.

There are frequent occasions when African Americans are expected to speak up and to develop, hone, and showcase verbal skills. These situations range from informal social gatherings to more formal situations such as church or public forums. It is therefore inaccurate to accept the stereotype that African American clients are deficient in verbal skills and unable to adjust to the verbal interaction of psychotherapy.

Spirituality and the Role of the Black Church

Many social scientists have long remarked that the most segregated time in our society is Sunday morning. The United States has a long history of people worshiping along racial divides. It is fairly ironic that despite the Judeo-Christian ideals of love and acceptance, most of the individuals who worship together are racially homogeneous.

The Black church is one of the few institutions that have been under the control of Black people. It is not surprising that the civil rights movement grew out of the Black church, because it was one of the few places Blacks could gather without being under the scrutiny of Whites. It is also chilling to think that because it remains one of the few institutions of Black control, power, and economic resources, majority members continue to target the church for fires, desecration, and random violence.

In addition to the allegiance many African Americans feel toward the organized Black church, many African American clients also deeply value a sense of spirituality. These feelings exist in many individuals regardless of whether or not they maintain regular attendance at a place of worship. Most African Americans have been exposed to the idea that there is a creator, a master plan, and meaning to the challenges of living. This strong sense of spirituality and harmony may be accompanied by numerous references to God, Jesus, the devil, angels, sin, temptation, and redemption. A client also may make allusions to God's Will that can appear to the uninformed therapist to represent fatalism, a lack of internal control, or both.

Because Black churches are almost exclusively composed of Black members, it is one of the few places where African Americans can feel comfortable about fully expressing their feelings. In the safety of the church, people can speak in tongues, sing and clap, verbalize a sentiment in support of a sermon or a song, and cathartically work out the burdens they carry. Majority culture often misinterprets this behavior as being immature, regressive, or naive, or as a sign of being out of control in a manner akin to psychoses. Such interpretations miss the point of what is valued by African Americans in their celebrations of faith.

Only recently have therapists begun to appreciate that the spirituality of many clients may be completely unrelated to pathology or to borderline or psychotic states. For African American clients, these strong religious values frequently are vehicles that they can use adaptively as a source of strength, support, and inspiration. We need to be alert to the fact that our clients' spirituality reflects a long-standing collective strength and resiliency that we should see as an asset and not a liability.

SIGNIFICANT MENTAL HEALTH AND TREATMENT ISSUES

There is considerable debate about the rate of utilization of mental health services by African Americans. Preliminary research suggests that African Americans are more likely to use these services than some other groups of ethnic minorities.[10] But these studies also make clear that African American clients who present for mental health services are more likely than other racial and ethnic groups to be hospitalized and to be diagnosed as schizophrenic. These findings have helped shape the perception of mental health workers that African Americans are somehow more disturbed and in need of restrictive mental health services than are other racial and ethnic groups.

Other analyses demonstrate inconsistent utilization rates for African Americans. These figures, which were derived from reviews of national statistics and of utilization rates at colleges, suggest that African Americans tend to underutilize mental health resources.[11] Research and clinical practice have consistently shown that African American clients are most likely to seek services in crisis situations and are less likely than European Americans to persist in therapy for more than one session.[12]

Ambivalence About Seeking Services

African American clients are cautious about seeking mental health services. They may recognize their need for counseling, but many have heard horror stories about the insensitivity of therapists and about being forced to disclose personal information and then having what was said in therapy used against them. Consequently, many African Americans are unsure that the potential benefits of help outweigh the potential risks of harm.

In addition, therapist bias against African Americans does exist. Too often, therapists have lumped Blacks into a category of clients who cannot benefit from verbal or cognitive therapies. The idea that these clients can't benefit from psychotherapy owes a lot to long-standing stereotypes and to therapists' own comfort level in working with Black clients.

There is no question that therapists feel most comfortable and confident when treating clients most like themselves.[13] As a result of their discomfort, many therapists distance themselves by recommending a group intervention or medication rather than individual, talk-oriented therapy. They justify this practice with the rationale that African American clients will not open up or that they simply don't have adequate verbal skills to benefit from therapy. Because these clients are different from the therapist, they are seen as more disturbed than other clients and must therefore be referred for medication.

When African American clients seek help, they are likely to be fearful, as are most other individuals. All clients are concerned that they will be held responsible for their difficulties, labeled as "crazy," or be misunderstood. Black clients must also overcome their historically legitimate fears of being blamed for their misfortunes. There have been too many occasions when they've been told, "You brought these problems on yourself," "You didn't work hard enough," or "Can't you just snap out of it!"

A special concern for African American clients is that they come from a cultural tradition that values people solving their own problems or at most seeking assistance from family and friends. To seek help from the formal mental health system can make most Black clients feel like a failure simply because of their need of assistance.

In many cases, clients seek services in response to external pressure rather than because they have decided for themselves that they want therapy. African American clients may be referred by school personnel because of problems with their children, by social services because of concerns about family dynamics, by the court or criminal justice system because of legal problems, or by health specialists because of psychological aspects of physical diseases. In all these situations, clients are apt to have realistic fears that how well they do in therapy may have significant consequences for their lives. It is difficult to trust either the authorities who referred them or the therapists who treat them. Often these clients know they do not have full confidentiality and that their progress or lack thereof will be monitored and reported.

Another subtle reason that African Americans are fearful of therapy is that they are aware of the occasions when Blacks have been referred to therapy simply because they didn't conform to White middle-class standards. Many of the difficulties African Americans face in work, school, and other societal settings arise simply because the structure of these settings is not designed to be responsive to their values, behaviors, and needs. The implicit message is, "Go to therapy because you are not like us. You need help so that you will be more like us and fit in."

When we do not respect difference, we are sending the strong message that one way of behaving is superior to another and that those who don't conform will not be accepted. It is not surprising, therefore, that African Americans are fearful that therapy is simply another technique to "shrink" them into more acceptable mainstream values and norms. Their hesitation to seek services from the majority culture is appropriate.

Paucity of Culturally Competent and African American Therapists

When I refer an African American client for therapy, the immediate question is, "Does this counselor understand Black people?" This is a loaded question. What this potential client is actually asking cuts across several dimensions: Does this therapist

- Understand that Black individuals and families are dis-tinct from other individuals and families?

- Understand that racism, classism, sexism, and other sources of discrimination are real issues for Black clients and not a sign that they're "too sensitive" or paranoid?

- Treat me as an individual deserving respect and at the same time avoid being biased or paternalistic or having a personal agenda?

- Know something about Black cultural expressions: val-ues, music, styles of speech, dress, mannerisms, and popular and classic music and literature?

- See me as deviant simply because I'm different from him or her?

If the therapist is Black or is another person of color, the client is likely to ask the following questions:

- Can he or she relate to me?

- Can this therapist understand the complexity of my life?

- Is this individual too distant from me because of differ-ences in our income or education or because of the need to be "one up"?

- Is this therapist as qualified or as well trained as a White therapist?

Basically, the client is asking if the therapist is culturally com-petent. Unfortunately, many therapists are not. Although many training programs address issues of cultural competence, African American clients can't feel confident that the therapist they are see-ing has met any widely accepted standards in this area.

African American clients and therapists from any racial and ethnic group can entertain stereotypes and biases about each other that can impede the process of therapy. Therapists who are demographically similar to the client, who are themselves members of an ethnic minority group, or who have experienced some form of oppression and identify with minority status can also belong to the category of culturally inadequate therapists. Unfortunately, in some cases minority therapists aren't any more likely than majority therapists to have been fully trained to be culturally competent.

In addition, many African Americans have been exposed to the view that White therapists receive higher levels of training and education than do other groups and are therefore more qualified and skilled. When African American clients harbor these feelings of internalized racism, they often challenge therapists of color to "prove their competence." These clients worry that Black and other ethnic minority therapists are also inferior to White therapists in the areas of power, prestige, resources, and connections. However, in situations where the therapist is viewed as very impressive, his or her array of credentials and skills may then intimidate African American clients. The bottom line is that therapists of color have to walk a narrow path with respect to proving their competence without intimidating their Black clients.

For some clients, the issue of cultural competence is not as important as the basic question, Is the therapist African American? Increasingly, clients understand how expensive and time consuming mental health care can be and rightfully express their right as consumers to have services from a therapist of their choice and who matches their racial or ethnic background. Because it is estimated that fewer than 8 percent of all mental heath workers are of ethnic minority ancestry,[14] statistically African American therapists are rare. African American clients are justifiably concerned about the availability of African American therapists.

Lack of Confidence in Therapy

For all the historical, political, and social reasons already mentioned, it's not surprising that Black clients are mistrustful of therapy. In addition, we also know that one of the biggest impediments to seeking therapy for African American clients is the basic question, Will it work for me? It's very clear that an essential ingredient for successful therapy is the client's belief that the process of therapy can and will help him or her.

African American clients historically have not felt confident about their interactions with therapists. It is therefore very important in a first session for us to consistently convey to our Black clients a realistic portrayal of the potential efficacy of therapy. It is vital that we develop and nurture clients' confidence in the process of therapy from the first session. We must be extra sensitive to African Americans' skepticism while at the same time being willing to give extra reassurance.

Reasons for Seeking Therapy

African American clients seek treatment for the same problems that others do. But we need to be aware that specific factors, such as race and class, can make their presenting problems more complex and may have strained any existing resources to cope adaptively. African American clients often feel that they should be able to handle problems without seeking outside assistance. Many of these individuals take pride in overcoming adversity and challenges. In addition, there has long been a perspective that "airing dirty laundry" reinforces negative cultural stereotypes about African Americans. Both of these factors are impediments to seeking help. Therefore, by the time a Black client seeks therapy, he or she has had to overcome long-held barriers and may be in desperate need of services because the difficulties are overwhelming. In many cases, it is a crisis situation involving the family that brings an African American client to treatment, because by definition these situations represent immediate danger and the risk of escalation.

Another circumstance that can precipitate treatment for African American clients is either an implicit or explicit directive from school, work, the court, or social services. Because so many African Americans view education as the key to advancement, reports of school problems can overcome the tendency to resist counseling.

Similarly, African American clients have a strong commitment to employment. Due to historical and current problems of unemployment, underemployment, unfair compensation, and discrimination in the workplace, work issues are very sensitive for African American clients. Work problems are challenging both to a person's sense of worth and to his or her basic survival. African American clients often are without additional economic resources beyond their salary, so any threat to their tenure or performance at work is taken seriously and can lead to involvement in therapy.

Statistics indicate that African Americans are disproportionately processed through the criminal justice system. Approximately one out of every four Black males is involved in probation, parole, or incarceration. As a result, African American men are often involved in treatment that is court ordered.

Domestic problems account for a significant number of referrals to therapy for African American clients. These problems include balancing multiple demands, coping with relationship difficulties, violence, abuse, substance abuse, and the challenges of caregiving to children and older relatives. Sometimes the decision to seek therapy is made after consultation with primary care physicians, clergy, family, and friends.

African Americans face many of the same pressures and problems that other individuals do. In addition, they also must contend with the challenges that result from the intersection of their cultural values with the dominant middle-class Eurocentric culture. A typical concern for African Americans can be how to help their children develop a healthy sense of identity and attractiveness when one of the major messages in the society is "White is beautiful."

In some cases, the problems African American clients bring to therapy are made more complex due to issues of race, class, gender, sexual orientation, ability status, and other demographic categories. We must be able to sensitively assess with the client whether issues of discrimination, trauma, and stereotyping may be present or whether they do not appear to be significantly related to presenting problems. I'll help you sort this out in the next chapter, which focuses on presenting problems.

With a strong grounding in understanding an African American client as both an individual and also as part of a family and an eth-nic minority group, we have taken significant steps to setting the right tone for therapy. In the next chapter, we'll review issues related to the presenting problems of African Americans and how these issues can be mediated by racial factors.

2

Racial Dynamics and
Mental Health Problems

African American clients present for therapy with diverse concerns and presenting problems. In some situations, racial dynamics play little or no role in the concern that the client brings to therapy. In other cases, we must be alert to how racial issues interface with common mental health problems. In this chapter we'll explore some of the historical factors that shape African Americans' decision to seek treatment. Next we'll review some of the most common problems that lead Black clients to seek therapy. We'll examine relevant background issues, psychosocial stressors, and risk factors. Finally, we'll describe the symptom pictures for a variety of presenting problems, including information on racial and cultural factors.

HISTORICAL ISSUES

In reviewing the literature on African Americans and mental health problems, I was surprised to learn that accurate incidence and prevalence data are not available. A significant problem is that data about Blacks occur in race comparison studies that focus primarily on Whites. Information on African Americans is poorly documented, and interpretations of these data can be misleading because findings on White individuals are not interchangeable with the Black racial and cultural experience. Even well-known classic mental health studies, such as the Midtown Manhattan and the New

Haven, Connecticut, studies, had less than 1 percent participation of African Americans in the entire sample. The majority of data reported on Blacks and seeking help focus on more severe and chronic populations found in inpatient facilities.

African American researchers have noted that the first documentation of mental health problems and Blacks occurred during the Reconstruction period following the Civil War. Statistics were deliberately falsified to indicate that mental illness was higher for those Blacks who had not had the "advantages and benefits" of slavery.[1] Many studies also attempted to portray Blacks as more pathological than Whites in an effort to promote and justify separatism, segregation, and differential treatment.

Many of us are also aware of the infamous Tuskeegee studies that began in the 1930s and extended through the 1950s. Blacks were recruited to participate in a study to examine the long-term effects of untreated syphilis. Even when penicillin became available as a quick and efficient cure, this medication was withheld from the participants so that the study could continue. This experiment left a very destructive legacy. It reinforced the paranoia of Blacks about participating in research studies with Whites and about receiving assistance from Whites. Because Blacks are reluctant to participate in mental health studies, most of what we know about this population comes from studying institutionalized, poor, and more vulnerable members of the community.

In the past, survey teams were composed mainly of White individuals who were often uncomfortable conducting interviews in predominantly Black neighborhoods, especially in the inner city. Other research efforts used mass mailings. Given the distrust that African Americans have for official forms, it's unlikely that this technique produced useful data.

REASONS FOR SEEKING CARE

It has only been in the last decade or so that results from more comprehensive national studies have begun to include more representative samples of Black Americans, although it's likely that Black men are still underrepresented. Now that we have more information on Black Americans, there is debate with respect to understanding the meaning of statistical trends and patterns, as well as to establishing the validity, reliability, and representativeness of the data collected.

There are few studies that comprehensively and systematically address the percentages of African Americans who seek mental health services for specific problems. The studies that are available list broad categories of difficulty that lead Black clients to seek help from outside their informal support systems. In a national sample of Blacks these categories included the following:

Interpersonal and adjustment difficulties	41 percent
Economic concerns	22 percent
Health and physical concerns	16 percent
Emotional distress	12 percent
Grief issues related to a death	9 percent

Typically, clients experiencing these problems did not seek help (51 percent). Those who did seek assistance relied heavily on contact with a physician or emergency room (44 percent), a minister (19 percent), or social services (8 percent). Only 4 percent sought services from a private mental health provider, and 4 percent turned to a mental health center. The other 11 percent sought assistance from schools, employment agencies, or lawyers.[2]

In addition, clinicians note that Black clients often seek services for problems in living and for child-focused concerns. In order to cover the variety of presenting problems suggested by therapists and theorists, we'll review the following presenting problems for Black clients:

- Interpersonal and adjustment difficulties

- Economic and work-related problems

- Affective disorders

- Anxiety disorders

- Posttraumatic stress disorders

- Alcohol and substance abuse

- Schizophrenia

INTERPERSONAL AND ADJUSTMENT DIFFICULTIES

We know that Black clients seek services when they encounter difficulties with self-esteem and identity, relationships, and school issues involving their children. We need to be sensitive not only to the racial dynamics involved in these situations but also to the need for evaluation of associated problems of anxiety and depression.

Self-Esteem and Identity

Many Black clients are aware of a link between feelings of low self-esteem, identity issues, and depression. For these clients, identity and self-esteem issues are of enough concern to lead them to seek counseling. In other cases, these issues of esteem and identity are secondary to other concerns.

Black clients may seek therapy when they're in a majority White environment and they experience feelings of doubt, inadequacy, or actual impaired performance. Black clients may feel that they're being treated unfairly or simply ignored. They may struggle to find a way to speak up and make a positive change in their environment, but they're often fearful that any response they make might result in their being labeled too assertive, aggressive, or sensitive. As therapists, we can help our clients explore how they can build a sense of self-efficacy as an antidote to feelings of low self-esteem.

In some situations we'll also face Black clients who are comfortable working in a White environment but may have to deal very explicitly with Black identity issues if they enter a predominantly Black environment. For these individuals, many of the behaviors and coping mechanisms that were adaptive in other environments are no longer as useful.

I once worked with a Black male professional, Mr. Phillips, who moved from an almost all White work setting to a predominantly Black setting. He enjoyed his new setting, but he sought counseling because he was forced to deal with several issues that he had never really experienced before. First of all, in his previous work environment, he rarely socialized with his colleagues outside of the workday. In his new job, he was expected to attend weekly social events in the evening and on weekends. He also had to deal with the fact that he met women in his new job whom he thought he might want to date, whereas he had never before had to figure out how to separate his potential romantic interests from his work life. Mr. Phillips was also teased about having gone to predominantly White schools and having worked in several prestigious White companies. His African American colleagues wanted to know if he could still relate to them as a "brother" or if he had lost his ability to "keep it real." He was also warned that he'd better not think he was superior to his coworkers because of his experiences and credentials.

The final area of difference for Mr. Phillips involved his new colleagues' open acknowledgment and discussion of racism. Mr. Phillips tended to minimize any potential racial factors in how other individuals related to him or evaluated him. In his new setting with other Blacks, his colleagues were comfortable pointing out the day-to-day hassles and insults they had experienced in White settings. They talked about how they were more comfortable not having to worry about being mistreated because of their race. Mr. Phillips got in touch with the fact that he had experienced periods of anger about racism in his past but also that he had never felt he could express these feelings because he had rarely worked with other people of color. During our first session, he indicated that he was angry with himself for ignoring his negative feelings for so long but was glad that he was finally able to express these emotions.

Multiracial Identity

Currently there are approximately ten million individuals in this country who identify as "other" or "multiracial." Controversy exists about whether they have the right to classify themselves. Many of these individuals have marched and protested for the year 2000 census to include a multiracial designation.

It's interesting that it's often African Americans and other members of minority groups who are uncomfortable with the move to identify as multiracial. Many Blacks feel that if multiracial individuals are not counted as Black, African Americans will lose power and resources that are based on population figures.

As the population of multiracial families grows, we see more clients who are interested in addressing issues of identity. We must always recognize the right of all individuals to define for themselves their sense of personal identity and culture. Although the majority of multiracial individuals have as healthy a sense of self-esteem as other individuals do, they may seek therapy because of the ways that other people respond to them. Therapy can be useful in helping these clients consolidate a healthy identity in the face of challenges from society.

Some families are anxious to gain assistance from therapists who are culturally competent as they try to parent their children and develop relationships with spouses and lovers who may be of a different race, ethnicity, or culture. This is particularly true when a family takes on the responsibility of adopting a multiracial child and receives a lot of negativity from people of color who are opposed to cross-race adoptions. Often these parents are very unsure of how to handle issues of identity and how to allow their families to be exposed to Black culture as well as White culture.

Relationship Issues

It's important for us to be aware that in cases where Black clients present with relationship issues as the focal concern, many of the other issues addressed in this chapter will have to be discussed as well.

Relationship difficulties for African American clients almost always have to be understood in the context of the unique cultural environment that Blacks in this country experience. Black couples will present with the issues that other couples face: separation, divorce, infidelity, communication issues, management of finances, relationships with friends and family members, abuse, and debates about roles and responsibilities. What makes these dilemmas more stressful for Black clients are the conflicts inherent in adhering to bicultural standards. Meeting the expectations of Black culture while also conforming to the standards of a White majority culture is a formidable task.

For example, African American men feel the same pressure to be successful economically in our society as White men, but they have fewer resources, networks, and opportunities to prepare themselves for these roles. In addition to having to play the dominant male role expected by the majority culture, Black men are expected as members of the African American culture to show flexible gender roles and help out with children and household tasks when needed.

Black women are expected to emulate White feminine behavior characteristics of passivity, submissiveness, helplessness, and making males feel strong and necessary. For survival reasons, however, Black women must also be strong, resourceful, independent, and able to support or help support the family financially. Having to live up to conflicting cultural messages places Black men and women under a great deal of stress.

In order to gain our Black clients' trust that we can be effective in assisting them, we must be aware of the multiple realities these couples face. Many of the relationship issues that lead Black clients to seek therapy involve racial, cultural, social, economic, and other demographic issues.

Sexual Relationships

Although figures are not well documented, many therapists believe that Black clients are increasingly seeking services to deal with issues of sexuality and sexual orientation. The years of sexual stereo-typing of African Americans have exacted a heavy toll.

Some Black men, particularly those with limited options to prove themselves in other arenas, experience major conflicts with their masculine identity when they can't demonstrate sexual prowess. Although few males are willing to seek services specifically for problems in sexual functioning, their partners often raise this issue in the context of couple therapy.

Some men experience changes in sexual functioning as a result of stress, aging, and medication. Not surprisingly these changes can also be associated with depression. In fact, many Black men have historically been unwilling or reluctant to use hypertensive med-ication because of possible side effects of reduced sexual ability.

The need to live up to a "macho" image also has the disadvan-tage of making some Black men hesitant to talk about their needs for love, understanding, and companionship beyond issues of sexu-ality. We have to listen closely in order to facilitate the expression of emotions that are difficult for Black males. In some cases these men are tired of the pressure to "run" women or to focus on sexual relationships; they would prefer to develop a serious and meaning-ful relationship but are unsure of how to do so. Some Black men use superficial relationships as a way to block feelings of depression and emptiness. We can be suspicious when we recognize that these males don't seem to show any real emotion or pleasure in their description of their relationships or when they sabotage relation-ships by engaging in behaviors so that their partners find out they're being unfaithful.

The relative shortage of Black men as compared to Black women (47 percent versus 53 percent) begins in the late teen years and early twenties. This discrepancy is a result of homicide, suicide, substance abuse, and the incarceration of Black men. Furthermore, beyond age thirty, Black males are at higher risk for a variety of medical conditions that further increase their mortality rates. This gender imbalance leads many heterosexual Black women to feel pressured to do all they can to win the attention and support of Black men. Some Black women stay in relationships that are unsatisfying, demeaning, or abusive because they're afraid they have no other options. Black women who are unable to feel good about themselves without being in a relationship may place themselves over and over again in abusive, demeaning, or sexualized relationships, believing that they can't have or maintain a relationship with a partner who will treat them well.

A continuing sense of tension, rage, and frustration exists for many Black women when they feel that they're not only competing with other Black women but they may also be competing unsuccessfully with White and other ethnic minority females. Black women who feel unable to attract and maintain a partner can become locked in a cycle of depression and self-blame.

Gay, Lesbian, and Bisexual Concerns

African Americans often have homophobic attitudes. Blacks are aware that although they are deemed inferior by virtue of their race, they can at least attain heterosexual privilege. To express a homosexual or bisexual lifestyle is an affront to many Blacks who believe that it just makes the Black race look more pathological. The fact that there are more Black women than Black men also leads to homophobia, as a gay lifestyle further reduces the population of heterosexual males.

Although we know that some African Americans are supportive of their loved ones' gay, lesbian, or bisexual orientation, many Blacks hold up the Bible and point to the current AIDS epidemic as justification for their prejudices against homosexual and bisexual individuals.

Black clients will present for therapy to work on clarifying their sexual orientation. In cases where an individual is secure in his or her orientation, we may be needed to assist the client in dealing with negative reactions from family, friends, coworkers, or society. Black clients who are gay, lesbian, and bisexual often feel they must choose between being closeted and keeping the acceptance of their loved ones or "coming out" and risking the loss of some of their most important relationships. The pressures that often accompany accepting one's sexual orientation and gaining the acceptance of others can be directly related to depression, anxiety, and possible substance abuse. Many Black lesbians have also noted that they feel that their dating and mating options are as limited and restricted as those of heterosexual Black women.

School-Related Difficulties

Throughout the school years, African American males and females are more likely than White students to drop out and to be subject to disciplinary actions, suspensions, and expulsions. Blacks have also been disproportionately referred to and placed in special education classes. Historically and currently, Blacks are often tracked into low-level classes and non-college-preparatory curricula and advised by guidance counselors that they are not college material or have little or no chance of reaching their vocational goals and should therefore aim lower occupationally.

Given these practices, it is not surprising that Black parents are frequently concerned about their child's development in school. One of the major reasons for Blacks to seek therapy is to secure guidance about providing their child with an optimal foundation for success. In some cases, cultural factors clearly play a role in negative evaluations of Black children. Many teachers contact Black parents because Black children are judged to be too talkative, assertive, mouthy, or aggressive. It appears that even young Black males in the elementary grades are being given a message by the school system that they need to be quieter and less threatening simply because they frighten teachers unaccustomed to cultural differences in play and self-expression.

I can never forget having a young Black couple, Mr. and Mrs. Brooks, call and ask to speak to me about a concern that their son's kindergarten teacher had raised with them. In their son's first parent-teacher conference, the teacher explained that their son, Kelvin, was too talkative and active in class and had trouble with his coordination and couldn't skip, probably because he was bigger than the other children in class.

The teacher went on to elaborate that problems in coordination were often associated with learning difficulties. The teacher concluded by saying that she knew that Mr. and Mrs. Brooks were well educated, but she wanted to warn them that in consideration of Kelvin's poor coordination and high activity level in kindergarten, she thought that attaining a college education might be a reach for him.

Of course, I didn't hear what the teacher said firsthand. I did know that the couple was shaken and that Mrs. Brooks was in tears. I told her that although I had no direct knowledge of her son's academic potential, it was utterly inappropriate for a teacher to make such a negative and long-term prediction based on so little data. I encouraged the couple to take a strong and active role in asking the teacher to document any strong opinions or predictions that she chose to make. I also advised them to ask the teacher to include the comments and reports of other teachers with whom Kelvin interacted to see if their views were similar.

Mr. and Mrs. Brooks soon determined that Kelvin seemed to be doing fine but that his teacher had a very rigid understanding of the characteristics of academically successful youngsters, and Kelvin's profile was not included in her repertoire. By accident I ran into Mr. and Mrs. Brooks at a social event recently. They were proud to report that Kelvin is a very well-adjusted honor roll student who is on track to attend the college of his choice.

In other situations, teachers detect real academic, behavioral, or emotional difficulties that need to be addressed. Many Black parents have little confidence in schools because of schools' treatment of Blacks in general. As a result of this distrust, parents find it challenging to evaluate what is a real problem as opposed to a manufactured issue that results in their child's being shoved to the margins of the school system.

We know that it's extremely important for schools and parents to work together collaboratively, and often therapists and counselors can be involved in making this arrangement work. When we meet with families around school issues, typically the parent takes the lead in explaining the concern. Younger children may be only minimally aware of the specific concerns, but they, like older children, may show anxiety, depression, and conduct problems when they're marginalized by the school system.

Part of the reason parents may seek therapy for a school problem is because they no longer feel connected to schools, teachers, and principals. Parents, educators, and community members have been concerned about the following disturbing trends:

- Few Black teachers

- An absence of Black male classroom teachers at the elementary school level

- White flight from urban centers into the suburbs

- Black middle-class flight into the suburbs

- The perception that White teachers are not as committed to the success of Black children as were the Black teachers of the past

- Segregated schools for Black children, which have fewer resources and lower school achievement than predominantly White neighborhoods and school districts

Parents may seek therapy for advice about testing and placement or to assist in negotiating with school personnel. As we in society try to build better linkages and supports for young children among their families, schools, and communities, therapists can play a significant role. As therapists, we need to be able to understand parents' concerns and reassure them that we'll work with them to help their children and families.

ECONOMIC AND
WORK-RELATED PROBLEMS

African Americans must live with the reality that their profile in the work arena reflects chronic unemployment and underemployment. They still face the age-old challenge of having to do more to get the same recognition that others receive. Increasingly African Americans are facing pressure to be competitive in today's technological job market when fewer than 12 percent have college degrees and the credentials that can lead to competitive salaries, stable employment, and possibility for advancement.

Even in the waning years of the twentieth century when overall unemployment rates were declining, Black men showed unemployment rates of 28 to 30 percent overall, and those who were employed worked largely in unskilled positions. For African American men in the eighteen- to thirty-year-old range, this figure was as high as 48 percent.[3] Black women are more likely to be employed than Black men, but they tend to work in female-dominated unskilled or semiskilled positions with low salaries and limited opportunities for salary increases or advancement.

According to labor statistics, approximately 17 percent of Black individuals work in managerial and professional occupations as compared to 27 percent of Whites. Blacks account for 23 percent of those working in semiskilled positions as compared to 14 percent for Whites.[4]

The long-term problems with unemployment have led many Blacks to turn to the military for jobs. African Americans currently account for approximately 20 percent of military personnel. Military employment also offers benefits in terms of education, training, and the use of commissaries.

Despite the benefits of military employment, Blacks in the military have learned that racism and discrimination still operate and that they often have less recourse to protest than in civilian society. Research has shown that Blacks in the military face problems with promotions and problems in the military criminal justice system.[5]

A prevalent myth is that affirmative action has created a level playing field for Blacks. The reality is that Blacks continue to suffer in the labor market. We need to remember that affirmative action and equal opportunity programs are under siege and have been legally terminated in some states, such as California.

Whether the job is with the military or in the civilian arena, African Americans still face stress at work. In all too many cases it is assumed that they are not as competent as White job applicants or that they were hired for affirmative action purposes. Blacks also feel subtle pressure to "sell out" and "act White" in order to get the best jobs, promotions, and benefits.

I have worked with Black clients who are treated in discriminatory ways, yet they are nonetheless still expected to socialize with Whites during lunch or at off-work social events. My clients have complained that there are too many "unwritten rules" that can block their success. They feel pressure to conform to White standards of speech, behavior, and mannerisms in order to fit in and gain approval.

Many clients feel they are always being watched and evaluated in an attempt to find any weakness and to punish them for it. Blacks have noted that they feel they have to be "on" at work and can't afford to just relax and be themselves. Oliva Espin has commented on the way some individuals have to switch from one group of cultural norms to another. She warns that people, like equipment, become much more vulnerable and fragile if they must constantly switch on and off.[6]

An enduring myth about Black females is that they are given advantages over Black men in the workforce. This belief stemmed from the practice of trying to steer Black females toward college to avoid the sexual harassment and abuses associated with domestic work. Although the rate of attainment of college degrees for Black women has historically been higher than for Black men, it's not true that Black women enjoy significantly higher status or earnings as compared to Black men. It's important for us to be aware of this myth in working with clients. Some Black men direct their anger toward Black women in the mistaken belief that they're the cause of their job-related frustration. Black men and women both suffer from work-related problems, but the interaction of gender and race produces unique issues for the female population.[7]

Black Women and Work

Since slavery, Black women have a tradition of working outside as well as inside the home. In addition to these two roles, most African American women are expected to assist in caretaking roles with the extended family and to participate in church, community, and civic organizations. It is no surprise that many Black women feel overwhelmed with responsibility. They are often guilty of taking care of others to the detriment of their own self-care—failing to comply with routine health checks, to get proper amounts of rest, exercise, and nutrition, or to attend to the health problems they already have.

One of the major problems Black women face in therapy is learning how to cope more adaptively with their strength. As therapists we need to be aware that many Black women exhibit the "superwoman syndrome." Black women are expected to handle enormous levels of responsibility by working outside the home and by playing a leadership role inside the home. They're expected to understand the challenges that Black men face to be breadwinners despite the obstacles that society poses. They're challenged to care for their children and inspire them to do well in school and stay out of trouble. Consequently we need to help these women develop stronger limits and boundaries.

Many Black women would like the option of not working outside the home, but the challenges of discrimination make financial stability almost impossible for most Black families without their paycheck.

Even though the majority of Black women work outside the home, 71 percent of these women earn an annual income under $10,000.[8]

In addition to the problems of dealing with multiple roles, Black women face multiple levels of discrimination in the workplace. Although both Black men and women face discrimination based on race, Black women must also face issues of sexism and sexual harassment.

When Black women seek therapy to talk about dissatisfaction with work or problems with productivity, it's important to find out whether or not they are experiencing some amount of harassment or sexism. This can lead to symptoms of anxiety and depression, but these women, like most others, are reluctant to come forward and complain. They fear retaliation if they speak up and are usually afraid to risk their job, despite any guarantees of protection.

Also, many Black women have experienced such chronic stress related to harassment, abuse, and sexism that they no longer feel empowered to stop it or even to take the steps necessary to protect themselves. In fact, in some cases we rather than the client will be responsible for labeling behaviors as forms of sexism or harassment.

Black Men and Work

Black men are under constant pressure to prove themselves in our society. They have been stereotyped as inadequate breadwinners for their families. The reality is that the spiraling unemployment of Black men is directly related to specific changes in the labor market. Up until the 1970s, when many Black men had the option to work in well-paying but unskilled jobs, they could earn enough to support their families. As factories moved to foreign locations or closed down due to technological innovations, large numbers of Black males lost their jobs and were not trained for the increasingly skilled jobs that were available.

As Black men lost their livelihood, they were sometimes put in the situation of choosing to leave their families so that the family could receive government support and services. As these labor force changes evolved, we witnessed a rise in single-parent homes and a decrease in marriage for Black men and women. With the prospect for employment so unstable, many Black men are opting not to marry. When Black men can't obtain a job in the labor market, some turn to illegal activities in order to make money. Many gangs in urban communities generate income for unemployed Black males.

Just as there are multiple expectations for Black women, there are multiple expectations for Black males. Black men have historically been more involved in sharing household responsibilities than have White males. Black men are also expected to be involved in social, civic, and church activities. In the wake of the Million Man March held in 1995, there's a new excitement about Black men working harder to be more responsible at work, at home, and in their communities. Many Black communities have started rites-of-passage programs, mentoring activities, and father-son activities to make Black men more visible as role models for their children.

When the work issue is one of unemployment or underemployment, it is most likely to come to our attention in couple or family work. Not many Black men are willing to come for therapy to discuss not having a job. But Black men in higher-level jobs as well as those in lower-level jobs do come for therapy to discuss issues of discrimination and problems with getting along with coworkers or supervisors. Often they have received encouragement to seek therapy from partners, friends, or a work supervisor. It can be amazing to observe how the feelings of rage, depression, anxiety, and impotence caused by unfair work environments transcend education, job level, and socioeconomic status. Often when Black men pursue therapy for work-related issues, there are accompanying problems with health, substance abuse, relationships, violence, or other psychological distress.

AFFECTIVE DISORDERS

Research on affective disorders in the African American population is sparse because earlier studies suggested that Blacks rarely suffered from depression and manic-depressive disorders. Approximately

5 percent of African Americans are reported to suffer from depression.[9] It has been difficult to gain a clear picture of affective symptomatology because African Americans, like other individuals, vary in the ways they express affective distress. Research and clinical practice suggest that Black males are more likely than other individuals to demonstrate verbal and physical aggression as part of their depression. The following are some of the expressions of affective disorder:

- Internalizing or repressing emotions

- Expressing anger, agitation, or violence

- Complaining of physical symptoms or illnesses

- Suffering from problems with self-esteem and identity issues

- Masking or self-medicating affective distress through the use of alcohol or drugs

Risk factors for depression for African Americans include young adulthood, unmarried status, unemployment, low income, and low education. As compared to other individuals, Blacks who are depressed express higher levels of impulsivity, violent behavior, homicidal ideation, hallucinations, and substance abuse. In general it appears that African Americans present for help with higher levels of agitation, somatization, and hostility than other racial groups. Some of these symptoms indicate possible bipolar disorders that are underdiagnosed in Blacks, but more frequently these symptoms are linked to schizophrenia or paranoid personality disorders.[10]

Symptoms of Depression

Because we know that many African Americans may be uncomfortable admitting they are depressed, we need to note the more subtle indicators of depression. Clients might present for therapy and complain of feelings of low self-esteem or about difficulties in work or school, in relationships, or in concentration, attentiveness, or productivity. In some situations our clients might say that their temper is shorter and that they're "flying off the handle" more frequently.

As we ask about accompanying symptoms, clients may or may not confirm the presence of anhedonia and vegetative indicators, such as changes in sleeping and eating patterns, weight gain, or weight loss. I've had some clients complain of an increased frequency of colds, sinus infections, headaches, and gastrointestinal distress.

Black clients, like other individuals, may not be aware that the symptoms they are complaining about signal depression. It actually may be more acceptable for a client to seek services for somatic symptoms than to recognize depression and seek mental health help. I've frequently listened to a recitation of symptoms from clients, and when I tell them "I think you're depressed," they seem surprised. They are somehow unprepared to realize that the distress of depression can have such far-reaching impact in so many areas of their lives.

Depression and the Elderly

Depression can be associated with both cognitive and physical changes associated with aging. Depression can also be related to the cumulative effect of a lifetime of coping with stressors related to race, gender, financial adequacy, safety, and obtaining basic life resources.

In some cases, elderly Black individuals suffering from depression will not present for therapy. These individuals may be too resistant to seek services. Instead, the relative who serves as a caretaker for an elderly individual will seek help and guidance.

In many situations the elderly relative is depressed by a series of losses, including the loss of loved ones, physical abilities, privacy, mobility to drive and get around alone, and home and possessions; in some cases they have experienced the loss of status and possessions because of their failing abilities. Many of these older Black individuals are reevaluating their lives, and some conclude that their lives have not been fulfilling, thereby reinforcing regrets about important decisions and outcomes. In some situations, the depression has grown to such an extent that suicide emerges as an option.

As therapists, we may need to help our clients who are caretakers ensure that the relative in question is evaluated for depression and any possible physical illnesses; we may also assist in securing medication and appropriate treatment.

Suicide

The suicide rate for African Americans is lower than national averages for Whites and several other ethnic minority groups, but the suicide rate for Blacks has been escalating since the 1960s. The biggest increase has been in the suicide rate for Black males in the twenty- to thirty-four-year-old range.

The fact that suicide rates for Blacks are increasing comes as a surprise to many clinicians and researchers. Historically, African Americans rejected the idea of suicide as a way to cope with problems and stressors. A cultural belief existed that Blacks should turn to their spiritual beliefs, religious advisers, and family and close friends if they felt a problem warranted outside assistance.

For reasons that are not completely clear, African Americans are now more likely to see suicide as a viable alternative. It is likely that the higher suicide rate for Black males is an indication that Black males of today

- Experience higher levels of stress than previous generations of Black males

- Face different stressors than the ones with which Black males historically have had to contend

- Have fewer coping resources available to them

- Are lacking in insurance and health care options, which means that mental and physical problems may go untreated and thus become significant stressors

We've talked elsewhere about how the Black community has historically used support systems composed of extended family members and close friends. Perhaps this generation of young Blacks no longer has as much access to these resources.

Only a generation ago, every Black community had what Elijah Anderson calls "old heads."[11] These were elderly Black men and women who were sought after for advice. Anderson believes that current values that glorify materialism and violence have led to a new breed of role models in the Black community. These new models are often involved in criminal activities and destructiveness. The "old heads" as well as other adults in the neighborhood are less inclined to give advice to young people because they fear violence from so many of these individuals. With less support and direction, young people may see suicide as a more viable alternative.

The high-risk activities of many African American clients reveal parasuicidal intent and include reckless criminal activities, high-speed driving, unprotected sex, sharing of needles, and abusing alcohol and drugs. The classic movie *Boyz N the Hood* depicts significant numbers of Black adolescents who feel that life isn't worth living. They sometimes choose to engage in activities to hasten their deaths rather than to commit suicide more directly.

ANXIETY DISORDERS

The limited data available on anxiety disorders and Blacks suggest that Blacks are at higher risk than are Whites for phobias, generalized anxiety, and posttraumatic stress disorders in Vietnam veterans.[12] In addition, some researchers have noted that a high prevalence of panic attacks appears to be associated with sleep paralysis in some African Americans.[13] It seems safe to assume that Blacks face additional psychosocial stressors related to race that compound the influence of anxiety on day-to-day functioning. The impact of anxiety on Blacks needs to be understood because it can have a significant impact on relationships, occupational functioning, substance use and abuse, and violent behaviors.

Racism and Emotional Abuse

In the last decade, more attention has been directed to understanding the role that racism plays in causing trauma, anxiety, and emotional abusiveness for African Americans. Obviously, such major events as a physical attack, being denied a promotion, harassment, or being fired based on being Black are going to cause trauma and anxiety. And unfortunately, there is no denying that Blacks are at greater risk for experiencing these difficulties. Moreover, therapists recognize that in addition to major traumatic events, the day-to-day hassles of discrimination can lead Black clients to seek services.

A. J. Franklin has eloquently described the trauma of being rendered invisible. Many Black Americans face this treatment when they are ignored even though next in line for service, when they can't get a cab to pick them up, or when people refer to them in derogatory ways or as though they weren't there. These microaggressions are a source of ongoing stress, anxiety, and depression because they're not under the control of the recipient and because these events generate feelings of frustration and anger.[14]

On the flip side, Blacks also suffer from hypervisibility when they are followed in stores by security agents, when Whites cross the street or exit an elevator to avoid contact, and when they're forced to give multiple forms of identification to make a purchase with a credit card or check.

Many Blacks describe these pressures as overwhelming, ongoing, and exhausting. It's hard enough to go through all the ups and downs in life that others go through, but having always to be sensitive to the potential for racial discrimination places additional strain on everyday functioning.

Health and Appearance Concerns

We know that Black clients frequently turn to physicians when they're experiencing distress. Even when health specialists diagnose a physical disorder, many of them encourage Black clients to seek counseling as a way to manage their stress and anxiety. There are a variety of physical illnesses that are common in the Black population and also have a strong anxiety component: ulcers, hypertension, chronic pain disorders, skin and hair diseases, and eating disorders, among others.

Black clients often experience anxiety related to dermatological disorders, such as hair loss, skin rashes, scarring, and diseases related to problems in pigmentation. Many Black clients have recognized that there are significant areas of life that they can't control. But they may resolve to give significant attention to those areas of life that they can control, such as their appearance. Thus many African Americans are deeply concerned about creating a positive physical appearance with respect to dressing well and highlighting healthy skin and hair.

Hair is a major hot button for many Black men and women. Historically, many Blacks internalized White racism and felt that for "Black hair" to be beautiful it had to be like "White hair": straight and long. Many African American men and women have finally learned to value "Black hair" and to take a great deal of pride in being able to sport a variety of hairstyles. Therefore, when Blacks develop disorders that result in significant hair loss or breakage, and anxiety is believed to be a component, they are usually very motivated to work on identifying and reducing the anxiety in their lives.

Therapists need to know that many Black clients devote considerable time, attention, and money to hair care and hairstyles. Even when finances are strained, weekly visits to beauty salons and barbers may be considered a necessity rather than a luxury. It's also typical for many individuals to invest several hours in a weekly hair appointment, especially if the procedure involves braiding or use of hair weaves.

African American clients report that when they wear more Afrocentric hairstyles, they are told that many of their coworkers often feel intimidated by them and are more comfortable when Blacks wear more Eurocentric styles. We need to be alert to any signs that our clients have suffered discrimination, embarrassment, or teasing about their hairstyles or about how short, long, thin, coarse, or straight their hair is. We can let our clients set the tone for discussion of hair. If they initiate a conversation, we need to be ready to understand that hair can be a source of considerable pride, shame, or ambivalence for our Black clients and is usually a central component of how they and others evaluate their attractiveness. If we listen attentively to our clients, we can learn what role hair may play in their feelings about themselves.

Appearance is also a very important component of positive body image for Black men. It's very difficult for Black men to adopt a "cool pose" when they feel disfigured by hair or skin problems.

Eating Disorders

Most of the literature on eating disorders has historically focused on White middle-class females. Only recently has attention shifted to exploring how these disorders relate to males and people of color across socioeconomic classes. What we have learned comes largely from case studies, as people of color are not typically included in larger-scale studies.

Case study reports beginning in the 1980s suggest that an increasing number of Black females present with eating disorder problems, but the incidence is estimated to be less than 5 percent of all cases of anorexia nervosa and between 1 to 4 percent of all cases of bulimia nervosa.[15] We're also starting to recognize that Black males involved in sports where weight control is a factor (such as wrestling) may also develop eating disorders.

Sociocultural explanations have been helpful in understanding eating disorders in relation to Black women. First of all, it's established that Black women and Black men embrace a larger ideal body size for Black women than White females and males do for White females. African American women have also been found to have higher levels of body image satisfaction than White females. Although this trend may provide some protection for Black women with respect to anorexia, they're at high risk for being overweight or obese and are just as vulnerable as White females to binge eating disorders, which in turn makes them vulnerable to a host of health concerns and complications.

Second, as the cultural standards for beauty become more universal, many Black women are becoming more vulnerable to duplicating the behavioral patterns of anorexia and bulimia, such as dieting, overexercising, abuse of laxatives, forced vomiting, and episodes of bingeing and purging.

We might become aware of a possible eating disorder with a Black client although that may not have been the presenting problem. For reasons that are unclear, some Black women with eating disorders may not show this behavior in early adolescence but may show it in their twenties or later. Sometimes they may not conform to a specific category of eating disorder but may fall in the "not otherwise specified" group. As long as we focus on understanding eating disorders only from a White middle-class perspective, we may miss understanding some of the possible subtle and complex ways that race, culture, and socioeconomic status may operate in the lives of Black women to promote eating disorders. For example, it may not be until a Black woman struggles with racial identity issues or acculturation or is urged to conform to White female body ideals that an eating disorder becomes a problem for her. This may occur at a later stage of development than it does for White females, who face these pressures from their first few years of school.

POSTTRAUMATIC STRESS DISORDERS

Because young Black males had not been afforded the educational deferments that White males obtained, they were more likely to be inducted into the military. And because of the limited work opportunities for young Black males, they often volunteered for military service. Many of these men were naive enough to be motivated by the higher pay of combat duty and so signed up for duty on the front line.

Black participation in the Vietnam War led to ongoing casualties in terms of deaths, physical injuries, and psychological problems. In addition, following the Vietnam War it was noted that Black veterans suffered from higher rates of PTSD symptoms than White veterans.[16] Therapists who work with Black veterans have reported that many of these individuals suffer from the typical PTSD side effects of war. But Black veterans also felt a strong ambivalence about fighting for freedom in another country while they were not treated as full citizens in the United States. The veterans also felt shame about attacking men, women, and children who were also oppressed minorities.

There are Black veterans who are still suffering from the PTSD syndrome of anxiety, hypervigilance, nightmares, and poor adjustment to society. In addition, many of these veterans have developed serious substance abuse problems, have difficulty maintaining employment, and are unable to function effectively in relationships.

The PTSD literature has expanded from discussions of war experiences and natural disasters to encompass the psychological effects of rape, abuse, violence, and either witnessing or experiencing crime. We as therapists need to be sensitive to assessing PTSD when we are told about presenting problems dealing with relationship difficulties, performance and productivity issues, and emotional expressions of anxiety, depression, and low self-esteem. In the following section, we'll review some of the risk factors associated with violence that can cause PTSD reactions in Black clients.

Violence and Injustice

In order to understand the lives of African American clients, we need to recognize that the world they live in is not as safe as it is for other citizens of this country. They live each day at high risk for violence, assault, rape, and murder.

Some therapists mistakenly believe that belonging to the middle or upper class protects Black people from crime, violence, and interactions with the criminal justice system. It's important to recognize that although being in a lower income bracket can enhance risk, it is skin color that makes all Blacks vulnerable to these problems. For example, most of us have heard about profiling—a practice used by many police departments across the United States, whereby Blacks are routinely stopped for questioning without a specific reason. They are halted for "driving while Black," that is, because they racially match the demographic characteristics of some criminals.

Clearly, being stopped by police and detained and questioned without cause can lead to feelings of frustration, rage, impotence, and depression. Although this practice has existed for years, it wasn't called into question until higher-status and more affluent African Americans experienced this humiliation.

In some cases, it's middle-class African Americans who may be more likely to seek services to address the trauma of having a negative experience with the police or criminal justice system. Some of these individuals believed that their jobs, status, or income would protect them from these random indignities. When they become a victim of abuse by the criminal justice system, it may violate the sense of order and control that they're trying so hard to develop in their lives.

The following are some of the statistics we as therapists need to know about African Americans and violence in our society:

- Of all homicide victims, 42 percent are Black.[17]

- The majority of homicide perpetrators are younger and male.

- Homicide is the leading cause of death for young Black males and females ages fifteen to thirty-four and the second leading cause for those ages ten to fourteen. This homicide risk is eight times that of their White counterparts.[18]

- In urban centers, the risk of homicide can be sixteen times higher than for White males.[19]

- Two-thirds to three-quarters of Black homicide victims know their assailants.[20]

- African American women are twice as likely as White women to be battered.[21]

- African Americans account for 45 percent of all spousal homicides and have a spousal homicide rate that is eight times higher than that of Whites.[22]

- Black women are at higher risk for sexual abuse and rape by a family member than are other women.[23]

- African American women are more likely than other women to wait until years later to report a sexual assault.

- Higher child abuse rates in African American families are related in part to harsher disciplinary practices.[24]

- Higher violence levels are associated with lower socioeconomic status.

- Participation in gang violence provides a mechanism for many African American men to prove their masculinity.

- Inner-city African Americans are at high risk for observing violence—43 percent have seen someone shot and 23 percent have witnessed a murder.[25]

- Of all hate crimes, 36 percent of the victims have been African Americans.[26]

- More vulnerable members of the African American community are at higher risk for physical and sexual abuse. This includes individuals who are gay, lesbian, bisexual, and those with mental and physical disabilities.

These statistics create a startling backdrop for the presenting problems of our Black clients. Violence is pervasive in the lives of

African Americans. It is encouraging that the media have begun to document the epidemic of homicide seen in young Black males, but they have not yet publicized the alarming rates for other groups, such as Black females, young children, and older males.

A great deal of the violence in the Black community is a reflection of conflicting gender role demands. Black men are expected to be strong, protective, and able to provide for their families. They feel rage and frustration when they find significant obstacles to fulfilling these goals in this society.

Research shows that men who are unemployed or working part-time are twice as likely to batter than are men who work full-time. Inability to secure rewarding employment is sometimes related to gang activities, promiscuity, violence, and sexual risk taking.

Barriers to Seeking Help

In most cases during an initial session, we will learn only indirectly of issues of rape, domestic violence, child abuse, and the trauma of witnessing violence. Given the high levels of violence in the lives of African Americans, what makes them so reluctant to report this violence and seek help? First, for young people involved in violence, there is a strong code of silence about turning other people in. In many cases this is a realistic response to the possibility that turning in the name of a perpetrator may lead to retaliation.

Second, African Americans understand that the criminal justice system is often harsh and discriminatory, especially with respect to Black men. Research clearly documents why Blacks are concerned about questionable arrest, prosecution, and sentencing procedures. It is blatantly obvious that Blacks have legitimate concerns about being treated fairly by the police and court systems in this country. Black males and females are more likely to be arrested, charged, and convicted of serious offenses than are Whites in situations of violence and abuse.

Religious doctrine also plays a role in Blacks' reluctance to report family violence and abuse. The Black church is a patriarchal institution despite high levels of involvement by Black women. Many churches and religious leaders teach Black women that the man is the head of the household and that women should obey their husbands. As a result, in many cases Blacks don't report domestic violence and abuse except in the most severe and life-threatening situations.

The consequence of protecting perpetrators is that the victim often experiences violation and trauma without the support, comfort, and acknowledgment of family and friends. It shouldn't surprise us that Black clients who are suffering as a result of domestic violence are very reluctant to seek protection. Part of being a culturally competent therapist has to include knowledge of safe places to refer clients for protection. We'll discuss this in our chapter on crisis management.

ALCOHOL AND SUBSTANCE ABUSE

Even though alcohol is a leading mental health problem for African Americans, White Americans show even higher levels of alcohol use and abuse up to age forty. After age forty, Blacks show rates similar to Whites. Some researchers believe that alcohol becomes a more significant problem for African American males beginning in their thirties. At this stage, heavy drinking for Black males is associated with binge drinking, dependence, tolerance, and loss of control in their daily lives.[27]

Overall alcohol use for Blacks is approximately 55 percent of the population, and abuse and dependence rates over a lifetime are estimated to be 14 percent. Heavy use of alcohol on a daily basis is estimated to be present in about 4 to 7 percent of the Black population. These figures must be interpreted with caution, as they rely largely on self-report information.[28]

Patterns of Usage

In the Black community, rates of illicit drug dependence or abuse are estimated at 15 percent, with the highest use by those ages eighteen to thirty-four (24 percent).[29] Marijuana is the most frequently used drug, followed by high usage of cocaine, crack, and crystal methamphetamine. Heroin use in the African American community showed a decline since the 1960s but has begun to increase in the 1990s. Both alcohol and drug abuse rates are higher for Black males than for Black females.

African American women show fewer problems with alcohol than do White women and Black men and show abstinence rates of about 46 percent. However, those Black women who do drink are more likely to show patterns of heavy usage and binge drinking. Although surveys suggest that Black adolescents are not nearly as involved with alcohol as are Whites of the same age, it's not clear that surveys have adequately captured representative samples of Blacks. It is possible that alcohol usage for Black adolescents is underreported.[30]

Risk Factors

Alcohol abuse is a risk factor for drug dependence and abuse, unemployment, poverty, violence, homicide, physical diseases, homelessness, and criminal activities. Both alcohol and drug abuse can exist with other psychological disorders and produce individuals with dual diagnoses. Substance abuse in African Americans most frequently is linked to second diagnoses of schizophrenia, mania, and, most commonly, antisocial personality disorder.

The ravages of substance abuse can certainly worsen mental illness and lead individuals to losses in their social support and their ability to work and to maintain a residence. As a result, many of these individuals with dual diagnoses become unemployed and homeless, which makes their ability to recover from their addiction and mental illness even more difficult. The existence of mental illness with substance abuse disorders makes issues of diagnosis and treatment more complex; some individuals are misdiagnosed and given improper medications that cause debilitating side effects.

Because African Americans are already at high risk for problems in living—obesity, diabetes, and hypertension—substance abuse can have such a significant additive effect in the presence of these disorders that it can trigger serious crises in the lives of clients.

In fact, many Black clients who seek treatment have admitted that it's often the harm that substances have in other areas of their lives that motivates them to get help. In a national study, Black clients said that substance abuse led to treatment requests subsequent to

Involvement with the criminal justice system	29 percent
Health concerns	24 percent
Relationship difficulties	52 percent
Financial difficulties	30 percent
Work-related problems	9 percent

(The clients were instructed to indicate all issues that applied, so the total is more than 100 percent.)[31]

It appears that Black men, like other males in our society, use alcohol and drugs as a form of self-medication. These substances dull the pain of anxiety, depression, anger, hopelessness, and frustration. Likewise, we certainly must acknowledge that alcohol and abuse occur in a positive social context.

As the majority population has shifted to drinking more wine and beer, liquor manufacturers have increasingly targeted Black consumers in radio, television, and magazine ads. Advertisements throughout our culture depict drinking as "cool" and masculine. This reinforcement fosters the denial that supports all addiction.

Treatment Issues

We know that treating substance abuse disorders is extremely challenging; the majority of individuals with these disorders relapse in the five years following treatment. Complicating the issue of seeking and receiving services for Blacks is that Blacks are less likely than Whites to seek treatment for substance abuse. We know that

African Americans are underrepresented in the Alcoholics Anonymous (AA) program. AA programs and most other alcohol and drug treatment programs are based on what works for White males. Blacks have good reasons to be distrustful of traditional substance abuse programs. In many cases they are pressured to enroll in these programs because of problems at work, in relationships, or with the criminal justice system.

Experts believe that Blacks will continue to be reluctant to seek treatment unless programs are designed to incorporate culturally sensitive and culturally appropriate modalities. Some Blacks, for instance, are more likely to participate in an AA group if the membership at the meeting is predominantly African American. Programs that seem to work for African American clients involve the following approaches, among others:

- Family sessions to gain a better understanding of the personality of the client in different life arenas

- Random drug testing with urine samples

- Isolation from a peer culture that reinforces use of drugs and alcohol

- Confrontation when appropriate

- Education about the nature of substance abuse

- Detoxification followed by inpatient or outpatient treatment

- Educational and vocational counseling

- Working with African American counselors and clients

Because African Americans have not always been successful in traditional counseling programs, many believe that they must solve their addiction problems with the help of religion, and many have in fact been successful. More specifically, the Black Muslim religious organization has claimed significant success in rehabilitating substance abusers by incorporating religious and culturally sensitive approaches to treatment.

As therapists, we need to be aware that Blacks who come to us for treatment of substance abuse may be doing so under duress. We also need to explore with them adjunct resources that relate to spirituality, and to use a treatment approach that is relevant and sensitive to the traumas and challenges that African Americans experience in this country.

SCHIZOPHRENIA

Researchers and clinicians have noted that due to racism and poor training, mental health workers have historically overdiagnosed Black clients as psychotic. In addition, research has suggested that Blacks tend to be overdiagnosed as paranoid schizophrenic. This appears to be related to the fact that African American clients report more auditory and visual hallucinations than do White clients. In addition, Blacks often show what many Black theorists and therapists believe to be appropriate suspicion and distrust of White mental health workers.

Historically, Blacks have been overdiagnosed as schizophrenic and rarely diagnosed as suffering from affective disorders. It has been hypothesized that this inappropriate practice of diagnosing is due to the following factors:

- Differences in cultures, speech usage, and mannerisms between African American clients and White diagnosticians

- Use of any evidence of delusions or hallucinations as a basis for a schizophrenic diagnosis even if other criteria were not met

- Misinterpretation and exaggeration of paranoid or religious ideation and verbalizations of Black clients

- Failure to recognize organic brain problems and symptoms associated with the abuse of alcohol or drugs,
  which may precipitate paranoia, psychoses, hallucinations, and delusions

- The presence of higher levels of hostility and aggression than are seen in White clients

As a result, Blacks evaluated for their functioning have often
been hospitalized in institutions for long periods of time and have
been given minimal therapeutic interventions. This situation led
Blacks to distrust mental health officials. They learned to tolerate
the mental illness of their relatives rather than subject them to
long-term hospitalizations with little hope for improvement.

Black families know that individuals with psychotic functioning can't deal with the challenges of day-to-day living. But these
families tend to seek services only when there's a crisis situation,
when the client poses a danger to self or others, or when the family can't cope any longer with the burdens of caring for the client.

As we know, delays in treatment can allow psychological diseases to become more entrenched and resistant to treatment and
can facilitate the development of accompanying problems, such as
depression, suicidal and homicidal ideation and impulses, and substance abuse disorders.

Grier and Cobbs coined the term *healthy paranoia* in 1968 to
describe what they believed to be a healthy sign of coping in Black
Americans.[32] Grier and Cobbs have argued that it is normal and
adaptive for Black Americans to have paranoia if they live in the
United States.

Blacks are not imagining that historically and currently they are
the targets for a wide variety of abuses in this society, including bias,
discrimination, and prejudice, and physical, verbal, and emotional

violence and maltreatment. What has traditionally been difficult for therapists from the majority culture to do is to establish when a Black client is showing normal paranoia as a Black person as opposed to an unhealthy and maladaptive level of paranoia that is indicative of psychotic functioning. We can discriminate between normal and psychotic paranoia by asking clients to describe real-life situations at home, on the job, at school, or in the neighborhood that might provoke healthy or understandable paranoia. We also need to inquire about any recent incidents of trauma or violence that could have provoked paranoid thinking. We need to ask directly if our clients have heard or seen anything that others have not, to see if there are signs of hallucinations or delusions. Only with careful questioning will we be able to accurately assess the role of paranoia in our clients' functioning.

As we can see from this discussion of presenting problems, many of the issues that lead Black clients to seek therapy relate to racial, cultural, social, economic, and other demographic issues. In order to fully understand the presenting problems of Black clients and make plans for treatment, we must know how to establish a healthy rapport. In Chapter Three, we'll talk about how to build effective working alliances with Black clients.

3

Establishing Rapport
and Forming an Alliance

From the first contact, we must demonstrate to clients from all cultural backgrounds our capacity to establish trust, respect, and empathy. Clients bring mixed emotions to the first session of therapy, and as therapists we need to orient clients by conveying the following:

- We have the knowledge, skills, and comprehension of cultural context to understand the client's concerns, regardless of whether or not we share the same background.

- We can appreciate that the decision to seek therapy is difficult.

- We are confident that the process of therapy can be helpful.

- We will collaboratively solve problems without taking ownership of the client's problems or decisions.

This chapter will describe how you can take the necessary steps to build a strong alliance and develop a sturdy rapport with African American clients during the first session. We'll explore areas of special sensitivity, barriers to rapport, focusing on the client's perspective, critical steps in building rapport, assessing rapport, and repairing ruptures.

AREAS THAT REQUIRE SPECIAL SENSITIVITY

Clearly, you as therapist play a vital role in building rapport, but there are many other factors that contribute to establishing a positive working alliance with African American clients that require special sensitivity. In the following sections I'll describe some specific "do's and don'ts" for building rapport.

Office Personnel and Procedures

The first contact a client has with a therapist is often not with the actual therapist. More typically, first contacts are with a receptionist or business manager. It doesn't matter how sensitive or culturally competent we are if our client's phone contact is insensitively handled by a culturally incompetent receptionist!

Many African American clients know that their style of speech identifies their racial and ethnic background. If they feel that the person answering the phone or greeting them at the office is rude or insensitive, they may associate us with that negative encounter.

Obviously counseling is a business, and information about insurance, fees, and payment must be secured by the office staff. Information relating to these issues needs to be discussed clearly and openly by the staff so that the client is fully informed of financial responsibilities. It is important that these matters are handled tactfully but in a straightforward way. Some of us may work in settings where insurance is widely used. Typically business managers may use the following comments or questions:

Do you have insurance?

Do you have a deductible, and has it been met for this year?

From my reading of your policy it looks like your responsibility for the first visit is . . . and for subsequent visits your copayment would be . . .

Do you have any questions about these financial arrangements?

Please sign this payment form, which details all the financial arrangements we have made. I will give you a copy for your records for you to refer to, and I'll be happy to answer any questions you may have now or in the future. My name and number are written right here. Your therapist will also be happy to answer any questions you may have.

Others of us may work in nonprofit settings and in community mental health centers, where payment is more likely to come from Medicaid and social service agencies. We also need to be prepared for situations in which clients are referred by other agencies. Here again, staff need to demonstrate cultural sensitivity and competence, but the questions are different. Our intake workers need to ask such questions as the following:

Do you receive any public assistance?

What is the name of your social worker?

Who is your probation officer?

Do you have Medicaid or any other type of insurance?

We need to be aware that because so many Blacks have suffered from generations of poverty and limited resources, they may have learned to feel that they're not justified in asking for services. In addition, some clients may have been treated in the past with rudeness and disrespect when they've revealed that they are on public assistance or can't pay out of pocket or with insurance. Black clients are no different than other clients in their right to receive and expect appropriate treatment with regard to financial matters. We need to insist that when staff members discuss financial issues with African American clients, they ensure privacy, they are respectful, and they allow ample time for discussion, questions, and clarifications. The following are some points to keep in mind as you handle financial transactions:

- The business manager should be respectful and patient with the client, as the process of coping with forms, insurance papers, referral issues, contacts with other agencies, and payments can be confusing and intimidating.

- The client should be informed of all financial expectations and any policies with respect to cancellations and late cancellations.

- A written copy of all financial arrangements, cancellation policies, emergency procedures, and office information should be provided to the client in a written form for subsequent review and clarification.

- The business manager needs to be sensitive to any cues that payment may be a problem and to take the initiative if necessary to discuss payment options, including a sliding scale if you use one.

Handling financial matters requires a great deal of tact and perceptiveness, because some African American clients may feel uncomfortable about the amount of payment but unwilling to raise this issue. If the payment issues appear unresolvable, or if the client gives any cues that he or she is not comfortable in prolonging the conversation, the business manager should consult with you for additional clarification, ideas, or resources.

Reception Area

As we discussed in Chapter One, many African American clients are very sensitive to nonverbal cues, ambience, and vibrations.

Upon entering your waiting room, they receive messages about your potential cultural competence. You need to ask yourself the following questions:

Does the artwork only depict European Americans?

Are there magazines, books, and toys that are oriented to African American culture?

What messages are conveyed by the musical selections or commercials that are audible via the sound system?

Is the overall atmosphere of the reception area welcoming or intimidating?

Are there personnel and signs readily available to greet the client and let the client know what to do upon arrival?

The bottom line is that we begin the process of building positive rapport by having office staff and office furnishings that reflect cultural sensitivity to African Americans. Having positive interactions with the office personnel and feeling welcomed and comfortable in the reception area can help Black clients develop a positive expectancy about the therapy process. It goes without saying that it would be reassuring for these clients to see a receptionist, business manager, or other clients in the waiting room who are also African American.

Qualifications and Competence

Certainly African American clients, like most consumers, want to work with therapists who are well qualified, competent, and professional. I have frequently noticed my clients observing diplomas, licenses, and certificates that are on display. Sometimes clients are reassured if they see a degree from a predominantly Black college or university. Not all clients use the same criteria when assessing the qualifications and competence of therapists.

Several years ago, I was treating a middle-aged African American female named Mrs. Garris. We decided that it would be useful to invite her husband to join us for a few sessions. Her husband was reluctant to participate and asked Mrs. Garris if I was a well-qualified therapist. I was very surprised to hear that she reassured her husband that I must be extremely competent because the clients whom I treated before and after her were always White!

I did not discuss this observation with Mr. and Mrs. Garris in their first joint session, as Mr. Garris was already hesitant about becoming involved in the therapy process. I was tempted to point out the internalized racism in the view that I was competent because White clients sought my services. But I restrained this interpretation because the first session is not typically the right time to raise a potentially sensitive issue without knowing more about the client's views and having a good rapport. I knew that I could follow up on Mrs. Garris's comment when she and I were in session without her husband.

Later on, Mrs. Garris and I actually had a productive discussion about her internalized racism. She explained that she wanted to have a Black therapist. But throughout most of her life she was taught that Whites were better than Blacks. According to Mrs. Garris, the fact that I was Black but still sought out by Whites made me ideal for her. It meant that she and I could relate to one another but also that I had to be well qualified in order to have a White clientele. Eventually we made some progress in helping Mrs. Garris think more broadly about competence and about how she had learned to be prejudiced against members of her own race.

Interpersonal Contact

African American clients value interpersonal contact. We enhance positive rapport when we spend a few minutes of "warm-up" time with our clients. Either the client or the therapist may make a brief comment on the weather, clothes or appearance, or the decor. It's not wise to attribute such comments to resistance. African American clients are interested in our ability to generate comfortable con-versation, even when we are not talking "business." It can also be considered in poor taste to bypass a short period of conversation before the formal session.

Very often therapists are trained to be "neutral" or like a "blank slate." But when they assume this stance, they miss the point that therapy is an interpersonal encounter. A therapist's refusal to inter-act in a few pleasantries can make Black clients feel uncomfortable and distanced. We must also understand that African American clients feel quite comfortable making the intake a mutual process of questions and answers. So as we ask clients where they're from originally, we may get the same question from them. These clients are really trying to determine if there is anything in our backgrounds that may make it easier for them to relate to us. When a Black client asks us a question during this initial period, I think it's impor-tant for us to answer the question unless we believe that to do so creates a problem in the therapy. So it is appropriate to respond to questions about where we grew up, our racial or ethnic background, whether we served in the military, whether we have children, or the like. Clearly we need to keep the focus more on the client than on us if we get questions about our sexual experiences or orientation, whether we've had problems with addiction, or whether we have had personal experiences with the same trauma or problem the client has. We can simply say that we prefer not responding to a particular question because we think that in our work together we want to focus on the issues and concerns of the client.

I make it a point to ask clients if there is anything I am doing that they don't understand. I also say to them, "I am going to try to explain what I'll be doing in our sessions and why. If you tell me something and I don't understand, I'll ask you to explain. I certainly want you to feel equally comfortable raising questions or asking me for clarifications. We're both going to need to be involved in this process of listening, questioning, and making sense out of what we hear. Is that OK with you?"

Therapist Presentation

How we present ourselves can have a significant impact on developing rapport. Clients can be intimidated by what they perceive to be a glaring mismatch in socioeconomic status. If we wear conspicuously expensive jewelry and clothing, clients might feel intimidated. It is also a turnoff if we overuse esoteric phrases or the jargon of therapy.

Several years ago I worked with Mr. Stanley, a middle-aged Black male who sought services after a disappointing experience with a White therapist. Mr. Stanley reported that he was turned off by his first and only session with his therapist because she never answered any of his questions. Instead, in typical Rogerian fashion his former therapist was fond of using such phrases as "It sounds like you're saying . . .," or "I feel like what you really want to know is . . ." Mr. Stanley still showed some signs of irritation as he recounted to me, "I knew what *I* was saying, but I never found out what *she* thought!"

As soon as it is comfortable in the first session, you should start out with a check to make sure that the client is ready to proceed. I typically ask the following questions:

Were there any problems with what I said?

Do you understand all the financial arrangements?

Are there any questions I can help with?

Were there any issues that came up with any of my staff members that I can help with?

These questions give me the opportunity to troubleshoot and to extinguish any early areas of discontent. Next I explain, "We'll spend about the next fifty minutes together so that I can get a better sense of what made you decide to come see me now." I find it important to establish the expectation that our session is for fifty minutes and not an hour so that clients don't feel that I've cheated them of ten minutes they have paid for.

I explain to clients that "I'll be asking some questions, and by the end of the session, I'll indicate if I feel I can assist with your concerns. If it makes sense for us to work together, I'll try to give you an idea of some strategies that I think we can try and a rough idea of how long I think we'll need. If you or I don't feel that I'm the right person for you, I'll be happy to provide you with some referral information."

I think a significant component of our interpersonal relationship with each client involves the issues of confidentiality and informed consent. I tell my clients that what they talk about is held in confidence. I tell them that the only exception is in situations when they are endangering themselves or others. It's especially important that we clarify issues of confidentiality when treating a couple and individual family members. Adult clients worry if we'll divulge personal information to their partners, and children and adolescents worry if we'll tell their parents what they have told us. We have to be clear in letting our clients know that we'll respect their confidentiality.

If we work in a community mental health center or inpatient facility or if we are involved in training activities, we need to let our clients know that there may be a variety of professionals who work with them and who share information about their treatment.

Because the world of African Americans is small, one of the issues I have to confront with clients is that I may see them in social, business, and recreational settings. I explain that I will let them initiate any contact and that I certainly won't reveal our professional relationship. This issue of confidentiality can even extend to the scheduling of appointments. I have received referrals from clients who ask for appointments that avoid their being seen by people whom they know.

In talking about informed consent, I focus on the fact that any sharing of information with other professionals requires the client's written consent. I explain to clients that I also will keep them appraised of the general information I share with any other professionals or agencies with which they are working. I find that addressing these issues early on can help the client see me as ethical and responsible.

BARRIERS TO RAPPORT

Rapport can't develop when a client suspects that the therapist harbors biases, stereotypes, and prejudices. In some cases, therapists have been surprised to learn that even "good" stereotypes don't work.

I remember Ruth, a graduate student I knew from our training program. I served as her academic adviser, and she had taken a class from me, so when she felt that she wanted to do some personal therapy, she asked me to recommend someone. I gave Ruth the list of community therapists who were willing to work with doctoral students because these therapists were not affiliated with the program. Ruth decided that she would have to work with a White therapist, because she worked with just about all the Black therapists in our area through her participation in a variety of professional, social, and civic groups.

After her first session, Ruth came to me in tears saying that she could no longer work with Dr. Miller, a White therapist whom she selected from the list. Ruth explained that she originally decided to see Dr. Miller because he had a reputation for being very knowledgeable about working with African American clients.

I was shocked to hear Ruth report that in her first session with Dr. Miller, he made such comments as "I know how strong you Black females are as compared to your men," and "Have you ever thought about singing to minimize your depression? I know that lovely voices run in your race."

Ruth was justifiably hurt by these comments. I was surprised that someone who I had heard was sensitive to multicultural issues apparently didn't get it. Although well intentioned, Dr. Miller failed to realize that there is no such thing as a positive stereotype. By trying to encourage Ruth, he fit her into a preexisting stereotype of Black women. He was not listening to her tell him who she was and what her individual concerns, strengths, and weaknesses were.

Ruth wanted to continue in therapy, but she didn't know what to do. She asked, "Am I supposed to educate Dr. Miller about Black people so that he can help me?" I told her unequivocally that it was not her responsibility to use her time, money, and therapy hour to educate her therapist. She then asked if there really were any other therapists available who could relate to her, or "Will they all be like Dr. Miller?" I told her that I was confident that there were culturally competent therapists in our area; we were able to get another referral for her with a White therapist who worked out well for Ruth.

PSEUDO-RAPPORT

Like other clients, African Americans expect their therapists to be professional. A therapist who doesn't look or sound professional or who tries too hard to be warm and friendly turns clients off. Conversely, it is difficult to develop rapport with a therapist who radiates an inability to be at ease. Therapists who try to accelerate rapport by appearing liberal or condescending, using Black English or Ebonics or by telling the latest African American joke will quickly discover that these behaviors are not appreciated.

I continue to be amazed by clients' stories about how some therapists try to hasten rapport by saying, "I understand Black people because I am . . .

From the ghetto or the "hood" too

Gay, lesbian, or bisexual

Jewish

A woman

An immigrant

Physically challenged

From a trailer park

A White South African

. . . and therefore I understand oppression too." It's a turnoff for Black clients to have someone parallel the experience of being African American to other types of oppression. Although facing one type of discrimination or oppression may make a therapist more sensitive to understanding these phenomena in general, it may not lead the therapist to be particularly knowledgeable or sensitive in understanding the unique experiences of the African American client in the therapy room. It's demeaning and insensitive to assume that oppressions are parallel and interchangeable.

FOCUSING ON THE CLIENT'S PERSPECTIVE

Every individual has unique values, perspectives, and experiences that shape every aspect of his or her being. As therapists, we must be able to suspend our own perspectives if we are to be successful in fully understanding African American clients. Listening from the client's perspective can be difficult when our closely held values are challenged.

At a conference on feminist therapy that I attended, several White female therapists were discussing their use of feminist therapy principles with African American women. The African American therapists in the group pointed out that it is unethical for us to try to get our clients to buy into our value systems, no matter how well intentioned our motivation. When a client seeks treatment because of domestic violence, it is not our right to orient the client to a feminist analysis of violence in this country. It is more important that we understand why she is making the decisions that she does and find ways to join with her as we help her problem-solve and protect herself and her family.

Black clients come to us with their own set of unique experiences, values, and perspectives. When a client is different from us on any demographic dimension, we sometimes compensate by either exaggerating or minimizing our areas of similarity or difference. I have heard some therapists say, "I have nothing in common with this client." Chances are, this is not true. I have also heard of therapists who try too hard to find an area of similarity with a client that does not lead to any real bonding.

For instance, Roberta is a friend of mine who was in therapy with a White female from her hometown in North Carolina. Roberta shared with me that the irony to her was that the therapist seemed to feel that their relationship would develop faster because they had this tie. Roberta actually felt a combination of distrust for and distance from her therapist, because although they lived in the same town and attended the same schools, their paths had not crossed. The experience of growing up Black subjected Roberta to a whole array of negative experiences about which her White therapist did not seem to have a clue.

What probably would have worked in this therapy interaction would have been for the therapist to ask Roberta, "What was it like for you to grow up in this town? I suspect growing up here as a Black female was different from my experience as a White female."

Discussing Difference

Cultural differences can make therapists feel insecure and defensive. In addition to cultural and racial differences, African American clients also show normal signs of resistance and discomfort in the therapy process. Therapists must negotiate the challenge of discriminating between normal signs of resistance and difficulties that are related to race and culture. Not every sign of resistance with a Black client is due to there being a demographic difference between therapist and client. The following are some possible signs of difference you may observe that may be due to cultural factors:

- High or low levels of animation

- Less frequent eye contact

- Discomfort in sharing negative affect and problems

- Difficulty in linking negative behaviors and attitudes with loved ones (for example, saying something negative about a mother)

- High commitment to protocol and etiquette

The following behaviors suggest normal resistance that is typically unrelated to racial and cultural dynamics; note these behaviors and, when appropriate, explore them with the client:

- A change in the client's level of involvement

- Refusal to make eye contact

- Withdrawn or defensive body language

- Minimal responses to questions

- Avoidance of certain topics

- Guarded facial expressions

- Stuttering or lack of fluency

- Silence

- Fidgeting

- Confusion

You need to be secure in the process and in your skills so that you can assess when a client's behavior is a sign of a racial or cultural misunderstanding and when it is not.

There are many subjects that are difficult to talk about, such as racial, sexual, cultural, financial, and socioeconomic issues. In addition, some therapists are simply not comfortable working with African American clients. For these therapists, it will be particularly challenging to talk about potentially sensitive topics, and the tendency may be to avoid these topics.

For instance, if a client is discussing a problem and the therapist wonders if there are any racial, ethnic, sexual, or gender overtones, it is appropriate for the therapist simply to ask if these issues are involved. The following are comments that I have used:

> "Marcus, are you saying that you think racial issues are related to your not getting the part in the school play?"

> "Mrs. Lucas, do you feel that this treatment is because you're one of the few females your company has employed?"

> "Ms. Reed, do you feel that this happened because people suspect that you're a lesbian?"

Dealing with Racially Sensitive Issues

Clearly it is difficult to talk about sensitive issues with any client. But these discussions have special meaning for Black clients because when they face a difficult situation, they have to sort out whether or not racial issues are involved. Sometimes our role involves helping facilitate a discussion of the role of racial dynamics. Our ability to bring up racial, cultural, and ethnic issues in a calm and matter-of-fact manner can help the African American client feel a stronger rapport with us.

We would be wise to heed the warning that when we are not comfortable with someone from a different cultural background, we can make two types of errors: (1) assuming sameness or (2) assuming difference. In many ways our training as therapists has taught us to assume sameness; we have been trained that people and families all follow universal rules.

For example, in European American families, the immediate nuclear family has primacy. But in African American families, the extended family is often just as important as the nuclear family. I have had many experiences of working with graduate students in supervision who feel that the African American families they work with are pathological. They reach this conclusion because Black families don't function the same way as White families. My students ask, "I can't believe how often the grandparents visit and share in the family decision making when there are major issues at stake. Clearly, I'm going to have to work with the mother and father and support them in telling the parents to stop this enmeshed behavior."

I then discuss with these students whether we're talking about a case in which this Black father and mother need help in being more assertive or whether they actually value and appreciate this parental input even though it makes decision making more complex. Given the diversity of African American families, in some cases it is appropriate to support the mother and father in asking for some space from parents or in-laws.

In contrast, we can also err by deciding that behaviors we are concerned about are just different from our culture but are acceptable for African American culture.

I witnessed this manifestation of assuming difference when I was supervising Don, a White graduate student. He was working with a young African American couple who were spanking their three-year-old son several times a day. I asked Don, "Have you explored other methods of discipline with these parents?" He replied, "No, because from what I learned in a multicultural class on families, I know that African American parents, unlike White parents, prefer spanking to other forms of discipline."

Don believed that he was demonstrating cultural sensitivity in his therapy and in his explanation. I saw him making the mistake of buying into "assumptions of difference." Although it is true that there was historically a tradition of spanking in the African American community, Don had decided that Black parents were so different from White parents that it wouldn't make sense to explore other discipline options.

During supervision I talked about the heterogeneity of parenting styles in the African American community. Don and I agreed that he could explore other disciplinary strategies with this couple in a way that was respectful and did not involve him imposing his values on the clients. We role-played some of the comments that Don could use:

- Mr. and Mrs. Clark, have you tried any other discipline?

- Have you tried time-outs, rewards, or punishment?

- What happened when you tried a different technique?

- Did you feel that any other techniques worked?

- It must be frustrating to have to discipline your son so many times each day!

- Let's see if we can figure out a way to get your son's behavior under control so that the three of you can have more positive time together.

Don was able to have a productive discussion about including other discipline techniques besides spanking, and the parents actually thanked him for helping them expand their repertoire of alternatives.

Dealing with Sexually Sensitive Issues

It can be hard for therapists to discuss sexual issues with Black clients because our society is rife with innuendo and stereotypes about the sex lives of African Americans. It also must be acknowledged that many Black men feel they have been so denigrated by society that they are ambivalent about *not* trying to fulfill the hype about their sexual prowess.

As I said earlier, even positive stereotypes are negative. We do a disservice to African American males when we back away from relevant discussions of sex or when we communicate that we view Black men as hypersexual. Trying to live up to all of society's sexual stereotypes for Black men has to be an exhausting process. In addition, viewing Black men as hypersexual does not allow us to see the complexity of Black males, their caring, humor, vulnerability, and resiliency, and their dedication to their important roles as family members, providers, and participants in the community.

So how do we bring up these subjects? These topics are delicate whether the therapist is African American or not. If we are working with a gay client who states that he likes to date other men although he is in a committed relationship, we need to ask him to tell us about why he feels this need. If I am working with a couple and I suspect from what they are saying that sexual issues are a problem, I have to be able to say, "Can you tell me what is happening to you two with regard to sex?" If this is met with silence, I can ask them individually if they are happy with the quantity and quality of their sexual experiences with each other.

In a similar fashion, African American women are also sensitive to how they have been portrayed sexually in our society. The life circumstances of most African American women are very different from other females. Black women have been criticized for showing the strength that helped foster the survival of the race. Because they are deemed as more assertive than White females, they have been stereotyped as too controlling and not "appropriately" submissive and deferential to men. The fact that African Americans were targeted for rape by white men has been distorted and used to project these women as somehow responsible for their violation. They have been portrayed in society as loose, immoral, and promiscuous to focus attention away from the sexual abuse they endured.

The widespread stereotyping of Black women has led many of them to feel very sensitive about issues of teenage parenting, female-headed homes, and not being married or in a relationship. It is therefore inappropriate and potentially damaging for therapists to compare African American women to White women or to somehow intimate that African American women are inferior or less moral because of some of the decisions or life circumstances they have faced.

Dealing with Financial, Socioeconomic, and Demographic Issues

Financial, socioeconomic, and demographic issues can also be challenging topics. We need to be vigilant about noting if these areas seem to be sensitive for the client. If there are problems in any of these areas, they must be explored and resolved.

I have had situations arise in which I feel that the first session of therapy went well, but the client declines a second session. I ask, "Do you feel comfortable continuing our work together?" If the nonverbal cues are positive but I also sense reluctance, I simply ask, "Are finances a problem?" Sometimes it takes getting to the end of the first session and establishing a positive rapport before the client can acknowledge economic pressures. In some of my work in mental health centers, we discuss a sliding scale of payment by my asking, "What do you feel you can afford to pay?" If necessary, I explain what the lowest allowable fee is, and we figure out if there is some way we can make the therapy arrangement work.

If the client indicates that he or she is unsure of our ability to relate based on some area of demographic or socioeconomic difference, we should discuss it. It's important to let clients express their feelings about areas of difference rather than derail the conversation because of our feelings of insecurity or discomfort.

For example, I worked several years ago in a local mental health center with Mr. Ferguson, who was a retired longshoreman. He had not completed his high school education. He said to me, "I'm not sure if I'm the type of person to be in therapy because I don't talk fancy like you." Although we shared racial similarity, Mr. Ferguson was aware of the disparity between us, and it made him uncomfortable.

After clients express their views, we need to get the sense of whether there have been some actual miscommunications or if the client is simply concerned about possible problems. I asked Mr. Ferguson if he thought I understood him. When he indicated assent, I asked him if he understood me. He responded in the affirmative. If we receive some assurance that there has been good communication and understanding so far, it makes sense to ask the client to continue in the same vein, with both parties being vigilant about preventing communication problems. If the client does not feel understood, we need to engage in dialogue with the client as to where the breakdowns have occurred to determine if it is possible to repair these ruptures. We will talk about this process later in this chapter.

When a discussion on differences unfolds, it is important for us to be sensitive to the client's discomfort with any of the obvious differences that may exist between the client and us. Taking the cue from the client's comments or nonverbal behaviors, it is certainly legitimate for us to say, "How does it feel for you to work with a therapist who is [White, female, male, African American, or whatever the case may be]?" In some cases, we may have done a good job of building rapport, but the client might say, "I just think that I would be more comfortable with an African American therapist or a female therapist." When this occurs, respect this view and, if necessary, discuss referring the client.

In many cases with which I'm familiar, African American clients can be somewhat cautious and may say something like, "Well, so far you're OK, but this is only the first session." In this case, I would simply explain to the client that I would continue to be sensitive to our areas of difference and ask for assistance in keeping our communication clear and open. I usually try to say something along these lines: "It's important to me that I clearly understand you and that you understand me. Please stop me if I say anything you want to ask me about, and I'll do the same with you. I especially need you to let me know if I say something that upsets you or that you think is off base."

Therapist's Ability to Understand

Another area that can be a barrier to rapport is that most often clients seek services from us when they are at the end of their rope. Clients can sense the incongruity of the crises in their lives and the professionally calm demeanor that we as therapists exude. I've had clients of all races ask me, "Can you really relate to how messed up my life is right now? You look like you have it all together."

When I get this question from a client of color, the inquiry is more intense because it signals a deeper question along the lines of "How Black are you really? Have you really struggled as hard as I have, or did things somehow come easier for you for whatever reason?" I fielded this question several times when I first started working in a community mental health center. I conducted intake and therapy sessions with African American clients who were typically facing problems in multiple areas of their lives. In my first session with Ms. Lattimore, she asked me, "How can someone like you help me? I have five children, no husband, I'm on welfare, and I'm a recovering addict. What can you do to help me?" I responded to Ms. Lattimore that she was right, that probably a lot of my experiences had been different from hers. But I was also able to say, "Although my experiences have been different, I think that my training and my clinical and life experiences will allow me to relate to your difficulties and work with you to see if we can make some improvements in the areas that you want to change." I assured her that if she felt that I couldn't help her, I would work to find a therapist who she felt could be of more assistance.

I think that all we can do with this question of relating to client concerns is let our clients know that yes, we do have our own struggles, and yes, we'll try to understand their unique situations and feelings. Beyond giving an answer along the lines I have suggested here, we simply must back up our claims that we understand our clients by doing so. The real proof is in building rapport with our clients.

CRITICAL STEPS IN BUILDING RAPPORT

First and foremost, we build rapport with our clients by being genuine, personal, and approachable. Good rapport is based on listening, empathy, and respect for all individuals across race and all areas of difference. We can promote positive rapport by demonstrating attentiveness, responsiveness, and good listening skills, all in the context of culturally competent practice.

Forms of Address

One thing to be especially sensitive to with African American clients is how we address them. I recommend that until the client suggests otherwise you use a formal designation, such as Miss, Mrs., Ms., Mr., or Dr., followed by his or her last name. African Americans have had a long history of being spoken to with disrespect by being referred to as "boy" or "girl" or addressed by our first names. Although our society has adopted more informality in the use of first names, many African American clients will expect to refer to their therapist using a professional designation, and we need to reciprocate.

As a rapport develops and the relationship warrants, either we or the client may ask if it would be acceptable to move to a first-name basis. Even with college-age individuals, I make it a rule to get permission to use their first name before doing so. According my clients this type of respect sends a signal that we have a professional relationship in which I will convey respect and an appreciation of appropriate boundaries in our relationship.

My use of surnames and formal titles surprises most of my White colleagues and students. I have found that they are much quicker to initiate the use of first names for themselves and their clients. Certainly, some African American clients are comfortable with first names at an early stage of the relationship. I still feel that it is better to err on the side of caution. It is easier to move from a formal address to an informal address than it is to repair a possible rupture to the rapport by presumptively using a first name.

Self-Disclosure

Self-disclosure represents a double-edged sword in establishing rapport. If we use it effectively, it can facilitate bonding. In contrast, if we use it artificially, insensitively, or prematurely, it can be a turnoff for clients. For the most part, I have found many African American clients to be responsive to appropriate self-disclosure. In fact, as I've mentioned earlier, in some cases they actually request specific information. For these clients, our self-disclosure reassures them that we've been there and that we can understand, relate, and help. Some self-disclosure that is helpful involves low-key statements like these:

> "I know how hard it is to get around after a broken leg."
>
> "Yes, I'm familiar with that part of the country. I have friends in that area."
>
> "I know how hard being a military family is, since my dad was in the navy."
>
> "Yes, I do belong to a sorority, but [smile] it's not the same one you belong to."
>
> "I know what it's like to raise adolescents, because I survived that stage. My kids are now grown."
>
> "No, my partner and I do not have children."
>
> "No, I've not been married."
>
> "Yes, I know how hard it can be to go through a divorce."

Self-disclosure doesn't work with African American clients when they sense it is gratuitous or unrelated to their issues.

Edna, a sixty-three-year-old African American colleague of mine, went to therapy to deal with some grief issues related to the death of her mother.

The therapist with whom she was working was White and in her mid-thirties. I asked Edna how therapy was going. She said, "Well, it's going all right now, but I had to get that therapist straight."

"What do you mean?" I asked.

Edna responded, "That Miss Jones tried to tell me that she understood what I was going through because she lost her mother when she was in her twenties. I had to tell her that's not like my situation at all. I had my mother for more than sixty years. The hurt I'm carrying around isn't the same that a young person feels."

In this case Miss Jones was trying to use self-disclosure to bond and offer support to Edna. Unfortunately, Edna felt that their circumstances were very different. She felt that her therapist's comments minimized and distorted what she was feeling and going through. Fortunately, Edna was able to point this out to her therapist. Miss Jones then realized that her self-disclosure in this instance was not helpful.

Nonverbal Behaviors

One of the best ways for us to assess the progress we are making in developing rapport is to monitor the exchange of nonverbal behaviors. We must acknowledge that many Black clients won't be able to bring up their discomfort in direct verbal ways, particularly if they feel incongruent with the therapist racially, in terms of ability to express thoughts orally, or in terms of socioeconomic status. We need to be aware of whether or not we are maintaining appropriate eye contact, focus, and emotional pacing with our clients. Is there reciprocity in terms of body movement, facial expressions, and verbalizations? We'll have clients who vary from the very active and excitable to those who talk to us in a reserved and laid-back manner. We have to find ways of responding that let clients know that we're with them, that we're focused on what they're saying, and that we understand, in ways that enhance our relationship with them.

Inviting Active Participation

In my orientation comments I usually include the invitation for clients to ask questions, raise concerns, disagree, and get clarifications. I explain, "We'll be able to do our best work together when we have clear and open communication. I'll have some ideas about what you tell me, but I'll need feedback from you to let me know if I am on target with any of my comments or observations." I then make sure I leave openings or make openings for questions and comments from clients.

Typically, this is when I might get a question from a teenager who wants to know if I will tell her mother and father everything that she says to me. This gives me an opportunity to revisit the issue of confidentiality. I also sometimes have an individual who is concerned about relationship issues but whose partner is unwilling to come for therapy. I use this inquiry to discuss that although it's ideal to have both individuals in therapy together, there's still work that we can do together while we encourage the partner to participate in therapy.

Use of Metaphors and Media

In recent years we have seen a growth of movies, books, and television programs that feature African Americans as central characters. As a result, I have begun to make reference to characters from literature or the media as a way to better understand an emotion that my client may be expressing.

For example, when the movie and book *Waiting to Exhale* were popular, several of my African American clients volunteered that they could identify very specifically with one of the characters or situations that were depicted. The use of these examples led to some very productive discussion more quickly and at a deeper level than we might have been able to reach ordinarily.

I also quote famous African American politicians, public figures, or such comedians as Bill Cosby, Eddie Murphy, or Sinbad. Using the comments and one-liners of these famous Black people can help develop rapport between me and the client. At the same time, it helps me gain insight into some of the thoughts and feelings of my clients. Just as important, my clients begin to see me as someone who shares their appreciation of Black cultural expressions and traditions. This technique can be especially useful for White therapists because it demonstrates their familiarity with African American culture in a comfortable and nonthreatening exchange. Again, therapists need to ensure that the use of cultural expressions is genuine and timely. A clumsy reference to foster quick rapport would be a turnoff.

ASSESSING RAPPORT

Therapists must monitor the interaction with their clients to make sure that they are in sync with one another. African Americans have to rely on their well-honed abilities to read character from nonverbal cues. Sometimes these skills were necessary during periods of acute danger; more routinely these talents were used to be aware of underlying bias or prejudice. As a result, African Americans often read others while at the same time hiding their true feelings. Just because an African American client is compliant and responsive in an interview does not mean that we have achieved rapport. African Americans have had hundreds of years of practice in dissembling feelings and pretending to "play the game," especially with White professionals in positions of authority.

So how can you tell if you are developing a true rapport with your client? Clients who demonstrate the following behaviors are showing signs of positive rapport:

- Comfortable body language

- Spontaneous facial expressions

- Willingness to share personal information at a deeper level as the session progresses

- Range of emotional expression, such as tears, laughter, anger, or disagreement

- Match between their speech and affect

- Active engagement and involvement in the process of speaking, asking questions, and making sense of the workings of therapy

- A shared responsibility for the success of therapy

- Genuineness, honesty, and ability to be straightforward

- Easy flow of communication and give-and-take

- Increasing ability and confidence to talk about differences and difficult subjects

- Willingness to look at themselves and others in new ways

REPAIRING RUPTURES

As we strive to develop a strong therapeutic alliance with African American clients, we must be pragmatic and acknowledge that sometimes we say or do something in our work that actually hinders the development of rapport or even rips a budding rapport to shreds.

I knew I was in trouble several years ago when I was having a first session with Mrs. Belton, a medium-built, brown-skinned woman. Before I could do my usual orientation to therapy, she jumped right in and said that she was concerned about discriminatory treatment at work.

Mrs. Belton was a janitor for the school system and felt that although she worked hard, she was being overlooked for promotion and pay raises. I said to her, "Well, that sometimes happens to African Americans." She pulled herself up to her full sitting height and announced that she was not African American—she was from Panama. It was clear to me that she was insulted by my thinking that she was African American.

I immediately apologized for my mistake and told Mrs. Belton that I recognized that there were major cultural differences between individuals from Panama and African Americans in this country. I then asked her if she could fill me in on some of her background so I could better understand her experiences and perspectives.

This experience taught me to be very careful in my use of racial terms. I now sometimes use a less loaded term like "a person of color," as it's impossible for us to know the racial and cultural background of our clients by simply looking at them.

Despite our training and good intentions, we all sometimes make mistakes. It is impossible for us to be aware of all the different issues to which a particular client may be sensitive, and we may offend a client without meaning to. If we are being vigilant in processing the verbal and nonverbal behavior of our clients, we should be able to detect that something is out of synchronization pretty quickly. If we suspect a problem, we must address it immediately. We can use the client's reactions as a basis for raising our concern that perhaps we have miscommunicated or said something offensive.

The following are some therapist behaviors that can lead to ruptures in the rapport:

- Not understanding the significance of material that the client has shared

- Missing client signals

- Saying something insensitive

- Being unable to support or confront when necessary

- Becoming too informal too quickly

- Violating the client's sense of timing by being intrusive

- Conveying boredom or disinterest through body language

- Demonstrating inappropriate affect

- Making administrative errors, such as being late, rescheduling, billing improperly, or double-booking appointments

- Making assumptions

- Failing to demonstrate active listening skills

When there has been a rupture, we want to enlist the client's support in clarifying our error, to hear the client's thoughts and feelings in response to what we said or did, and to receive permission to apologize and, ideally, repair the rupture.

Strategies we can use to repair ruptures include the following:

- Apologizing

- Explaining our error if appropriate

- Rectifying our mistake by getting further clarification

- Ensuring that we don't make the same mistake twice

- Modeling good communication and problem-solving skills

Our best defense in handling ruptures to rapport is the good offense. Our most effective offense is to be respectful and culturally competent. If we can convey that we have spent time and energy learning about the lives of African Americans, many of our clients will give us some leeway to learn about their unique needs, interests, and sensitivities.

———————

Developing rapport and a strong therapeutic alliance is at the heart of conducting a successful first session with African American clients. In the next chapter we look at how we will build on our relationship with our clients as we focus on how to conduct effective assessments and evaluations in the first session.

4

Assessment and Evaluation

The assessment process involves both an art and a science. The science of assessment is enhanced when we as therapists address the unique needs of African American clients. We can't simply apply majority culture perspectives to Black clients. We must recognize the roles of societal forces in shaping the difficulties that African Americans face.

But knowing some of the facts and figures about working with Black clients is not enough. We also must become proficient at the art of assessment with Black clients. We must learn to use ourselves as instruments to understand behaviors, verbalizations, and patterns that we can use to formulate and test hypotheses. Clients often present material to us in a piecemeal fashion, and it's our job to integrate the information they give us into a coherent whole. For us to appropriately process information during a first session, we must look for patterns but not rely on stereotypes and biases.

Although the assessment component is critical to the first session, many African American clients are especially fearful and uncomfortable about cooperating in this process. In the past, assessments have often been used to label Blacks as crazy, retarded, incompetent, ineligible for jobs or gifted educational placements, unfit as parents, or in need of interventions from the criminal justice system.

This chapter gives you information that will help you conduct efficient, useful, and valid assessments of your Black clients. We'll talk about using both the art and the science of assessment to establish a climate of trust, develop psychosocial histories, assess risk, conduct mental status examinations, and arrive at a global assessment of functioning and diagnosis in order to plan for treatment or other options, such as additional evaluations and referrals.

ESTABLISHING A CLIMATE OF TRUST

All clients need to be treated with sensitivity and respect, and we've talked throughout this book about how vital it is to develop a strong rapport and good communication with our African American clients. In this section we'll discuss what we can do to establish trust with Black clients as we conduct assessments in the first session. We'll highlight

- The rationale for assessment

- Rights and record keeping

- Biases and stereotypes

- Cultural competence

The Rationale for Assessment

We can foster trust in our African American clients and facilitate the assessment process by explaining why we need assessment data. Our Black clients are more likely to be responsive to our questions when we tell them something like this: "The questions I'm going to ask you will help me understand what's going on in your life now. I'm going to try to learn what other problems you're facing and what you see as your strengths and weaknesses. I want to hear your impressions of stress you've gone through recently. I also want to gain an appreciation of what have been important issues in your background as well as information about your family. As I listen to the material you give me, it will help me better understand the nature of your current difficulties, which will assist me in developing a comprehensive treatment for you."

Black clients will typically be more accepting of the intrusive nature of assessment questions if they understand why we're asking these questions and how we plan to use the information. It's also important to explain to clients that we will not be asking them any "trick questions."

Many Black clients believe that the real purpose of an assessment is to gain access to information they don't want us to have. Clients are often on guard and suspicious that our queries are designed to look innocent but actually have a deeper meaning and will be used in harmful ways.

Many of the questions about the psychosocial history are fairly straightforward, but when we move to the mental status exam, clients sense that these questions are different, and they may become anxious. It's important that we explain to clients at this point of the session, "I am not concerned about your trying to get these questions right or wrong. What I'm going to be interested in is how you respond to these questions so that I'll be able to gain a clearer idea of what strategies you and I can use to work together."

Client Rights

Although we talk about issues of confidentiality and informed consent at the start of the session, African American clients may raise these issues again as we begin the assessment process. It's therefore useful for us to take the initiative and review these issues as the questions become more personal.

We must address whatever working arrangements we have made so far. If social services, the criminal justice system, or an employer has referred a client to us, we need to acknowledge to our clients that we'll be providing these referral sources with some type of report based on our work together. We have an ethical responsibility to let our clients know the limits of their confidentiality with us.

Increasing numbers of clients are more frequently raising questions about whether or not their employers will have access to information about their visit with us. Even if our clients are not directly referred by their supervisors, we must inform them of possible disclosure if they are using third-party payment options, be it insurance or funding from a public agency.

We need to advise clients that it's possible that information about their diagnoses and number of treatments as well as their progress may be made available to their employers or referral sources. Although this information may have been discussed at the beginning of the session when clients signed payment forms, it warrants repeating. Clients must be fully informed of how information we collect may be used by others so that they can make an informed decision about what they want to reveal.

It's also vitally important that we let clients know that they're unlikely to shock us with what they may say. We need to convey that we've worked with a wide variety of clients (if this is the case), including individuals who faced issues similar to theirs. We are therefore optimistic that we will be open to hearing whatever they choose to share that will enable us to develop an effective treatment plan.

African American clients may also ask us about our process of note taking or show nonverbally that they're concerned about what we are writing. We must let our clients know that we maintain a written record of our session for several reasons. First, it allows us to document and keep track of important events in their lives for our review. Second, we're sometimes in situations where we depend on these notes to forward to third-party sources. We can explain that in some cases our actual notes are requested for review; in other cases, we use our notes as a basis for a report.

I make a point of ensuring that my note taking does not interfere with my ability to maintain eye contact. As clients see that I'm attending closely to what they say and only occasionally jotting down notes, they often relax.

In some cases it can actually be therapeutic to engage in note taking with Black clients. If we come to a point in the discussion when clients are struggling with some difficult emotions or material, taking the focus off of them for a few seconds to write gives them some space and time to regroup.

Biases and Stereotypes

Although we'll look closely at countertransference issues in Chapter Seven, it's important to stress that our attitude can play a major role in how the assessment process unfolds. Clinicians can set up negative reactions to clients if they convey that they think their African American clients are

- Pathological

- Dangerous, hostile, defensive, sensitive, or paranoid

- Beyond their ability to help

- Unlikable

- Untrustworthy

We also need to realize that therapists can show positive biases toward African American clients and still do harm in the assessment process. Expressions of these positive biases include the following:

- Avoiding appropriate interpretations and confrontations

- Minimizing difficulties or problem behaviors

- Demonstrating inauthentic positive regard

- Making excuses for the client due to race, gender, class, or other demographic factors

- Talking down to the client, making jokes, or oversimplifying complex issues in order to foster rapport

We've talked about the fact that Black clients are often very attuned to nonverbal behaviors. It's likely that African American clients will pick up on therapists' negative emotions or a display of overly positive attitudes or behaviors. In the latter case, Black clients will conclude that the therapist is trying too hard and is not being honest, genuine, or sincere.

Black clients do not expect to become "best friends" with us in the first session. They expect to be treated with professionalism, respect, and honesty. If Black clients sense strong positive or negative emotions from us during assessment, we no longer have a valid record of the client's behavior. We can't rule out that anything a client says or does is in response to our underlying attitude.

Cultural Competence

Although Chapter Seven discusses self-awareness and cultural competence in detail, we need to especially be aware of the importance of cultural competence in doing assessments with Black clients. We must constantly maintain an awareness of what we're feeling and what our clients are pulling from us with respect to emotions or behavior. The more experience and practice we have in working with Black clients and in using ourselves as an assessment tool, the more skillful and accurate we'll become in making sense of what is occurring.

We'll sense when we need to ask, clarify, support, or shut up. We become more adept at using both minimal verbalizations and subtle and specific nonverbal behaviors. Perhaps most important, we'll learn the language of the client in the room with us. We'll understand what special meanings the client ascribes to words and behaviors. We'll be able to convey that we understand by our eye contact, nods, and body language. We'll demonstrate that we're in sync with our clients.

PSYCHOSOCIAL HISTORIES

Collecting information for the psychosocial history is a major element of the assessment process. As our clients tell us about their lives, we're better able to put their current problems into an appropriate context. Although we usually don't have time in the first session to do a comprehensive psychosocial history, we need to collect some information in the following areas:

- Demographic indicators and issues of self-esteem and identity

- Family-of-origin history

- Socioeconomic status

- Developmental history

- Significant relationships

- Health and physical status

- Psychosocial stressors

Demographic Indicators, Self-Esteem, and Identity

It's important for us to ask Black clients about their ethnic background or race. How a client views himself or herself is just as significant as how others may classify him or her. We want to be sensitive to whether our clients identify as Black, African American, multiracial, or some other designation. Usually the way we gain this information is by asking questions about where they are from and where their parents are from.

I sometimes say something like, "Are most of your relatives from that part of Florida?" We may think that our client's racial background is obvious, but in fact, many clients who we think look Black are actually of Latin, Caribbean, Indian, or multiracial descent. The only way we can find out how they identify is by asking them about their background and how they view themselves with respect to racial and cultural identity.

As we process how clients view themselves, we need also to be sensitive to whether our client looks racially ambiguous. Many Black clients who have straight hair, fair skin, or finely chiseled facial features have gone through years of having to explain their racial background to others. Clients who have European-appearing features often describe how humiliating it has been to hear White individuals make derogatory comments about Blacks in their presence because they were unaware of the client's Black heritage. We can ask clients what kinds of reactions they get from others of various races and whether these reactions have posed any difficulty for them.

Some clients report that they have at times been singled out from other Black individuals, and people have complimented them on their more European-looking features by saying, for example:

"You have beautiful hair; it's so long and straight."

"What gorgeous hazel eyes you have."

"How unique, a Black woman with blond hair."

These comments may cause discomfort for the Black person involved because there's no one way that Blacks look. Also, in some cases there is a very clear implication that the European features are perceived to be better, prettier, or more attractive than African features.

We also need to be sensitive to the fact that Blacks have been exposed to White beauty standards all their lives. As a result, many Blacks themselves have negative or ambivalent feelings about having broader features, kinkier hair, and fuller figures than Whites. These attitudes of internalized racism can have a profound impact on the self-esteem of Blacks. Some Blacks think that their "best" feature is their straight hair and feel shame if they have dark skin.

These issues also get played out in families, jobs, and friendships, where individuals believe, and in fact it may be true, that preferences can be based on hair and skin color. Both males and females can experience bias based on skin, hair, and features, but such bias tends to be more pronounced for Black women, because our society still emphasizes physical attractiveness as a major asset for all women.

This discrimination can work in two ways. In the more classic situation, an African American woman experiences bias based on having more African features; she has been made to feel second class compared to Black women with lighter skin and straighter hair. I've also had clients with more European features who complain that other Blacks have had negative reactions to them because of expectations that these women are "stuck up" or "think that they're better than others."

These issues of attractiveness are still virulent in the African American community. There's a legacy of anger and frustration associated with historical practices of giving preference to Blacks who looked more like Whites. We need to remember that this discrimination still occurs and is practiced not just by Whites and people of other races but by African Americans as well.

Black individuals with dark skin, broader features, and kinky hair can achieve positive self-esteem but also recognize that they're still discriminated against in our society. This discrimination can occur in job placements; entrance to sororities, fraternities, and social and civic groups; school admissions; and, just as significantly, in relationships.

Meanwhile, Blacks who appear to others to look more "White" often deal with anger and slights directed toward them from Blacks who resent them for what they assume to be a rejection of their Black heritage.

Family-of-Origin History

Some of the most useful information for us to obtain in the first session is a sketch of our client's family background. We know that African Americans have diverse experiences and perspectives, and we want to avoid making assumptions. We want to try to develop a sense of the client's family's basic philosophies and acculturation as a way of understanding the client's values and perspectives. We can gain some idea about what the client's early attitudes were about Black pride and identity and what the family's experiences were with Whites, with people of other races and cultures, and with discrimination and racism.

Was the family more or less encapsulated in a predominantly Black world with respect to schools, jobs, or experiences? Was the family one that grew up largely with frequent contacts with Whites? We also need to be sensitive to the effects of regional differences as well as Caribbean, West Indian, French, Portuguese, or Spanish cultural influences.

Many Blacks are raised with a strong participation by extended family members, godparents, and fictive kin. (As you recall, fictive kin are individuals who don't have a blood tie to an individual but are treated as biological relatives.) African American families sometimes explicitly tell their children that if there's an issue or problem that they don't want to talk to their parents about, then they can turn to a member of the extended family.

We can ask our clients about their family tree, and they'll describe mother, father, and siblings. We need to make sure that we ask whom they lived with or were raised by because they may not have been with their parents or siblings.

In many cases historically and currently, grandparents or other individuals raise Black children. This situation may occur because the parents need to work long hours away from home, because the parents cannot support the children, or, in recent years, because the parents are addicted to substances or are incarcerated.

In some cases a Black person has been raised by a mother and father but considers a grandmother or grandfather to be his or her true parental figure. Clients in this situation may feel they received more of what they needed—such as consistency, support, discipline, religious training, identity, pride and self-esteem, and values and philosophy—from the grandparents than from their parents. We need to listen closely to understand to whom our clients feel close and toward whom they feel any dislike, ambivalence, or distance.

I often ask clients which relative they felt closest to and why. I also ask if their parents or parent figures had any "favorites," and if they did, I ask them what the basis was for this perception. I ask clients to tell me how they got along with any siblings in the past and what their relationships are like now. It's also important to gain a sense of our clients' relationships to family members currently. Are there close emotional ties? Do family members live close by? To what extent is the family a source of stress rather than a source of support?

We finally want to make sure that we understand our client's current family dynamics. What are the client's relationships with partners, children, and other significant people? What are the strengths and what are the weaknesses in his or her family relationships?

Sometimes family relationships include stepparents, stepsiblings, and half brothers and half sisters. We need to listen with special sensitivity as we hear family dynamics to detect possible "family secrets." We may see our client become silent, more agitated, or confused as a prelude to explaining a secret, such as a pregnancy before or outside of a marriage or a child in the family who is a product of an extramarital relationship. Other possible secrets that we must listen for and ask about involve violence, abuse, sexual assault, abuse of or addiction to substances, and any family history of mental illness.

Clearly, we must note both verbal and nonverbal cues to assess how far we can go in asking about sensitive issues in the first session. If we think that these family secrets are vital to a crisis issue, we need to find a careful way to explore these secrets. We can say, for example, "I know that what we're talking about now is very private to you, but I think that in order to help you and your family with the crisis that's going on now, I need to hear more about this period of violence and alcoholism in the early years of your marriage." If the client seems resistant, and we feel that we need to develop more rapport and trust, we can make a note to ourselves to revisit sensitive issues.

African American clients can still have difficulty acknowledging mental illness in the family. It's often easy to deny or be confused about the presence of mental illness because of the tradition of keeping relatives in the home. Many clients talk about someone in their family who is like "Uncle Pete," a character in the movie *Soul Food*. This is an individual who is definitely strange and can't interact with others or take care of himself, and he simply lives in the home but apart from the rest of the family that provides care for him.

I ask clients how their parents met and what their parents' relationship was like. I use this information to gain some idea of what early messages about relationships the client may have been exposed to. Sometimes clients report such messages as "You can't trust men, so you better get an education and be able to take care of yourself" or "All females are just out for what they can get from you, so don't be too easy at giving them your love."

I also ask about parental educational levels and occupational status. Many African Americans use their parents' accomplishments as a baseline. They may have been encouraged and supported to make sure that they surpassed their parents with respect to educational, financial, and occupational attainment.

Socioeconomic Status

Therapists must be able to assess important differences in socioeconomic status and values in Black clients in order to be effective. It's interesting to ask clients what their socioeconomic status was when they were growing up and what it is presently. Usually it's more difficult to place African Americans neatly into one category than it is to place Whites. Blacks may not have access to the same jobs, salaries, and housing as Whites with comparable education and training. African Americans also frequently note with wry humor that even though they consider themselves to be middle class, if they were to lose three months of their job income, they would fall into the lower income bracket.

This statement reflects the fact that even some middle-income Blacks may not have economic cushions like stocks and bonds, savings, or relatives with real estate or extensive assets from whom to borrow. It may be more important to focus on the notion of economic adequacy and learn from the clients if their families were able to meet basic needs and if there were resources available for extras.

We also need to be mindful that we will work with some African American families who seem to move in and out of middle-class and working-class status at different points in their lives depending on their educational and job status. Part of the lack of economic stability that African Americans face is due to their tenuous job stability, to "last hired, first fired" employment practices, and to the fact that culturally, many Blacks are expected to help give financial support to extended family members, even if their own finances are strained.

We also may work with Black clients who come from families with several generations of college-educated members. These clients may have issues with self-esteem, identity, and acceptance that can be very different from the issues of Blacks who are less well educated and financially secure.

I once worked with Mr. Deal, who came from a very prominent upper-middle-class family. His presenting problems centered around his certainty that he could not exceed the accomplishments of his parents and grandparents. His grandparents were well known for establishing a highly successful restaurant, and his parents had established a nationally known consulting company. Mr. Deal was fairly accurate in his perceptions. He could find a well-paying job, but he wasn't interested in or motivated toward accomplishing any major projects in his lifetime. To be "average" in his family made him abnormal, even though his family didn't try to force any of their ambition or drive onto him.

Sometimes those Blacks who have been more advantaged suffer from attacks and harm from other Blacks. I've frequently worked with Black adolescents who are teased or even pushed into physical altercations by Black peers for talking too "White" (as in speaking Standard English), getting good grades, doing well at school and getting along with Whites, gaining the attention of the opposite sex, having more money to spend on cars, hairstyles, clothes, entertainment, and jewelry, or generally having access to more privileges.

We also need to know how our clients feel about their current economic status and how their position affects their status with family members and peers and in the church or community. If clients are doing better than their parents or other family members, we can ask them if they feel proud of their achievements. In some cases these clients may have ambivalent feelings. They may be pleased, guilty about their success, or angry with other family members for not also succeeding, and they may feel responsible, resentful, or indifferent to providing assistance to others.

We need to be sensitive to situations in which our clients feel that they have not upheld family traditions in terms of education, occupation, or status. When clients share information that indicates they have achieved less than their parents or family members, we need to ask them if comparisons are made in the family and if so, how that makes them feel.

It's also difficult for some African American clients to have to relinquish roles of authority and prestige that they have worked hard to attain, as the next case illustrates.

I worked with Mr. and Mrs. Jeter, a Black couple in their late fifties. Mrs. Jeter had persuaded her husband to come for therapy because she felt that he was carrying his position as an elder in the family too far.

Mr. Jeter explained that his father had been the oldest son in his family and that he was the oldest son in his generation. His father had started the tradition of providing emotional and financial support to his extended family whenever they were in need. Mr. Jeter had tried to carry on that tradition, but he had been in and out of the hospital with flare-ups in his sickle cell anemia condition.

Mrs. Jeter felt that her husband was no longer being objective about how much money he could afford to give or lend to relatives. Mr. Jeter greatly valued the respect and admiration he received for helping his relatives financially. Our work in this first session revolved around how much of their income could be shared with other family members, given the Jeters' concern about retirement in a few years and Mr. Jeter's medical concerns. We also had to help Mr. Jeter adjust to a new role in his family whereby he still gave his time and attention but was willing to consult more with his wife before committing their money to others.

Developmental History

We'll probably learn something of clients' developmental history as we ask questions in other areas. But we also should spend a few minutes asking clients about their growth and development.

We want to learn if they showed typical or atypical attainment of developmental milestones. Did they or members of their family suffer from physical or emotional illnesses or difficulties? Did any members of their family suffer any major traumas, stressors, or deaths?

We want also to be sensitive to whether clients experienced poverty, whether they were on welfare or had food stamps, or whether they endured threats to their safety and well-being at school, home, or in their neighborhood. Did our client feel ignored or unloved?

We want to ask African American clients if they had friends as they grew up. Did they live in the same area, or did they move around? We want to find out if parents or parental figures were consistent in their lives and if they lived with them. Did they always have a place to stay, or were they ever homeless? Did they ever live in a shelter or foster home? Did they or any family member experience incarceration? What external agencies were involved in their lives—social services, the criminal justice system, schools, churches? How did they do in school?

We want to explore whether our clients were actively involved in school or turned off. Did they participate in sports or extracurricular activities? Were they popular? Were they ever retained or given special services? We want to ask our clients what kind of grades they earned and what their best and worse subjects were. It's always interesting to ask clients what they aspired to be when they grew up and to connect these plans with where they now are occupationally.

We can also use this discussion as a segue to talk about clients' work history and whether they are comfortable with their occupational and educational attainments. We can explore whether they're satisfied with their current employment situation and why or why not. At this point in the interview, I listen closely to hear if clients feel that discrimination or racism has played a significant role in their life. I don't initiate this question unless clients bring up information that suggests that these issues are of concern to them.

As we ask questions about work and school achievements, we can integrate this information with what we're hearing from clients to make some global assessment about their intellectual capabilities and skills.

Although we may not have time for discussion of all the aforementioned areas in the developmental history, as therapists we must decide which of these areas is important to pursue. In general I try to follow up on issues related to the presenting problem. Typically, we'll look at a number of factors, including the following, to help us determine which issues to investigate:

- The presenting concern of the client

- Nonverbal cues that indicate that a topic is important

- Our dialogue with the client to understand other significant areas that need to be explored

Significant Relationships

A routine part of our assessment is to ask clients about their relationship status. We want to understand something about the history of their relationships, what factors affect their current
relationship status, and what our clients think about the quantity
and quality of their relationships. As we listen to our clients, we
want to discern any possible patterns of behavior, such as seeking
unattainable others or consistently being in an abusive relationship.

If the presenting problem relates to a relationship issue, we obviously may want to focus more on this section of the psychosocial
history so as to get a better understanding of relationship dynamics.
We know that Black couples must contend with all the issues that
other couples do, but in addition they also often have to live up to
bicultural expectations of male and female roles and deal with social
forces such as racism, unemployment, and underemployment, with
fears about safety and being treated fairly, and with concerns about
how to support and nurture family members to feel good about
themselves.

In my work with Black women, one of the most frequent presenting problems is dissatisfaction in their intimate relationships.
Our job is to understand the source of this discontent. Part of the
assessment is to help the client distinguish the issues of her partner
from her own scripts or patterns that lead to troubled relationships.

It's rarer for Black men to initiate a therapy contact for a relationship issue. I more frequently see men when there's a problem
with a child or a job. When a Black man comes for couple therapy,
it's usually when problems have really escalated and the threat of
the relationship ending is very real. It's critical to find out why a
couple chose this time to come for therapy—what's happening right
now. Sometimes it's because of the suspicion or reality of an affair,
escalation of arguments to violence, or one of the partners wanting
out of the relationship. In many cases, Black men feel that their
partners don't appreciate how hard their day-to-day lives are. They

often feel misunderstood, unappreciated, and unnecessary to women who have been taught to be strong and self-reliant.

As I assess problems in relationships, I almost always begin by asking clients how they met. Usually there's a visible lessening of tension as the couple recalls happier times. I also ask what it was that attracted each of the individuals to the other. Often it's the very quality that attracted a partner that is causing problems now. For instance, the woman who admired the ambition and drive of her partner now is unhappy that he's a workaholic and never at home. The man who admired his partner for her ability to make him feel important and in charge is now angry at her dependence.

I try to get the couple to describe the dating relationship, how they made the decision to have a more committed relationship, and when problems first emerged. We try to develop a chronology of the relationship while understanding any critical incidents and the strengths and weaknesses of the relationship. I also try to get very explicit descriptions about what each individual sees as the problem areas and what the expectations are for a resolution.

In the first session we also try to understand our clients' sexual orientation. This subject may become clear as clients talk about their relationships. If a client is not forthcoming about the gender of his or her partner, we may need to give the person more time to develop comfort and trust with us before he or she feels able to come out. I find that using nonheterosexist terms like *partner* or *significant other* can help create a climate in which our clients know that we're not making assumptions about their sexual orientation. I feel comfortable in not asking about sexual orientation and letting my clients tell me in their own way and in their own time.

Recently I worked with Mr. Howard, a twenty-nine-year-old Black male who worked for the city's transit system. Mr. Howard said that he came for therapy because he was an only child and his parents had been teasing him about getting married and bringing them some grandchildren. They told him that they couldn't understand why he was still single. After all, he was good looking, had a good job, and didn't drink or do drugs.

Mr. Howard said that he too was wondering what was wrong because he really wasn't interested in dating and getting married. He reported that he'd always been shy and had never dated very much. On several occasions, his parents fixed him up with the daughters of their friends for proms, but nothing ever came of these dates. I asked him if he had ever had a crush on anyone special. He paused, then said no. I got the impression that he wanted to say yes at first but decided not to.

I wanted to get Mr. Howard to focus more on how I could help him, so I said to him, "You've told me what your parents want for you, but I'm not clear on what you want for yourself in terms of relationships. Do you think that you're a loner and not cut out to be in relationships?"

"No," he said, "but I still don't see myself as the marrying kind." I told him that I was unsure if he was telling me that he was interested in relationships but just hadn't met the right person yet. He said, "Yeah, something like that. But what if the person I was interested in isn't the kind of person my parents would want for me?" I asked him how he could tell beforehand that his parents might not accept his choice. Again, Mr. Howard was silent.

The line of conversation and Mr. Howard's silence and agitation made me think it was possible that he was gay or bisexual. I also suspected that his real reason for coming for therapy was to start exploring his sexual orientation. In this case I felt that Mr. Howard wanted me to help him to get some of these issues out in the open. I made an overture by saying, "People vary in their interests in relationships and in sex. Some people are not very interested in relationships at all. Others are more attracted to and more comfortable with females and others are attracted to and comfortable with males. Do you have a sense of where your interests are in terms of relationships?" As Mr. Howard gave me steady eye contact, he paused for several seconds and said, "I think I may be more interested in males for relationships. But how would I know? I've never had a serious relationship with a male or a female."

From this opening, we went on to discuss some of Mr. Howard's questions about whom he was attracted to and how he could sort out his plans for learning more about his sexual orientation. We talked about his fears of losing his parents' approval, but he also talked about what a relief it would be if he could be himself and find other people who had some of the same questions and concerns that he had.

On occasion, we as therapists will work with individuals in therapy who have either had consensual or forced same-sex contact earlier in their lives. These individuals sometimes need us to give them support as they sort out how these experiences affected them in the past and whether there are any current unresolved issues about their attraction to men and women.

Because of prevalent homophobic attitudes in Black culture, gays, lesbians, and bisexuals often experience higher levels of depression, anxiety, substance abuse, and suicidal ideation and behaviors. They often feel isolated, alone, and misunderstood. As more individuals identify, not as heterosexual or gay but as bisexual, they're also at risk for rejection and emotional distress. Several of the clients with whom I work are individuals who have been married or in long-term relationships but decided at some point that they prefer a relationship with a same-sex partner.

These individuals are justifiably concerned about the reactions of their partner and children and have to decide how much of their lifestyle they're willing to share with others. We should ask these clients about their feelings and whether they have a support system, and explore with them any concerns about being gay, lesbian, heterosexual, or bisexual.

As we explore issues of sexuality, we need to be prepared to ask our clients if they have any sexually transmitted diseases. We know that Blacks are one of the fastest-growing ethnic groups with respect to HIV-positive status and venereal diseases.

Health and Physical Status

In addition to asking about any sexually transmitted diseases, it's important for us to ask clients about their overall heath status. Any ongoing physical condition can be a drain on our clients' abilities to problem-solve in other areas and may be a significant source of stress. We know that African Americans are at high risk for such medical conditions as obesity, heart disease, glaucoma, hypertension, diabetes, stroke, cirrhosis, obesity for Black women, and cancer of the breast, prostate, cervix, and colon. We need to find out if our clients have these diseases, if they are under the care of a physician, or if they are at high risk for these diseases due to their family histories.

I've frequently worked with African American clients who are stressed because they have a family history of a disorder but are afraid to go to a physician to be evaluated lest their fears be confirmed. Most of these individuals don't consider the possibility that their fears could also be allayed.

Sometimes African American clients are vague in answering our inquiries about their health. I've found that some clients are reluctant to see a physician because they know they smoke too much, are overweight, or are not eating properly, and they don't want to have a physician confront them with their need to adopt a healthier lifestyle. I ask Black clients what activities they use to fight stress and about alcohol and drug usage, smoking, nutrition, and exercise patterns.

Depending on the presenting problem, I may or may not address the mind-body connection in the first session. An important part of our work with Black clients involves helping them understand the diverse sources of stress in their lives and teaching them how to incorporate healthy stress-fighting options, such as exercise and good nutrition, and to limit or eliminate smoking, drinking, and the use of drugs.

We also need to know if our clients are taking any prescription or nonprescription medications. Often Black clients have already consulted a physician and may have been placed on antianxiety or antidepressant drugs.

Psychosocial Stressors and Resources

From what we've learned in the course of the assessment in other areas, we may have learned of clients' psychosocial stressors. It's important to include in our first session a specific question about whether there are any other factors that are bothering them at this time. If they haven't dealt with this issue so far, we can gently probe about the issue with respect to relationships, work, home, and any dealings with external agencies and services.

As we explore clients' affiliations, we can ask, "Do you have a church home or any strong spiritual beliefs?" This allows us to gain some insight into our clients' basic philosophies and to see if religion or spirituality may be a possible resource for them.

We also need to assess whether church or religious experiences are a source of pain, conflict, or contradiction. Problems can arise for women if they feel religious pressure to remain with an abusive partner or to keep secrets about violence and sexual abuse, or for gay, lesbian, and bisexual individuals who want to be a part of their church but feel rejected and excluded.

We need to review with our clients whom they typically turn to for support and help and how adequate that system is. It's likely that if the client has sought our assistance, he or she feels or someone else thought that we could help this person in some way that his or her usual support system couldn't.

Sometimes when I'm dealing with a couple issue or a family problem, my African American clients tell me that someone in the family has admonished them for seeking help from a therapist rather than simply taking their problem directly to the Lord or to their pastor or spiritual leader.

When I worked with the Williams family around communication problems, it was clear to me that Mr. Williams wanted to work with his
pastor and not with me. Mrs. Williams told me that she preferred
working with a therapist who didn't know the family and who would
not be in contact with the family after the counseling was over. Further, she indicated that some of her friends had worked with the pastor before, and she was concerned that his orientation was very
supportive of the idea that "a man is the head of the house and
women should be obedient to their husbands."

Not surprisingly, Mr. Williams had no problem with the pastor's
orientation. I suggested a compromise whereby the Williamses would
continue to work with me but also talk to the pastor. This way, Mrs.
Williams felt that she had someone who could be more objective than
the pastor, and Mr. Williams felt reassured that he would also have
support and the church's blessing. I told them they were free to talk
with their minister about anything that I said to them or that we discussed together. Over the next few sessions, the minister approved
of our work together, and the Williamses jointly made the decision to
work with me alone.

In another situation, I worked with a Black female who was a lesbian.
I asked her if she had a church home that could give her any support. She explained to me that she had a church home and planned
to continue to worship there, but she knew that her minister would
not be supportive of her sexual orientation. She felt that she had
enough support from her friends and lover to be able to enjoy the
benefits of her church membership even though she knew that she
could not be open about her lifestyle in the church setting.

It's important that we understand how our clients' support system functions so that we can support and supplement these resources. We need to determine if support comes from friends, relatives, work colleagues, neighbors, or associations with civic and community organizations.

We must be careful not to communicate a message that we're in competition with or feel superior to our clients' resources, lest we scare clients away from us. The bottom line is, however well or poorly the support system is functioning, it has longevity and a history that we don't yet have with our clients.

ASSESSING RISK

Another critical area of the assessment process is determining if our clients are involved in the use of drugs and alcohol and understanding their risk status with respect to violence and suicide. We already know from our review of presenting problems that African Americans as a group experience significant difficulty with these issues.

Drug and Alcohol Abuse and Addiction

As therapists, we know that denial is an integral part of drug and alcohol abuse and addiction. Therefore, unless our clients are seeking assistance specifically for drug and alcohol problems, we can expect that those most at risk will not readily cooperate with our quest to assess their use of substances.

A variety of clues can give us information about possible substance abuse. We need to be sensitive to the fact that many African Americans are very adept at projecting an image. These Black clients may do a wonderful job of covering over, rationalizing, and "getting over" authority figures by fooling them about their involvement in maladaptive activities. We need to be alert to possible "con" behaviors on the part of Black clients. We can become suspicious about abuse if we notice any of the following:

- Disorientation

- Inappropriate and labile emotions or behaviors

- Spotty work history

- Problems in relationships

- Erratic motivation and attention

- Accidents

- Criminal activities

- Arrests

- Belligerence and violence

- Disturbances in sleep, appetite, and sexual functioning

We may not be able to come to a definite diagnosis of substance abuse in a first session. Our role may be restricted to collecting information and testing the waters to see if our clients are willing to discuss and confirm our suspicions. We know that Black clients may be slow to confide in us. Consequently, whether or not clients confirm our concerns, we need to be firm in asking specific questions if we think that alcohol and drugs could be a problem.

We can begin by stating, for example, "I certainly am not interested in judging your behavior. I've already mentioned that what you tell me is confidential. I know that you're feeling a great deal of pressure in your life right now from your family and job, and you don't feel like you have anybody on your side. I can best help you if you tell me all the factors that might be relating to your wife's leaving you and your problems at work. I think I can help, but I need you to answer some questions about your drinking."

Because many African American women were brought up in traditions where they're not expected to drink, it may be very shameful for them to admit to having problems with alcohol. We can say to our Black female clients, for example, "If there are times when you're losing control over your drinking, I know that this would be hard to talk about with a stranger. If you can answer some of my questions, I think we can figure out how to get you some support so that you can deal with your anxiety and depression. We'll also work on getting you some assistance as you try to cope with the children, the finances, and your job."

The following are some of the questions I ask:

How often do you drink?

What is your drink of choice?

How many drinks do you have at a sitting?

How can you tell when you've had enough to drink?

Have you ever used any drugs?

What drugs have you used?

How frequently do you use drugs?

What is your drug of choice?

How do you pay for your alcohol or drugs (or both)?

Have you experienced blackouts?

How has your alcohol and drug use affected your job and relationships?

Potential for Violence

As we assess our clients' potential for violence, we're concerned about harm to our clients as well as about our clients harming others. In Chapter Two we reviewed the statistics showing that African Americans are at high risk for violence in their daily lives. In our first session we need to listen closely to any indications that our clients might harm others or are at risk for harm. The following are some of the issues about which we need to gain more information; we need to know whether our clients have

- A history of violence either as a perpetrator or a victim

- Access to weapons

- Problems with substance abuse and impulsive behaviors

- Strong feelings of anger, entitlement, or revenge

- A background of adjustment problems, schizophrenia, mania, or borderline and antisocial personality disorders

We also want to determine if our clients can verbalize a fear of hurting someone else or of being hurt. Obviously we're going to be particularly concerned if we have clients who are threatening to harm others or who visibly demonstrate fears that someone will harm them. We are ethically bound to focus our attention on any potential for violence in our clients to determine the proper intervention.

In my work with Mr. and Mrs. Brown, they readily admitted that the reason for therapy was escalating violence. I immediately focused my assessment questions on the relationship and what had been happening. I asked Mr. and Mrs. Brown to describe the fight that had led to their decision to get help. Both Mr. and Mrs. Brown started talking at the same time, and neither was willing to listen to the other. I stopped the conversation and asked if I could speak with them individually and then meet again together. Mr. Brown said, "Let her go first and tell her lies, and then I'll come back and set the record straight."

As I spoke with Mrs. Brown, she explained that she had a college degree and worked as a teacher. Her husband had gone to college but had dropped out because of financial pressures. He had a son from a previous relationship whom he supported financially and with whom he maintained a close relationship. Mrs. Brown felt that after they married and had two children in two years, the financial pressures mounted. She thought that her husband, who worked for a mail courier company, felt threatened by her professional status and education.

Mrs. Brown admitted that she sometimes complained about the fact that her husband didn't make more money and that he came from a family background that differed from hers, because most of her family had college educations and professional jobs. She said that their fights had gotten more physical and that she had shoved and pushed her husband; she was frightened because although he claimed he was just restraining her, she felt that he was trying to over-power her and harm her.

I asked Mrs. Brown whether her husband had ever threatened her, and she said that on several occasions he had said that he would never let her embarrass him by leaving him, although he never explained what he would do.

I asked Mrs. Brown if her husband had any weapons or knew people who did. I also asked her if he had ever harmed or threatened the children. She said that he had never done anything threatening to the children but that she felt at times that his threats to her about leaving could also involve the children.

Mrs. Brown said that she hadn't talked to her family about what was going on in the marriage because they were already ambivalent about her husband and weren't sure that he was the right person for her given his previous relationships, his son, and his limited educa-tion. I asked her if she had ever called the police when the arguments became physical. She explained that she hadn't because she was afraid that if her husband were arrested, he could lose his job and their financial situation would be even worse than it already was.

We spent the remainder of our time together discussing her options. Mrs. Brown said that she loved her husband and wanted to try to save her marriage. I pointed out that he had frightened her with his threats and that for the sake of herself and her children, she needed to have a contingency plan. I gave her information about two domestic violence shelters that she could use for safety. We also talked about strategies she could use to keep the violence from escalating. As we talked, Mrs. Brown felt that one other resource was her husband's uncle, to whom her husband might be willing to talk and listen.

When I talked to Mr. Brown, he was immediately defensive and asked, "So what did she tell you? I guess I'm the bad guy in all of this." I reiterated to him that I wouldn't share what Mrs. Brown said but I did want to hear his perspective. I said, "I know from what the two of you said earlier that Mrs. Brown can really push your buttons and make you angry. What do you do when you start losing it in your arguments"? He told me that he had never struck her, but he admitted to grabbing her, shoving her, and restraining her tightly enough to bruise her.

I asked him if he had ever threatened her. He admitted that he had told her he would never let her leave him, but whereas she took it to mean that he would harm her, he meant that he would simply do all he could to keep her with him. I emphasized that his threat seemed serious to me as well as to his wife, considering that he had been so physical with her on several occasions. I told him that I was willing to work with him and his wife but that there would have to be an end to all the physical violence and that we'd have to work on their communicating in less aggressive ways.

I asked him if he would be willing to join a group that focused on anger and aggression and was run by a Black male therapist. He told me that he really didn't want to discuss his business with a lot of other people, especially other Black men. He said, "Look, I know I've messed up. But I love my wife and kids. That's why I'm here today. I wouldn't have come in here and have us tell you all that we did if I wasn't serious about making some changes."

I indicated that I could respect those feelings. I was also concerned, however, that if he and his wife didn't get some help right away, we were looking at the possibility of more violence, police intervention, and loss of his family, job, and reputation. He agreed to weekly sessions with his wife and me and to at least trying the men's group. In this case both Mr. and Mrs. Brown kept their commitment to therapy and were able to first decrease and then eliminate the violence in their arguments.

Part of the assessment I had to make in this situation was how honest I could be with Mr. Brown about letting him know the seriousness of the situation that he and his wife were in. Any information I shared had to be balanced against whether Mr. Brown would retaliate against his wife or family outside the session. No matter how sincere the promise to change may be, we need to make sure that our clients have several plans to get help and to leave on short notice if necessary.

Suicide Potential

We've noted that suicide is a growing problem in the African American community, especially for Black males. In some cases we'll detect suicidal ideation in statements of helplessness and hopelessness. In other cases our clients may be fairly direct in stating they don't want to live anymore.

We also may be exposed to a large number of Blacks, particularly the young, who engage in risky behaviors that are life threatening. These activities include engaging in unprotected sex, fighting, carrying guns, and combining and abusing alcohol and drugs.

Our priority in our assessment is to determine how serious a suicide threat is for a particular client. Although we have a variety of demographic predictors that tell us who is most at risk for suicidal behaviors, these statistics are not always useful in determining if our client is at risk.

The following questions may be helpful in determining the potential lethality of suicidal ideation:

Have you thought about how you could kill yourself?

Do you have access to the weapon (or drugs or sleeping pills)?

Have you made previous suicide attempts?

Do you have trouble controlling your urges to do something?

Have you thought about giving away or have you given away anything valuable to you?

Do you ever visualize how your death might affect other people?

Do you have any problems with substance abuse?

What are your relationships like? Are you having any problems?

Have you had anything very traumatic or upsetting happen to you or someone you are close to?

How often do you think about suicide? Do these thoughts interfere with what you're trying to do during the day?

Have you been seen for emotional problems before?

Have you ever been depressed?

Have you ever had problems with the police?

Have you ever felt like you were "losing it"?

Some of these items are designed to see if there's any evidence of behavior consistent with affective disorder or antisocial or borderline personality disorders.

If we determine through our questioning and assessment that a client shows multiple risk factors and appears serious about making a cry for help or about not living, we are responsible for developing a plan to keep our client safe. We'll talk more about handling issues of violence and suicide in Chapter Six, which focuses on crises.

MENTAL STATUS EXAM

We can't arrive at an accurate assessment of our clients' functioning without including a mental status review. The basic components of a mental status include an examination of the client's

- Appearance

- Speech and language

- Thought process and content
- Affective functioning
- Insight and judgment
- Cognitive functioning

We'll now review these categories as they pertain to working with African American clients.

Appearance

Usually the first thing we notice about our clients is their appearance. Assessing appearance is critical because it gives us a chance to look at what clients are communicating about themselves to others. It gives us a chance to see what messages we pick up about our Black clients, and we can eventually learn whether how we see them is how they see themselves.

Although there's a great deal of diversity in how clients look, we should first focus on basic issues, such as whether the client is clean and appears alert and oriented. By doing so we get immediate input about the client's ability to be well groomed and make a positive impression. It also allows us to be alert to possible problems with substances, orientation to reality, or borderline or psychotic functioning.

In terms of clothing, Black clients will vary along a continuum with respect to how conservative or trendy they are in their style as well as to what extent they adopt more of a Eurocentric rather than Afrocentric style. Clients with an Afrocentric style may sport braids, dreadlocks, Afros, or head coverings. They may wear African-inspired garments and jewelry and brightly colored clothing and hair. We can note our clients' style, but we certainly can't form any automatic associations about our clients' politics, self-esteem, problems, or perspectives by looking solely at their dress.

It's important to note, however, that people, including therapists, often are intimidated and have an automatic bias against seeing these individuals clearly. Many African Americans, Whites, and members of other ethnic minority groups often treat those individuals who adopt more Afrocentric or trendy hair and dress styles with more suspicion and distrust. If job problems are an issue, we can ask clients if they feel that people are put off by their style of dress.

In contrast, we can meet a Black client who has a prestigious job and is well dressed, very articulate, and well educated, and we can lose our sensitivity to detect possible problems with alcohol, drugs, abuse, or violence. Sometimes we'll work with Black clients who are able to look so well put together that no one hears their cries for help. We need to listen and look for signs that an individual doesn't know how to reach out to others for support.

We want to assess whether our clients look to be about their stated age, whether their weight is proportionate to their height, and whether they have any unusual or distinguishing physical characteristics. In addition to our visual perusal of our clients, we need to ask them something along the lines of "Are you comfortable with your appearance?" Usually I ask this question in the context of dating relationships or in discussions about self-esteem.

Sometimes a client who appears overweight to us may have a very positive body image; many Blacks have not internalized the same beauty standards of thinness that many Whites have. In other cases, we may observe a person who looks normal but may view himself or herself as too heavy. We need to ask about these issues as a first step in detecting problems with eating disorders or body image.

I also ask clients what messages they received about how they looked from their family, friends, and the broader culture as they grew up. We know that sometimes this feedback was helpful, but in other cases it has led clients to feel negative about their appearance despite the fact that others may now see them in positive ways. I generally use these discussions to get some beginning ideas about self-esteem, body image, and where the client falls with respect to his or her Black identity and feelings about racial issues and racial groups.

Speech and Language Functioning

We can gain information about our clients' internal state by observing their use of speech and language. Is the speech pressured, incoherent, slow, or disconnected? We need to examine speech patterns for signs of agitation, anxiety, or depression. We also want to note if our client is tangential or if the content is inappropriate or bizarre, suggesting that we look closer at potential problems such as substance abuse, issues of organicity, and psychotic functioning.

We need to be aware of the tremendous diversity among Black clients in terms of their speech and language. For example, individual family and geographic characteristics can cause natural variation in the speed with which Blacks speak. We also need to be aware that some Black clients may use terminology that is unfamiliar to us or have deep accents that are difficult for us to handle. It took me awhile to figure out that when clients from the South said, "They came past my house," it really meant someone had come to their house, or that "making groceries" meant going food shopping.

I have also been in situations where the word or phrase the client said made no sense until I realized that I was simply confused by an accent. In these situations I try to put the client at ease and apologize for being a little slow in catching on to what he or she is saying. If I feel that I've missed a critical word or phrase, I fall back on asking a client to spell it or write it down.

In addition, we need to know that some African American clients are more fluent and comfortable with the use of Standard English than are others. Blacks who are not as fluent may be self-conscious about their speech and be fearful of fully participating in the session. Sometimes a Black client will start the session with formal English but under duress or when comfortable will revert to less standard usage. One of the tasks we have is to decipher how much anxiety might be due to limited education, the novelty and pressure of a first session, and the tension of communicating in Standard English rather than to presenting problems. Usually this becomes clearer as we help our clients feel comfortable in the session. Sometimes we can make our clients feel more comfortable by speaking more informally and being sensitive to not using a great deal of jargon or sophisticated language.

Thought Process and Content

As we evaluate the thought processes of our African American clients, we're basically trying to determine if they show any evidence of a thought disorder or of psychotic processes. We need to ask directly if they hear voices, see things that other people do not, or have any other unusual experiences.

We also have to consider that culturally, African Americans are often comfortable saying they can hear or sense a departed relative, God, Jesus, or the devil speaking to them. These admissions by themselves are not enough to qualify as symptoms of a thought disorder. We need to make sure that any unusual experience reported by our clients relates to their being out of touch with reality rather than to feeling more comfortable with a type of spirituality that is not endorsed by White middle-class standards.

Affective Functioning

As we interact with our clients in the first session, we'll have an opportunity to observe their range of emotions. Do they have a predominant mood, or are they emotionally labile? Are they in control of their emotions, and do their emotions match the content of their communications? We also want to note if they show any problematic affect, such as extremes of anger, depression, or mania.

Again we have to acknowledge the possibility of confusion with respect to cultural norms. Although Blacks vary in how they express emotion, many African Americans are often more comfortable about showing the full range of their feelings as compared to some racial and ethnic groups. As therapists, we need to work to understand what a normal level of expression is for the client with whom we're working, before we assume that he or she may be demonstrating excessive emotions.

Insight and Judgment

At first glance it would seem that assessing insight and judgment in African American clients is straightforward. We want to know whether our clients see their problems accurately or whether they use a variety of defensive behaviors, such as denial, minimization, or projection. Does the client show good perception and judgment? If so, perhaps we're looking at a situation that may take less time to resolve than it would with a client who is lower on these two dimensions.

The problem is that insight and judgment are culturally determined. Our personal, cultural, and racial experiences shape our decisions about what is appropriate such that therapists can be inaccurate in assessing the judgment of an African American client if they are unable to understand the client's worldview. First of all, we need to be aware that family values, religious beliefs, lack of formal schooling, homelessness, and coming from an isolated rural background can mediate issues of insight and judgment.

So as we talk to Black clients about their children, for example, and they discuss practices with respect to safety measures and discipline that in our opinion might seem excessively restrictive, we need to understand certain realities. Many Black parents live in unsafe neighborhoods, they know that racism is a given in their lives, and they feel compelled to teach their children that the consequences of breaking rules are much worse for them than they are for other groups.

We've talked some about hostility and paranoia and how it's actually adaptive for African Americans to be vigilant about what is happening around them. They can't afford the luxury of assuming that they live in a just world and will be given all the rights and privileges that members of the majority group receive automatically. Our job as therapists is to note the level of any hostility and paranoia we see and, through our questioning about jobs or relationships, determine how much of these reactions may be adaptive and justified and to what degree they have become maladaptive.

We need to be aware of the reality of guns, drugs, and sex and parenthood at a young age in some African American neighborhoods. We need to use cultural sensitivity as we ask Black clients such questions as these:

> I can understand that you live in a dangerous neighborhood. What made you decide to bring a gun to school?

> You've told me that your boyfriend has been pressuring you to smoke crack for awhile. What made you decide to try it?

> The guys who hang out on your block have all been arrested for something. They're trying to get you in on what they're doing. How have you been able to resist?

> I know that you don't have many options for baby-sitting, and it sounds like your eleven-year-old son does a great job in taking care of the younger three children. When did you start letting him baby-sit, and what made you think he was ready to do this? Are there any neighbors or relatives to help him out?

> You've mentioned that all your friends in ninth grade have already had a baby. Why was it important to you to get pregnant?

It would be easy for us to conclude from our vantage point that many of the decisions our Black clients make are faulty. If we suspend our judgments and assumptions, we can learn whether what we're discussing is a difference in perspective and life experiences or whether we've hit on a situation with which a client needs additional help. A client who believes that it's OK to rape his girlfriend, an individual who is abusive to a child or another adult, and those who feel it is their right to steal from others are showing impairment in which we need to intervene.

Cognitive Functioning

We examine cognitive functioning in order to see how well a client is functioning with respect to memory, attention, and orientation. In most cases, we don't have to assess for severe distortions in cognitive functioning. Often we have all the data we need to determine whether a client is appropriately oriented to time, place, and person.

If a client seems to hear or see something that we don't, or if his or her thinking and language appear confused, distorted, or unusual, we need to ask the client a few basic questions. We need to be aware that even if a Black client has some problems with cognitive functioning, he or she may very well recognize our concern that something is wrong. We can say, for example, "I noticed that you keep turning your head to the corner of the room. Do you see or hear anything?" If we get the impression that there are problems in cognitive functioning, we need to proceed with a more formal mental status exam. We can try to minimize clients' nervousness and agitation by explaining that we need to ask some questions to gain a better sense of their strengths and weaknesses. We then may ask such questions as these:

What is today's date, including the year?

What is your birthday, and how old are you?

Please name the current president of the United States and continue to give all the names you can remember in sequence.

Please count backwards by sevens beginning with one hundred.

Please explain the meaning of the following two proverbs: One swallow doesn't make a spring, and A rolling stone gathers no moss.

In asking these questions and evaluating our clients' responses, we're looking to see if they are in control of their thoughts, if they are capable of abstract thinking, and if they are in touch with reality. No matter how considerable our skills as a therapist, if a Black client shows evidence of cognitive impairment, our first intervention may be most appropriately aimed at referring our client to a psychiatrist and to a specialist for a medical evaluation or for additional psychological testing (or both).

GLOBAL ASSESSMENT OF FUNCTIONING AND DIAGNOSIS

By the close of the assessment component of the first session, we should have a good idea of our clients' overall level of functioning. Using the *Diagnostic and Statistical Manual of Mental Disorders* (4th ed., *DSM-IV*), we begin to formulate diagnoses. As we go through the diagnostic process, we need to be aware that the *DSM-IV* reminds us that culture is an important component of the process. We are warned to be cautious about misdiagnosing and over-pathologizing when we work with individuals of different cultures, races, and ethnicities. We must be alert to the fact that some diagnostic criteria don't always apply in diverse cultural settings.

Our major or Axis I diagnosis should address the presenting problem of the client. Here we want to make sure that we don't simply look at the obvious issue of delinquency, acting-out behaviors, or hyperactivity without investigating the possibly more subtle presence of depression and anxiety that can be masked in African Americans.

On Axis II, we note any personality disorders or, for children, any learning or developmental difficulties. We need to be attentive here to distinguishing long-term maladaptive behaviors that our clients may be demonstrating from behavior that is actually helping an individual survive. For example, if we're working with a twelve-year-old child who transports drugs for pushers in order to help pay for rent and food, our focus may be less on diagnosing this behavior and more on getting this family better financial support.

On Axis III we record any medical problems. We need to be aware that Black children and families are at high risk for the following:

- Infant mortality and birth defects due to inadequate prenatal care

- Infectious diseases due to poor immunization histories

- Lead poisoning

- Fetal alcohol and drug addiction syndromes

- AIDS

We've noted that African American adults are at high risk for hypertension, heart disease, diabetes, cancer, strokes, cirrhosis, and obesity (for Black women).

On Axis IV we indicate any psychosocial stressors the client is facing and the severity of those stressors. We know that part of what we need to evaluate for Black clients are the effects of the following social conditions:

- Racism

- Sexism

- Poverty

- Homophobia

- Bias with respect to age and ability

- Violence

- Unemployment or underemployment

- Homelessness

- Interactions with the criminal justice system

- PTSD caused by multiple chronic stressors, losses, and inadequate resources

Finally, on Axis V, we offer a numerical representation of overall functioning. This number ranges from a low of one to a high of one hundred. We also try to indicate the client's highest and lowest levels of functioning over the course of the last year.

As we tabulate the data we have amassed in conducting our assessment, we should be able to share our findings with our clients. We can explain to them our diagnostic impressions, their stressors, and their resources. We can relate presenting concerns to our findings and begin to develop a proposed treatment plan for our clients' review.

As a result of the assessment, we may decide that we need additional information and need to refer a client for a physical evaluation or a psychiatric evaluation to consider medication. We may decide that the client requires a further evaluation of intelligence, personality, or neuropsychological functioning. We need to explain to clients what our questions are and how these additional evaluations will be useful. We must let clients know that we will stay involved with them during this process of evaluation to help answer any questions and to be a source of support. We can make clear that we'll be available to review any additional findings and to help develop an intervention plan pending these results.

Finally, we may decide that we can't proceed with a client because there isn't a good client-therapist match. If we as therapists feel that we don't have the requisite knowledge, competencies, skills, or insights, we must make a more suitable referral. We also may have to recognize that we can't proceed any further because the client is unwilling to cooperate and work with us or doesn't feel comfortable with us. At this point we can discuss alternative arrangements. We'll talk in greater detail about interviewing strategies for a first session in Chapter Five.

5

Interviewing Strategies for First Sessions

This first case example illustrates the challenge of using the first session to full advantage. We must listen to what the client is telling us now, but we have more to do. Frequently we hear a variety of concerns, and we must assist clients in giving their presenting problems a focus. We also need to know how to zero in on racial concerns competently and sensitively.

Ms. Wallace, an attractive forty-three-year-old African American female, was referred to therapy by her employee assistance program (EAP). Ms. Wallace worked in the human resources department of a large company as the director of multicultural and diversity training, and she had to travel throughout the United States. Several months earlier, while traveling to a training assignment, Ms. Wallace was injured in a minor car accident and sustained a neck injury. Although she had been treated and cleared to return to work, she still experienced discomfort in her neck that the doctors could not account for.

In addition, she felt anxious, tense, depressed, and unable to fulfill her work requirements. Ms. Wallace had to cancel several training seminars because she felt so fatigued and irritable. After two sessions with the EAP counselor, she was referred to see whether therapy would help with the distress and work impairment that she was experiencing.

Ms. Wallace provided the aforementioned information in her first session with me. We established a positive rapport. As Ms. Wallace and I tried to sort out her presenting concerns, we tried to figure out what stressors might be contributing to her persistent emotional and physical problems. I asked her if she felt that her work was stressful. "Only if you consider teaching White managers and employees to stop being racist every day," she retorted. As we talked, Ms. Wallace said that she felt more and more frustrated that her majority audiences had such difficulty understanding diversity issues. She said, "The material I teach is so obvious. How hard can it be for people to learn to treat others with basic respect? Can't they see that the world is changing and that people can't still get away with all that old boy's network crap? I don't know what else I can do to get through to people. None of them want to hear about targets, quotas, or lawsuits, but they're so unwilling to think about things differently."

In addition to her ongoing stress at work, Ms. Wallace said that the pastor of her church had recently retired and that this stirred up a lot of issues for her. When she was nine, a family friend inappropriately groped and kissed her. She finally worked up the courage to tell her parents, who while horrified, were unsure what to do. They decided to talk to the pastor, who simply advised them to pray for the molester but to forgive him. The pastor said that, after all, there was no proof of what Ms. Wallace had said and that if it were true he knew that God would handle the situation.

Ms. Wallace didn't fully understand what was happening at the time of the molestation. I asked her how she felt about the situation now. She was silent for a moment, then replied that she now was in touch with how unsupported she felt by her parents and pastor. Because they chose to take no further action, she felt that she, not the molester, had done something wrong.

We talked about how turning solutions over to God without earthly interventions could at times be an unsatisfying option. I asked Ms. Wallace what she could do now to feel better. She said she didn't think there's was much to be done except to share her feelings with me. She thought that neither her parents nor the pastor would be able to see why the way they had handled her molestation was so upsetting to her.

The last issue that surfaced was that Ms. Wallace had become serious about a male who was thirty-three. She was very hurt that her family teased her about robbing the cradle, going through a midlife crisis, or trying to "get her groove back" by dating a younger man. She was angry that when her brother married for the second time, the family felt that it enhanced his status that his wife was twelve years younger than he. Ms. Wallace felt that it was very hard for a well-educated Black woman to find a BMWJ (a Black man with a job). She was the oldest female in the family, had been supportive of all her siblings and their families, and couldn't fathom how they could be so unsupportive now that she had finally found someone to be happy with.

Although Ms. Wallace's presenting problem related to work impairment and emotional distress, over the next few sessions, I worked with her on the following issues:

- Feelings of anger she had in training White employees

- Posttraumatic stress related to the molestation

- Lack of support for dating a younger male

- Anger at her parents and pastor

- Strained relationships with siblings

Our job in the first session is to collect information on presenting problems. If we're able to be responsive, listen closely, and offer support, our African American clients are more likely to trust us. They'll tell us about the network of problems they are facing, and they'll collaborate with us in solving their difficulties.

In this chapter, we'll explore effective interviewing strategies for first sessions with African American clients. First, we'll focus on some of the protective devices that Black clients use when discussing their presenting problems. Next, we'll explore some of the communication styles that African Americans may use in the first session. I will provide therapists with important information in understanding some of the racial dynamics that may influence why a client adopts a particular way of communicating and how to make sure that therapists can respond to a variety of client presentation styles with sensitivity and cultural competence. The third area will highlight ways to effectively explore presenting problems. Finally, we'll review typical first-session challenges and accompanying strategies that can help Black clients be more comfortable in discussing their presenting problems.

PROTECTIVE DEVICES

As we indicated earlier, African Americans have learned to be cautious in dealing with authority figures. As a result, they may use a cadre of protective devices during their initial sessions. In this section we'll talk specifically about defensiveness and stoicism and about minimizing problems. These protective behaviors are designed to keep others from seeing clients' true feelings and motivations. Underlying these devices is usually the fear that if the clients were honest and forthcoming, they would come to harm because of others' judgment and subsequent treatment.

It's important that we as therapists be alert to these protective devices. We need to be cognizant that Black clients are often justified in being cautious because of the racism and discrimination they have experienced. Our empathy with and awareness of these diversionary tactics can help us understand our clients and their presenting problems with less distortion.

Defensiveness

As African American clients relate their present concerns, they may be motivated to protect their own images or those of others. For example, clients may be sensitive to revealing that either they or a loved one is not fulfilling a role as a wife, husband, mother, father, breadwinner, or protector, especially given the many negative stereotypes that exist about African American families. We've talked earlier about the difficulty many African American clients have in airing what they perceive to be dirty laundry.

In addition, it's often culturally congruent for African American clients to feel that they don't have the right or authority to discuss their serious problems or those of others such as the following:

- Illegal activities

- Violence

- Abuse

- Incarceration

- Problems with substances

- Mental illness

- Physical illness

What I'm suggesting here is simply that, although most clients try to present themselves in the best light, this tendency may be stronger for African American clients. Because of their history, it is realistic for them to feel that revealing problems to authority figures may have more negative consequences in their lives than it would for White individuals. If we're effective in developing a trusting relationship with our clients, we can help them understand that we need them to be open and honest with us. If we demonstrate that we're not going to judge them, they're more likely to believe that we're not going to judge those individuals whom they're worrying about protecting.

Stoicism

Another cultural expression that some African American clients exhibit to protect themselves from revealing problems or asking for help is a strong sense of stoicism. They take the attitude that "Hey, life is tough. What can you expect but problems?" Sometimes this is expressed in the context of religion. The message that some African Americans glean from their religious experiences is that they will have challenges to overcome as a test of faith. There is a feeling that to ask for help from therapists shows a lack of faith in God. Hence, some African American clients are resistant to describing their problems and asking for help. The reason I'm commenting on this attitude is that it sometimes leads clients into

- Taking too much responsibility for others

- Refusing to ask for or accept help

- Placing unrealistic burdens on themselves

- Losing touch with how much they're in distress or suffering

As therapists we may be surprised to find an African American client who has agreed to come in for a first session but then is not forthcoming in describing problems and appears unwilling to accept any suggestions for problem solving. For instance, researchers and clinicians have noted over and over that when Black women are feeling overwhelmed and are given the following options: (1) cutting back on their schedule, (2) asking for help from others, or (3) making themselves do more by getting up earlier or going to bed later—they usually select the third option.

Minimization of Problems

Some African American clients may admit in the first session that they are grappling with a specific problem, but then they choose to minimize the impact of their concern on their life. These clients might describe their problem as "no big deal" and that they just want some advice or hints about their

- Use of drugs or alcohol

- Fights with their spouse

- Problems on the job

- Trouble restraining themselves when disciplining their children

These clients typically report that their problem behaviors don't occur very frequently, aren't severe, and don't have much impact on their lives, even though they may have been pressured into therapy by family members or external agencies and their failure to demonstrate progress may result in serious consequences.

Again, although clients across race may try to minimize their problems, African American clients may feel that their ability to maintain a family and a job and avoid legal problems is so tenuous that they are afraid to acknowledge the seriousness of their difficulties. As therapists, we need to help our Black clients relax and open up about the full extent of their problems. We can let them tell us their stories at their own pace and recognize that, as they experience our patience, skill, and acceptance, they will learn that they can be honest with us.

HANDLING PROTECTIVE DEVICES

We need to be alert to how we can facilitate the client's ability to describe the presenting problem. We have seen that African American clients may exhibit a variety of protective and defensive strategies in the first session. What can we do to manage potential barriers successfully?

First, we can verbalize to the client that it is difficult to disclose personal information to and ask for help from a stranger. It's important for us to normalize the client's feelings of hesitancy, shame, discomfort, and embarrassment about needing assistance and about their perceived lack of control.

Second, we can react calmly to clients' protective behaviors. Clients need to hear us say something supportive like the following:

> I can see why it may be hard for you to talk about your problems.
>
> It would be hard for anybody to put up with all that you have gone through in the last year.
>
> It sounds like you've done a wonderful job of trying to solve this on your own. At this point, if we work together, I feel confident that we can fully resolve this situation.

We can help clients feel comfortable in sharing their honest thoughts and emotions by being calm, nonjudgmental, and respectful. We can convey to clients that we admire their courage in telling us their problems and seeking help. We can work collaboratively with clients so that they recognize that as consumers of our services they have the right to agree or disagree with anything we suggest and that we do not control their lives—they do.

COMMUNICATION STYLES

We've just reviewed a variety of behaviors that African American clients may use to protect themselves in first sessions. Although Black clients, like other clients, vary in their styles of communication, it's important that we understand the racial and cultural meanings that may be associated with different communication styles for African Americans. Sometimes these communication styles are reflected in the process of relating presenting problems. These communication styles and how they are interpreted by others may also make up part of the content of the presenting concern as well. In this section we'll explore two examples of communication styles that are important for therapists to understand in working with African American clients in the first session: (1) emotional expressiveness and (2) internalization and externalization.

Emotional Expressiveness

As our African American clients reveal their presenting problems, we may see a variety of levels of emotional expressiveness. Some clients are so emotionally expressive and unrestrained that therapists become uncomfortable and feel that the client is out of control. Other clients may maintain a firm reserve that is designed to mask feelings not only from us but from themselves. This facade may crumble when emotions escalate. In other cases, the more disturbing the affect, the more reserved the client becomes.

The case that follows illustrates the behavior of African American clients who have been taught that being emotionally restrained and in control is desirable because this style is associated with appropriate Eurocentric standards of behavior, whereas being emotionally expressive is undesirable as it is associated with inappropriate Black behavior.

I recall working with Mrs. Redd, a thirty-nine-year-old accountant with a successful law firm, who was confronting serious marital difficulties. She sought therapy because of her concerns about her marriage. In her first session she was able to provide background information in a very calm and dispassionate manner. When I asked her to tell me what she wanted to have happen in therapy, her reserve began to crack. She admitted that she wanted her marriage to continue but that her husband was unwilling to participate in therapy.

When I asked her if she thought he might be involved with someone else, she looked at first as though she might cry. Instead, she reined in her emotions and stated in a very detached manner, "Well, that is a possibility. We don't have sex anymore, he comes in late regularly, and he's accepted more out-of-town work assignments than he's ever had in the past. He tells me that I don't open up to him and that we never really talk. All we're doing is going through the motions of a marriage."

I asked Mrs. Redd if she could give me some history of her relationship with her husband. She told me that she and her husband met in college and began dating. Mrs. Redd indicated that both she and her husband had come from families where their parents often argued. Mrs. Redd's parents eventually divorced when she was twelve. Due to the ongoing tension between her parents, her father stopped initiating contact with Mrs. Redd and her sister.

Mr. Redd's parents were still married. He hated to visit them, however, because the fights were still as frequent as ever. Both Mr. and Mrs. Redd had resolved that their marriage would be different from their parents' marriages. They would find ways to talk and disagree without the arguing, shouting, and loss of control that they saw in their parents. Both Mr. and Mrs. Redd felt that losing control of one's feelings was vulgar and immature.

It seemed that Mrs. Redd had learned to restrain her emotions too well. I gently confronted her with my impression that she worked very hard to keep a tight hold on her emotions. She explained that she found that other people took her more seriously if she always came across as calm, detached, and businesslike. She said that she practiced this style all through her academic career and at work as well. There were several other African American women who worked at her company; they were known for being assertive and direct and for letting people know exactly how they felt.

Mrs. Redd felt that this direct style was perceived as confrontational by her conservative firm, and she definitely didn't want to be identified as having a style similar to these other Black women. She acknowledged that she was friends with these women but said that they teased her by saying she wouldn't get very far in the organization if she continued to be passive and expected her good work record to speak for itself when it came time for promotions.

I wondered with Mrs. Redd if her strategy of restraining her emotions was really paying off for her at home or at work. I asked her if she had ever let her husband know how upset she was about what was happening in their marriage. Not surprisingly, she hadn't. We were able to have a useful discussion about figuring out when Mrs. Redd needed to hold in her emotions and when she needed to take the risk of letting those close to her see what she was really feeling. We also talked about how she needed to release the stereotype that any show of emotions was bad and that restraining emotions was always good.

Mrs. Redd felt that her marriage was at a critical point. She asked how she could find a way to tell her husband what she really felt without replicating the anger and out-of-control behavior both of them had seen in others. We talked about how there was a lot of middle ground that she could use to express her feelings that was neither passive nor out of control.

The other side of the emotional expressiveness continuum involves cases in which our African American clients lose control of their emotions. In telling their stories, some clients are overcome with an escalation in feelings of anger, sadness, or hostility that have been too long buried.

I once worked with Ms. Rice—a Black woman whose eight-year-old daughter died suddenly and unexpectedly from a rare disease. All during her daughter's illness, burial, and memorial services, Ms. Rice remained calm and composed. She didn't seek therapy until more than a year after her daughter's death. Ms. Rice appeared shaky and tense in the first session and in trying to recount her daughter's death she frequently sobbed, voiced anger at God, and told me that she couldn't forgive herself for not recognizing sooner the seriousness of her daughter's illness. She confessed that her family had insisted that she seek therapy at this time because she was overwhelmed with bouts of anger, helplessness, guilt, grief, and sadness.

As we talked she admitted that she had been afraid to let any emotions out at the time of her daughter's death because she felt that she had an obligation to her family to remain in control and to go on with her life. Ms. Rice felt that in her roles as wife, mother, and daughter she needed to give support to her husband, her other children, and her extended family members. She didn't understand how she could have held herself together for so long and only in the last few weeks fall apart.

It was important for me to let Ms. Rice know first, that although feelings of guilt were very common in illnesses like her daughter's, as her family and the physicians had reiterated, there really was nothing more that she could have done for her daughter. Second, I explained to her that everyone finds his or her own way and time to express grief. There was nothing wrong with her decision to wait until she felt that she could safely express her feelings. I also let her know that now that she was in touch with her emotions, she could take her time to explore all the complex feelings she was encountering. It is common for some African American clients to be more concerned about taking care of others than taking care of themselves. In these cases, we may need to support clients in giving them permission to get in touch with and express their feelings.

For many therapists, seeing African Americans express strong negative affect is frightening. It is a violation of gender roles for females to express strong negative emotions like anger and outrage. I have been involved in many student and peer supervision sessions when non-Black therapists have been blown away by the anger of Black women.

I've advised my colleagues not to become defensive or confused by this anger. We need to remain present and find out what is upsetting our Black clients. As we sit and listen nonjudgmentally, we can help them experience some catharsis. We can also help them develop strategies to express their anger as it develops rather than saving it up until it explodes. We can focus on adaptive ways to express anger and on finding "safe" people with whom clients can express strong feelings.

Historically, our society has always struggled to allow Black men to express their anger. It's as if the majority culture has always known that Black men have good reason to be angry since their forced arrival during slavery and so has gone to extreme lengths to control them. These practices have included incarceration, unemployment, limiting voting rights, entrapment, negative publicity, and developing assistance programs for Black families that are linked to the absence of fathers.

We must be attentive to the context of the emotions expressed by African American clients. If a Black male has an outburst, this behavior is sometimes pathologized and therapists frequently see these clients as out of control. Black clients often use therapy as a safe place to express the pent-up rage and frustration accumulated from years of unfair or discriminatory treatment. Clients express feelings of rage as they recount situations in which they wanted to tell someone off, hurt the person or system that harmed them, or exact revenge.

The norms for Black behavior violate the expectations of middle-class White culture with respect to emotional control. I remember working with Al Roberts, a very bright and articulate graduate student. Al was by no means shy in expressing himself in the first session. "You're not going to believe the bull they've been putting me through in my department," he declared passionately and loudly when I asked why he had sought therapy. Al had been warned by his faculty adviser that he needed to show more emotional restraint in his interactions with faculty and peers and rely more on calmness and logic in making his opinions heard. He was frustrated because the faculty welcomed debates and an exchange of ideas but when he and his Black peers expressed their real feelings, problems developed.

When Al and some of his Black friends debated points, he noticed that White classmates became silent. When he and his Black peers became excited and engaged in the discussion, their voices became louder, they interrupted each other, they traded insults, and in general had a great time.

White students and professors had told Al's adviser that they were afraid that a fight was about to ensue. Al knew that just because he was a Black male, these students and faculty expected him to be violent. He was disillusioned and frustrated to find that in the midst of a classroom debate at a predominantly White university, his cultural style could still be perceived as threatening.

I certainly saw in the first session the high levels of animation and passion that Al was being admonished for, but I didn't find it intimidating because I was used to witnessing and participating in discussions using a style similar to Al's. I first affirmed to Al that I understood and respected the passion and excitement that he exhibited in the first session and in the classroom. I next acknowledged that some individuals were intimidated and uncomfortable with open displays of emotion because they associated this emotionalism with out-of-control behavior. I pointed out that I knew that he was in control of his emotions and behavior but others did not.

Al only needed one session to decide that he could use his experiences to talk about different cultural styles of communication in his classes with faculty and students. Al followed up on this action and found that it was useful, but when I ran into him one day on campus he told me that he felt some resentment for being in the position of always having to be on guard and being in the position of "explaining and making myself acceptable to others."

Although Black clients may feel frustrated about having to explain their styles of communication, they're often receptive to our asking them to look at what effect their styles have on others. If the communication is not working, they are often willing to work with others to find a way to communicate more effectively.

We need to validate our clients' real frustration about wanting to be able to express feelings without others expecting them to act out society's negative stereotypes about anger and violence. And in some cases we need to note that the client's ability to express emotions is blocked. For example, some clients express depression and sadness instead of anger, whereas other clients express anger to avoid getting in touch with feelings of sadness or vulnerability.

We can facilitate our clients' abilities to connect with and express emotions by letting them know that they don't have to be strong or stoic in our presence. We need to create an environment in the first session in which our African American clients understand that it is safe for them to let down their armor and use whatever emotional style they wish—to share their hope, fears, and vulnerabilities.

Internalization or Externalization

Another area for us to focus on is how much responsibility clients assume for their problems as they describe their reasons for seeking therapy. Obviously African American clients vary in their personality characteristics. It's important for us to understand the degree to which Black clients feel responsible for the difficulties they are currently confronting. We've already seen that many African Americans believe the only way a Black person can be successful in this country is to have a high level of internal control. These individuals usually find asking for help in therapy very demoralizing. They may see their inability to cope on their own as a serious weakness. They may experience guilt, shame, and embarrassment about developing problems and not solving them.

For these clients, it's important for us to let them know that all people can benefit from help and support at some time. We can tell them that they're still in charge of their lives and that our work with them doesn't imply that there is something wrong or lacking with them. Many Black clients are receptive to the idea that seeking counseling can be viewed as seeking professional consultation when one has a specific problem to be solved. Just as clients tend not to feel stigma about seeking help from health professionals or business specialists, clients can come to see that counseling is a positive and adaptive response.

In contrast, other African Americans correctly surmise that they are in a racist society and that external forces hamper their opportunities for success. Some of these individuals assume that they are therefore not responsible for their problems but that they are simply the victims of racism or discrimination.

I remember working with Ms. Johnson. She had received a poor work evaluation, and her supervisor suggested that therapy could help solve interpersonal difficulties with her colleagues. Ms. Johnson wasn't inclined to seek out therapy until the supervisor intimated that she would place Ms. Johnson on probation unless she saw positive improvements in the next three months.

When I met with Ms. Johnson, she was somewhat reserved. She did say that she was glad to have a Black therapist because I would understand what she was up against. I asked her to clarify what she meant. Ms. Johnson said, "You know, the way that Whites pick on us Blacks for every little thing but let other Whites get away with everything."

During the first session, we explored Ms. Johnson's work performance. It became clear that she had problems with punctuality, absenteeism, and meeting deadlines for work projects. As we talked even further, I realized that Ms. Johnson, rather than taking responsibility for her difficulties, blamed them on racism. She was unsure of how to handle her work assignments. She felt isolated from and intimidated by her coworkers. Rather than asking for help, she became more discouraged and hopeless, which was reflected in her low performance. When I ran these ideas by Ms. Johnson, she seemed relieved to admit that she needed help at work. With a new understanding of what was happening, we were able to proceed with clear problem-solving strategies.

African American clients will vary on this internal-external continuum, and it is helpful for us to explore where they fit on it. We may also need to help the clients do reality testing about how their present difficulties are related to internal and external forces.

Clients who are too internal may need to understand that they actually can make themselves feel worse when they blame themselves for situations that are out of their control. In contrast, therapists may eventually have to help clients who are unable or unwilling to take appropriate responsibility for their situation.

We have a responsibility to understand what our clients' views are. But we may also need to work with them to develop more realistic and adaptive self-expectations.

EXPLORING THE PRESENTING PROBLEM

One of the significant challenges of the first session is to enable our African American clients to explain why they came for therapy. As therapists, we know that our ability to create a safe climate will help our clients fully express their concerns.

After developing rapport and giving some brief orientation to the first session, we're ready to ask the client, "Can you tell me what made you decide to come in today?" Our job is to help clients focus and define their presenting concerns.

On many occasions, Black clients come for help with a particular issue of concern but are unclear about the specific factors that may relate to their distress. Over the years, I have worked with many Black clients who say their presenting problem is low self-esteem, a lack of confidence, or feelings of anger and frustration about their lack of recognition in work or school.

For many of these clients, the first session is spent on recognizing to what extent their negative feelings are due to their own behavior as opposed to external factors. In many of these situations, it's important for me to reframe and normalize negative affect. I often help clients understand that there are factors outside their control that have slowed or limited their progress. I look to see if clients are sabotaging their progress with "internal racism" by intrinsically adopting the majority culture's stereotype that they somehow can never measure up. I help them develop a realistic self-appraisal while at the same time discouraging negative and distorted thinking. This process allows us to gain a clearer understanding of the client's strengths and weaknesses. We are then in a much better position to assess the presenting problem and develop an appropriate intervention.

We want to make sure our clients know that we're open to and accepting of whatever information they are prepared to share. We recognize that there are layers to the presenting problem. The way we react to the client's verbalization can determine whether we stall at a superficial level or can help our clients get in touch with other issues that may be even more crucial for us to address than the client's stated presenting problem. The following case illustrates how we can help clients identify their most salient problems and concerns.

Several years ago I received a referral for a twelve-year-old Black male, Johnny, who was showing a pattern of declining grades. In the first session Johnny's mother accompanied him. I invited the mother, Mrs. Grant, to meet with me initially to provide some background information. I asked Mrs. Grant to tell me what was occurring at school and at home with Johnny that made her decide to seek therapy. Mrs. Grant wasn't able to recount more than a few statements about her concerns about her son before she began crying. After giving her a moment to compose herself, I asked her, "What's happening now? What's making you cry?"

Mrs. Grant replied, "I just can't keep taking care of everyone in this family. I'm working long hours; my husband has gone to work by the time that I get home; and all I do every day is work at my job and work at home to handle everybody's problems. I have no time for me. I have no time for a relationship with my husband."

Mrs. Grant's opening statement was similar to what I often hear from Black women. They are willing to seek therapy for a relationship issue or out of concern for another family member. It's hard for them to acknowledge their own burdens.

I stated to Mrs. Grant, "It sounds like you're overwhelmed." With this invitation Mrs. Grant went on to explain the mounting financial pressures, the marital tensions, and how all these problems were pulling them away from spending time with their usual network of family and friends.

I asked Mrs. Grant if she could tell me more about the financial stress that she and her family were encountering. Following this discussion, we went on to explore her feelings of disconnection with her husband and her inability to meet her own needs due to the demands of her family. Mrs. Grant could see that Johnny was probably being affected by all the emotional undercurrents and preoccupation that he sensed around him. We knew that we would have to explore what was happening to Johnny in greater detail, but we agreed that first we needed to take some time to focus on Mrs. Grant in order to decrease some of the tension that was affecting Johnny and the whole family.

In essence, as we hear the presenting problems of our clients, we want to listen attentively and use minimal prompts to elicit

- Details of the problem

- Accompanying symptoms

- History of the presenting problem

- Strategies the client has employed

- Triggering events

- Psychosocial stressors

- Resources

- Why the client chose to seek help now

- Ideas about optimal solutions

In the following sections, I'll outline some ways to gain useful information about presenting problems. I'll also offer some case examples that illustrate culturally sensitive ways to address racial issues that are intertwined with presenting concerns.

Details of the Problem

Clients usually tell their story from the perspective they think is important. Sometimes we hear the general issue but miss significant cues that alert us to what clients may be comfortable about doing to solve their problems. It is our job as therapists to hear their point of view and retain the information and emphases our clients impart.

For instance, I worked with Mrs. Webb, a middle-aged Black women who worked as a practical nurse. Her seventy-year-old mother had recently been diagnosed with Alzheimer's. Her mother was home alone during the day and was causing problems by misplacing mail, hiding important papers, and forgetting to tell the family about vital phone messages. More significant, Mrs. Webb's mother left a pan in the oven following lunch, which ignited just as Mrs. Webb came home from work. Although Mrs. Webb's arrival prevented more serious consequences, she recognized that she had to take action to safeguard her mother and her house.

Mrs. Webb had consulted with her mother's physician. She knew that she could no longer leave her mother home alone. What she emphasized to me, however, was, "I don't want my mother put away in a nursing home."

What I learned was that placing her mother in a residential hospital was unacceptable. At this time, Mrs. Webb was only willing to consider allowing her mother to attend a day treatment program or to have a nurse come care for her mother in their home during the day.

As clients become comfortable, we can question them about acceptable solutions. We do this by suggesting courses of action or decisions that others have made in similar situations and inviting clients' feedback. We listen for opinions about expected outcomes. We notice when clients become silent or show ambivalence. We help them explore relationships between their stated attitudes, values, and actions.

Accompanying Symptoms

As we develop a full picture of what our clients are facing, it's important to find out how their presenting problem is affecting their lives. We need to ask them the following questions:

> Do you have any physical symptoms that recently began or became worse?
>
> Are there any problems with your appetite or sleep schedule?
>
> Has this problem had any impact on how you feel about yourself?
>
> Has there been any connection between your current concern and your ability to function at work, at home, or in relationships?

In some cases, it's the severity of the accompanying symptoms rather than the identified problem that precipitates the visit to the therapist. This was the situation when I treated Mrs. Agbu.

I received a referral from an internal medicine physician to work with Mr. and Mrs. Agbu. Mrs. Agbu had been seen by the internist on three different occasions over the last seven weeks. She complained of heart palpitations, dizziness, mental confusion, and excessive sweating. Mrs. Agbu felt certain on each occasion that she was having a heart attack. All diagnostic tests indicated that her heart was functioning normally.

Mrs. Agbu was unhappy about seeing me because she was convinced that she was suffering from a serious physical problem and that the physician was unwilling to continue to work with her because he claimed she didn't have a physical illness.

As I talked to Mr. and Mrs. Agbu, I explored what else had been happening over the last several months. I learned that Mr. Agbu's mother was from an island in the West Indies and had come to visit the family for the Christmas holiday but had stayed for over three months after the holiday had concluded. Although Mr. Agbu's mother was critical of Mrs. Agbu's cooking, housekeeping, and care of the children, she had decided to extend her stay indefinitely in order to be of support to her son and the children.

In this first session, Mr. and Mrs. Agbu were very uncomfortable discussing the length of his mother's visit. It was more acceptable for Mrs. Agbu to focus on her physical symptoms than her anger, anxiety, and depression. By asking questions, I was able to help them make the connection between Mrs. Agbu's physical problems and her mother-in-law's extended stay. After the issue of the mother-in-law's visit was made explicit, Mrs. Agbu was surprised to learn that her husband was also uncomfortable about the length of his mother's visit. Over the course of this first session, both Mr. and Mrs. Agbu came to feel that it was acceptable to solve this problem together by having Mr. Agbu respectfully ask his mother to leave.

History of the Presenting Problem

We want to have the client tell us when he or she first became aware of the presenting problem. We also want to learn something about the severity, stability, duration, frequency, and impact of the problem and its symptoms.

By asking questions we learn a great deal about clients. We'll see that some clients have sought treatment as soon as a problem manifests, some come as a result of a crisis, and others are only willing to come because of some external force such as a doctor's recommendation, the insistence of a family member or an employer, or some change in family circumstances.

Early in my training I received a referral to work with a thirty-year-year-old African American female named Ms. Davis who, although just recently admitted to an inpatient facility, showed signs of long-term schizophrenia. I met with Ms. Davis's parents to gain some insight as to why they were finally bringing her to a hospital.

Mr. and Mrs. Davis explained that their daughter was their only child, and they did not have her until they were in their early forties. They recognized by the time Ms. Davis graduated from high school that she had significant emotional problems, but they wanted to try to care for her in their home for as long as possible. They realized, however, that their own health was declining and knew they had to make some more permanent arrangements for their daughter because they did not have any friends or relatives who were able to assist with Ms. Davis's care.

Triggering Events

We can work more effectively with our African American clients if we try to understand with them the precipitating factors related to their presenting problems. We have to recognize that it can be confusing for African Americans to recognize triggering events. When they feel that they're experiencing a problem, especially if it relates to race, they may frequently have difficulty in getting others to validate their perceptions. They sometimes then begin to discount their thoughts and feelings or internalize anger at not being acknowledged. I have worked with several Black men who told me they had sought therapy to help with a problem they had with "anger." I'll use the case of Mr. Reynolds as an example.

Mr. Reynolds was typically a quiet and laid-back person. He came from a small, rural community where most Blacks still worked at a local paper mill that was owned and supervised by Whites.

Mr. Reynolds was a bright individual from a low-income family. He never received much encouragement to pursue a college education, although his academic credentials suggested that he would have been successful. Mr. Reynolds felt that he had no realistic work options after high school except to work at the paper mill. He had impressive work records for attendance and punctuality, but lately his supervisor complained that Mr. Reynolds was developing an "attitude problem." I asked Mr. Reynolds to explain what this term meant.

Mr. Reynolds told me that it had been easy for him "to go along with the program and do what I was told" when he was a new employee fresh out of high school. He stated that he was more and more frustrated because he had been at the job for over twelve years and he often knew more about day-to-day operations than the newly hired supervisors. These supervisors were invariably White and had some college education. Mr. Reynolds stated that these supervisors "liked to throw their weight around and tell everyone else what to do. They aren't willing to listen to any suggestions or innovations from those of us who've been here for years."

Mr. Reynolds repeatedly was shut out and "put in his place" after trying to make some suggestions to help out the supervisors. He recognized that he was reacting negatively. "Yeah, I guess I do get an attitude sometimes. I tell them what they can do with their work orders to me."

As I talked with Mr. Reynolds, it became clear that we were looking at a circumscribed anger problem that related to years of racism at work and probably to the lack of encouragement he received in school as well. I asked him if he felt that he lost control of his temper at work. He helped me understand that he was really quite in control of what he was doing and was actually taking a stand to communicate his displeasure in how he was being treated.

We were then able to reframe the presenting problem into the following issues: (1) he felt that his talents were not being adequately utilized; (2) he was disillusioned that he had not been asked (as were some White employees) to consider taking courses to become a supervisor; and (3) he needed to think seriously about making a job change to a situation in which there were more possibilities for advancement and self growth.

Previous Strategies Employed

It is condescending for us to assume that our clients have not tried to solve their problems in some form before they sought services with us. We want to find out what strategies they've already tried and what happened. We're more likely to be efficient if we know what our clients have done so far.

I recall working with Mr. and Mrs. Evans and their fifteen-year-old daughter, Kenisha, who had been skipping school, lying about her whereabouts, and sneaking out of the house at night. Kenisha wanted time to spend with her boyfriend, Jason, a nineteen-year-old high school dropout who Mr. and Mrs. Evans felt was unsuitable for Kenisha to date.

Mr. and Mrs. Evans explained that Mrs. Evans became pregnant with Kenisha when Mr. Evans was seventeen and she was sixteen. He was able to graduate from high school, but she had to return to school for a general equivalency diploma. The Evanses can still recall how heartbroken their families were when they announced the pregnancy.

Mr. and Mrs. Evans had both been good students and before the pregnancy had planned to go to college. They got married but resolved to beat the odds against teenage marriages surviving. They decided not to have any other children so that they could get decent jobs, become financially stable, and give their daughter a supportive and carefree period of growing up. They tried to let her know how important it was to stay focused on school and to stay away from sex, drugs, and the wrong crowd. They couldn't believe that after all their sacrifices their daughter seemed to be rejecting their plans for her to go to college, meet a nice young man, and get married and have children only when she was well prepared. They knew first-hand the stigma of being Black and teenage parents, and they badly wanted Kenisha to fulfill their own unrealized dreams.

The Evanses reported that they had already had several stormy sessions of yelling and shouting; they had grounded Kenisha from all social activities, and she no longer was allowed phone privileges. I was quickly able to establish how frustrated the whole family was feeling by checking out what had transpired so far. I knew that I needed to help this family come up with new interventions and ways of communicating to break the impasse the family was now in.

I met alone with Kenisha in that first session for about twenty minutes. She told me that she loved her parents but was furious at them. All her life they had pressured her to get good grades, be active in church, and be an example of good behavior to all her friends. She had heard over and over how she had changed and maybe had ruined her parents' chances of going to college. She also heard, "If a Black woman is going to make anything of herself she needs to keep to her books and leave the guys alone."

But as Kenisha asserted, "I'm not my parents. I'm me. I wish they'd stop trying to make me live their lives through me. Yes, Jason dropped out of school, but he's smart, he's nice, and he has a good job. Why are my parents so prejudiced against him? You'd think that after all they went through they could relate to the fact that Jason has had some problems in his family. He didn't have supportive parents who helped him stay in school. I think my parents should back off and let me make my own decisions. They got married young and are still together. Why do they automatically think I'm going to mess up?"

When I brought the family together and asked Kenisha to share her feelings, her parents were able to admit to her that she was right about how much pressure they were putting on her to have a different adolescence than they had. They told her they were really concerned about her and that the only thing they thought they could do was forbid her to see Jason.

We were able to talk together about the value of Mr. and Mrs. Evans meeting Jason and having more involvement in his and Kenisha's dating. We talked about the Evanses sitting down with Jason and explaining their concerns to him. Although Kenisha wasn't excited about this idea, she was willing to try this in return for the ability to date Jason openly. We recognized that we would need to talk more about helping the Evanses understand that they could not relive their lives through their daughter, despite their desire to protect her from all the problems that they felt young Black females faced.

Psychosocial Stressors

To fully understand the context of our clients' difficulties, we must know what other stressors they are facing. Even if the client has coped successfully with the presenting problem in the past, current stressors may have depleted his or her capacity to cope. Furthermore, additional stressors may have added to the presenting problem, making the whole situation more traumatic, complex, and resistant to treatment. Questions that we can use to assess the level of psychosocial stress include the following:

> Are there any events going on for you in your life now that makes it harder for you to problem solve?
>
> What else is happening?
>
> What kind of impact are these events having on your life?
>
> Are there other people that you're worried about at this time?
>
> Do you have any pressing financial, work, relationship, or health issues at this time?

Mr. Frazier's case is a good example of how multiple stressors can operate. Mr. Frazier sought therapy after a routine physical exam revealed that he was seriously hypertensive. He was placed on medication. Although Mr. Frazier knew that many African Americans suffer from hypertension, he had experienced no warning symptoms. Mr. Frazier stated that he came for help because he had told his physician that he felt he was no longer able to be as focused and effective at work as he had been in the past.

Mr. Frazier had been fairly happy with his job as a high school social science teacher. He had been asked to consider moving "up" to an administrative position, but he had always declined in the past because he enjoyed his interactions with students in the classroom. Mr. Frazier had been divorced for seven years and had a good relationship with his ex-spouse and his sixteen-year-old son from that marriage. He had been dating a woman for the last two years, and they had begun to discuss marriage.

His girlfriend had never been married before and had no children; she had let Mr. Frazier know that she definitely wanted to have children once she was married. As Mr. Frazier and I explored the stressors in his life, he came to realize that he felt serious financial pressure to earn more money. He had promised to help pay his son's college expenses, and he knew that it would be expensive to marry and to raise another child. His ex-wife had accused him of not being ambitious enough in the past but he had always been able to meet his financial obligations and keep the job that he loved.

In order to realize his goal of marrying his girlfriend, Mr. Frazier recognized that his current salary would not accommodate these expenses and those related to his son. We were better able to clarify what was happening with Mr. Frazier by capitalizing on his desire to move beyond his physical diagnoses of hypertension and trying to understand how stress might be affecting his decreased focus and effectiveness at work. Once we identified the myriad of stressors he was facing, we then were able to develop an effective treatment plan.

Resources

Another dimension to understanding the presenting problem is recognizing that the client may have an array of resources that can be of assistance. We can affirm the client's self-efficacy and confidence if we review potential areas of strength that can support his or her problem-solving abilities. We also need to know how the client feels about any potential resources. This conversation can be affirming for some clients and difficult for others, depending on how they perceive their strengths and resources. If we learn that a client does not have a good support system, it's a signal that one session of therapy may not be enough and that one of the auxiliary goals of therapy may focus on developing such a network.

I worked with Mrs. Wright, who had five children, worked as a teacher's assistant, and had been married for fifteen years. Over the last eight years her husband's occasional binge drinking developed into alcoholism. After repeated warnings, Mr. Wright lost his job as a school janitor. Mrs. Wright lived in a low-income neighborhood and had to turn to public assistance to care for her family.

Mrs. Wright was referred for therapy when she told her social worker that her son had recently been suspended from school for drinking. She felt overwhelmed with her family responsibilities and felt that she had no available support system.

After she told me in our first session that she had no network of support, I was able to contact her social worker, and together with Mrs. Wright we arranged for the children to attend an after-school tutoring session at a neighborhood recreation center. We also were able to contact a neighborhood Black church that expressed an interest in supporting and mentoring local families. In this case, we were able to develop a very necessary support system for this family.

It is interesting to note that once the family received additional support, Mr. Wright was able to complete a rehabilitation program and regain his job.

I have worked with other clients who had resources they were not using. In some cases clients found that it was useful to spend some downtime talking to or visiting an old friend or relative who might reside out of town or out of state. When I have worked with clients who were struggling with alcohol, substance abuse, grief work, and physical and sexual abuse, they have sometimes been open to participating in support groups that work on these issues. Whatever the potential resources, one of the most useful strategies in therapy is to encourage and support clients to nurture and take care of themselves.

To assess the functioning of a support network, the following questions can be used:

What are some of the strengths you have been able to use in the past in problem solving?

Do you have a good support system?

Who is in your support system?

How regularly do you turn to others for help?

Do you feel that your support system can help you with your present concerns?

Explanation of Timing

We know it is essential for us to understand why a client chose this particular time to come for therapy. In some cases the answer is straightforward. The problem has just begun, it is causing a great deal of distress for the client, and the client is unable to cope any longer. In other situations the presenting problem has existed for a while but recently became worse or even reached a crisis level.

As we have discussed elsewhere, it is not unusual for African American clients to attempt to cope with problems on their own. Sometimes it takes another person or an external agency to insist that services be obtained so as to avoid additional negative consequences. In many of these situations, clients know a problem is developing but minimize or deny the difficulties they're facing. My work with Ms. Banks fell in this latter category.

Ms. Banks, a twenty-nine-year-old mother of two, had been in an abusive marriage for eight years, and had been divorced for two years. She had been living with her boyfriend for the last year along with her sons, ages six and eight.

Ms. Banks knew that her boyfriend, Mr. Willie, worked from eleven at night until seven in the morning. She also knew that sometimes he stopped with friends to smoke pot or have a few drinks before coming home in the morning. Ms. Banks relied on Mr. Willie to be at home by seven-thirty in the morning to wake her sons and get them ready for school. She waited until he arrived, then left in order to get to her job as a bank clerk by eight.

On many occasions, Mr. Willie didn't come home until after she had to get the boys to school herself. Consequently, she was late to work. Ms. Banks was afraid to challenge Mr. Willie about his lack of responsibility because he helped with rent, utilities, and food expenses. She also was afraid that if she tried to confront Mr. Willie he would either leave or become abusive, as her ex-husband had done in the past. It wasn't until the bank notified Ms. Banks that she stood to lose her job that she decided she had to figure out what to do about her relationship with her boyfriend, her children, and her job. She then sought therapy.

Clients' Ideas About Optimal Solutions

We learn a great deal about clients by asking them what needs to happen in order for their problems to be resolved. We can't make assumptions about what they want.

For example, I once worked with a young African American couple, Mr. and Mrs. Trent. They sought help because their marriage was in trouble. When I asked Mrs. Trent what she wanted as an outcome for therapy, she had very specific ideas. She told me, "I want my husband to spend more time with me and less time at work and with his friends. I want him to listen more attentively to me so that we can work out our issues and stay married."

When I asked Mr. Trent what he wanted from therapy, he replied, "I just want her to get off my back and leave me alone. At this point,

I don't care if the marriage continues. In fact, I think I'd be happier if we could work on how we can end this marriage and go our separate ways."

As it turned out, the Trents clearly had very different ideas about how to solve their marriage conflict. Mrs. Trent thought they still had a relationship to work on, but Mr. Trent was sincere in his belief that there was nothing he could do to make his wife happy. He said that he had loved her when they first got married but he felt they had grown apart. He wanted them to separate, and he wasn't willing to do any couple therapy at that time. Mrs. Trent was surprised at the depth of her husband's feelings. I saw her alone for several subsequent sessions as she came to terms with the marital separation.

The Trents' case reminded me that we can't be responsive to our clients without finding out what they consider to be a helpful and useful resolution to their concerns. We also must note that in some situations, clients recognize that they feel bad but are unclear about what could make them feel better. Therapists can then help clients clarify what is causing them distress and what steps can be taken to help them feel better.

TYPICAL FIRST-SESSION CHALLENGES

We know that accomplishing an effective first session is a demanding task. In addition to being sensitive to protective devices, handling diverse communication styles, and exploring presenting problems, therapists must also be prepared for those first sessions when we must work with involuntary or resistant clients. We also need to actively solicit client expectations and encourage their involvement as we help orient Black clients to the therapy process. The following sections discuss how we can best handle these first session challenges when we're working with African American clients.

Involuntary Clients

Some Black clients are referred to therapy or mandated to attend therapy by an external source. These individuals usually are ambivalent about the mandate to "get better or else." Consequences often range from losing a job, a relationship, or custody of children to facing a jail sentence.

As therapists, we must recognize the issues we face with involuntary African American clients. Individuals who are forced into therapy feel resentful, resistant, and uncooperative. Clients in this situation usually view therapy as aversive but come because the consequences of not participating are worse. We need to be straightforward in asking the client to explain how he or she feels about being mandated or advised to enter therapy. We can acknowledge and support clients' anger and ambivalence, and we can be sensitive to any racial factors that they feel are involved. It may be challenging for us to hear clients' negative feelings about coming for therapy, but it's impossible for us to develop trust without laying these feelings on the table. We can then take the next step and explain to clients that, although they have come for help under duress, therapy can help in the following ways:

- Get the probation officer off their back

- Reduce a court sentence

- Regain visitation rights with their children

- Give them another chance at work

- Convince a partner that they are serious about making some changes

- Make progress in the area that they've been asked to address

It's imperative that we clarify with whom we have our therapy contract. Frequently, we are responsible not only to the client we're working with but also to the external agency that instigated the original referral. We have an obligation to get a release of information signed so that information can be shared with other individuals. We must let clients know from the very beginning that our working relationship won't be completely confidential. We need to be clear with the agency about what material it expects to receive, and we need to inform our clients of what information will be shared.

Our ability to be straightforward in discussing issues of limited confidentiality accomplishes several goals. It lets our clients see that we're willing to be honest about difficult issues. It alerts them to how the information in therapy will be used, and it starts us on the process of collaboration and relationship building even when the client has been mandated to therapy.

Resistant Clients

Some African American clients feel so threatened or uncomfortable by the therapy process that they are actively or passively resistant in the first session. These clients may come late in order to allow less time for the interaction. Other clients may keep the conversation at a superficial level to avoid talking about the presenting problem. Another tactic resistant clients may take involves limiting their participation by refusing to answer questions, offering monosyllabic or minimal responses, or giving us the silent treatment.

When we encounter resistance in African American clients in the first session, we have to address this behavior tactfully but firmly. If we allow Black clients to resist the process of therapy, they're unlikely to benefit from the session or return. On the other hand, we don't want to confront African American clients in ways that promote embarrassment or discomfort. I usually allow the client to engage in the resistant behaviors long enough for me to feel confident that what I am observing is truly resistance and not a communication style of shyness, anxiety, or some serious psychological dysfunction.

Once I feel confident that I am dealing with a situation of resistance I develop a sentence along the following lines:

I can appreciate how hard it might have been for you to come in today. Although you've given me a lot of details about your job, I need you to help me understand exactly why your supervisor required you to come for therapy.

I notice that you seem to have difficulty opening up to me and answering questions. Is there anything I need to know about what you're feeling right now? Is there anything I can do to make this first therapy session more comfortable for you?

I know that this is your first time talking to a therapist and it may feel awkward. I believe that as we spend more time together you'll feel more comfortable, and it will be easier for you to see how, if we work together, we can make significant progress with the difficulties that you are experiencing.

If our African American clients tell us about a specific basis for their resistance such as concerns about finances, transportation, shame or discomfort, coercion into therapy, our qualifications, or our demographic or personality characteristics, we can openly address their concerns and questions. If we get the impression that the resistance is too entrenched for us to be effective with a particular client, we need to discuss and plan referral options.

Client Expectations

Client expectations for therapy and the therapist relate to what the client views as the ideal solution and what the client expects from the therapist. These expectations could be shaped by a variety of factors. Some clients may have had friends, relatives, or colleagues who have had positive experiences with therapy. These individuals may bring a positive expectancy to the first session and in telling their presenting problem they are confident that they will be helped. In fact in some cases African American clients may see us as such effective authority figures that they have unrealistically positive expectations. In these situations Black clients may expect too much from a first session of therapy. They may feel that we can somehow quickly solve their problems for them. We need to help clients understand that solving problems takes time and requires them to collaborate with us.

In contrast, other individuals may have heard negative stories about what happens to African Americans in seeking therapy and may be very guarded, fearful, and pessimistic about the therapy process. We need to take time with these clients to help them develop an accurate idea about how therapy works and what might be realistic accomplishments, given their concerns.

Clients who have been referred or mandated to therapy by an external source may feel hostile at worst or ambivalent at best about participating in the therapy process. They may have been presented with the mandate to "get better or else," which clearly can have a chilling effect on their enthusiasm for therapy.

For all clients, if we demonstrate that we want to hear their feelings, validate their concerns, and help them develop effective solutions to problems, we have a good chance to create positive expectations about therapy and us. We can explain to involuntary and resistant clients that we think some good can come of therapy despite external pressure. We can let them know that we've worked with others who had been pressured into therapy and that many of these individuals ended up feeling good about the gains they had made in therapy once they decided to participate. Whatever the client's motivation for seeking therapy, the first and subsequent sessions of therapy can proceed more smoothly if the therapist notes the following about the client:

- Feelings about coming for therapy
- Ideas about goals and solutions

- Reactions to us as a therapist

- Willingness to engage in therapy

The following case illustrates how I helped clarify client expectations for therapy, validated realistic concerns, and helped this couple develop some achievable treatment goals.

Several years ago I worked with Mr. and Mrs. Carter in a situation where Mr. Carter was an involuntary client. Mr. Carter was a sailor in the navy, and Mrs. Carter sold cosmetics part-time. They had been married for three years. Over the last year they had more frequent arguments about money, and on two occasions Mr. Carter had pushed and shoved his wife. On the first occasion Mrs. Carter was reluctant to get outside help because she was afraid to get her husband into trouble. On the second occasion of violence she called the police, which also resulted in this incident being reported to his supervisor at work. As a consequence, Mr. Carter was ordered to go through some required anger management sessions run by navy family services and was "advised" to participate in marriage counseling with his wife.

When I met with Mr. and Mrs. Carter, it was easier to establish rapport with Mrs. Carter. She indicated that she wanted the violence to stop or else she planned to leave the marriage. Mr. Carter was passive, quiet, and hostile. I decided to meet briefly with each of them alone. When I met alone with Mr. Carter, he explained that he was embarrassed to be in a position of being ordered to get therapy, he was afraid of losing his wife, and he was fearful of how his work record would be affected by his arrest and his progress in therapy. He also knew how angry his wife was at home and worried that if she didn't cooperate in therapy, she could disrupt the process of therapy and make him look bad to his supervisor.

My major objective in that first session with Mr. Carter was to keep him focused on why he had been forced into therapy: his violent and abusive behaviors toward his wife. I validated his concerns that he was in a precarious position with respect to work and his marriage. I helped him understand that unless he was able to (1) become actively involved in the therapy process and (2) indicate that he was willing to learn new ways of responding to his wife, she might very well be uncooperative and leave him, and yes, his job was at stake.

Although Mr. Carter continued to have some anger and resentment about being forced into therapy, he was able to tell me that I had at least "given him the bottom line" on what his options were. He became more involved in therapy, and both he and his wife felt that they learned some more adaptive ways of communicating and solving problems.

Encouraging Client Involvement

Many Black clients will be unclear as to what their role in therapy is supposed to be. In Chapter Three I described in detail the comments that I use to orient African American clients to the therapy process and help establish a good working relationship. Most of us expect our clients to show up, talk, and actively collaborate with us in problem solving. However, many African American clients are used to seeing friends and family members get help from clergy and physicians. Their exposure to the mental health system may have come from children's services, probation and parole offices, or other court services. Whether their experiences were positive or negative, Blacks have often felt impotent in these circumstances, which leads them to assume that the doctor is in charge of therapy and that they are to follow directions.

Some African American clients believe they can tell us their problems in the initial session and that by the end of the session we'll have a solution. They think therapy will be a variation on the way a physician hears about a symptom, makes a diagnosis, writes a prescription, and then says, "Go home, take these pills for ten days, and you'll be fine." We know however that, whereas some problems can indeed be solved quickly, others will require more time.

As a first step toward understanding how we can best encourage and engage our clients in the therapy process, we need to listen attentively to clients as they describe their presenting concerns so that we can determine

- How motivated the client appears to solve problems

- How involved the client is in the intake process

- Whether the client appears willing and able to play an active role in therapy

- How open the client is to exploring alternative view-points and strategies

The following case illustrates how I encouraged the Williams family to be involved in the therapy process.

I saw Mr. and Mrs. Williams and their fourteen-year-old daughter, Gail, on a crisis basis. Gail was the identified patient. She had taken about a dozen painkillers following an argument with her boyfriend. The argument related to pressure that the boyfriend had placed on Gail to have sex with him. I met with Gail and her parents after the hospital emergency personnel and the mental health crisis worker had seen her. Gail had contracted for safety and had been referred to me for outpatient follow-up work.

Gail and her parents were obviously still shaky and in shock. The parents were angry with Gail for making the suicide attempt and couldn't believe that she would jeopardize her life for the sexual demands of her sixteen-year-old boyfriend. Gail was angry at her parents, who she felt were always too strict and never cared about what was important to her. After trying to deescalate some of the high emotions, I collected some background information.

Toward the end of the session, I explained to the family that I thought Gail would need some individual sessions with me and that family sessions were also warranted. The parents were stunned. They told me, "You need to do something with her now. We can't wait for you to fix her in a couple of weeks!"

I had to explain to the parents that the problems the family was facing had developed over time, and it would take some time for us to work them out. I let them know that I had no magical solution that would transform Gail from the angry and frightened young person she was into the easygoing and conforming daughter they wanted. I told them I needed to work with all of them so that they could hear and respond more supportively to what was going on with one another and that this process would probably take months. I explained that I could understand why they wanted a quick fix, but it wasn't possible. We needed to work on Gail's perception that her parents were too strict and we needed to help Gail develop less impulsive and dangerous responses when she was upset and frustrated. They did agree to follow-up therapy, and we made good progress on our mutually developed goals.

This chapter has outlined interview strategies for effective first sessions with African American clients. In Chapter Six, we'll expand upon our repertoire of skills with African American clients as we explore crisis intervention strategies.

6

Crisis Intervention Strategies

We know that significant numbers of African Americans don't seek mental health services until they're in a crisis situation. Even when crises and emergencies occur, Black clients turn first to family members, ministers, or individuals in their normal day-to-day environment for help. Typically, these clients believe that turning to therapists will lead to their feeling misunderstood, humiliated, or even less in control of their lives.

Black clients who come for a first session in a crisis situation vary with respect to their problem, age, socioeconomic status, coping ability, and risk factors. Some of these individuals will have struggled with a chronic difficulty that they can no longer handle, whereas others will seek services due to situations with a sudden onset.

When we interact with these clients in a first session, we have very specific goals that we must accomplish in a time-limited fashion. We need to

- Understand the specific crisis and its ramifications

- Convey our respect, concern, and ability to help from the first interaction

- Develop a healthy rapport and communication pattern

- Work collaboratively to empower clients to mobilize their resources

- Determine the client's potential for harm

- Develop, evaluate, and implement a plan to solve the client's immediate concerns and to stimulate some growth and development in order to prevent crises in the future

One of the challenges that we have as therapists is to efficiently explore any possible role that racial or cultural dynamics may have in a crisis situation. Many Black families have learned to tolerate high levels of stress, so when they present for assistance they may be struggling with multiple, long-term stressors as well as acute situations. For some Black clients, the stresses and struggles of their daily lives are so challenging and their resources so stretched that they are unable to cope with a situation that families with more resources could absorb with less harm.

In this chapter we'll focus on the racial issues that therapists need to be sensitive to as they attend to the crisis situations of their African American clients. Specifically, we'll look at assessment guidelines, intervention strategies, and crisis situations involving health issues, interactions with law enforcement services, and domestic problems such as infidelity and violence.

ASSESSMENT GUIDELINES

Our assessment begins when we first interact with the client either by phone or in person. We must immediately try to understand any potential danger, harm, or risk. We note the emotion, agitation, and quality of thought displayed by the client. We're alert to any indications of active substance abuse or borderline or psychotic functioning. We're already processing whether we're in the midst of an active emergency that involves self-inflicted harm, the possibility of harm to others, the inability to self-care, trauma, battering, or abuse, especially of children, the elderly, and the disabled.

Once we have concluded that we are dealing with a crisis situation with a Black client, we begin to process what is happening with the client as we

- Ask the client to be honest

- Listen and validate client concerns

- Maintain an attitude of calm

- Identify potential resources

- Formulate possible interventions

In the case to follow, I illustrate how we can conduct an assessment in a crisis situation while developing a relationship with a client and beginning to formulate and implement problem-solving interventions.

I received a call from my answering service at five-thirty A.M. on a Sunday morning. When I called the number, I reached a Mr. Blake, a thirty-eight-year-old Black male. He told me that he had gotten my name from a friend but had never bothered to call until now. Although I don't know for sure, I believe that Mr. Blake called me in part because he knew I was Black and also because I was probably the only resource he could think of, although we had never met.

Mr. Blake reported that he was already on probation for a fight he had gotten in at a bar when someone made a pass at his girlfriend. The previous evening, after a few drinks and when driving home in a rainstorm, he went through a red light to avoid sliding. Although he didn't slide, he did collide with another vehicle. As a result, Mr. Blake was bruised and shaken up and later had to be patched up at the local hospital.

When two White police officers came to investigate the accident, he felt that they were belligerent and rude. They took a statement from him, conducted a blood alcohol test, and then told him to return to his home after he went to the hospital. They told him they would come talk to him by midday after they had talked to other witnesses.

He did not know how seriously injured the driver in the other car was. He knew that if he were charged with reckless driving, given his police record, he could lose his license and receive jail time. Because hunting was one of his hobbies, he had a variety of weapons at his disposal; he told me, "If I'm charged with reckless driving or if I seriously injured the other driver, I would rather kill myself than live with the harm that I caused."

It was clear that Mr. Blake was in immediate danger due to the fact that he had been drinking and was fearful about what would happen to him. Also, even though we know that they're fearful of psychiatric diagnosis, medication, involvement with social services or the court system, we must ask our Black clients to be honest with us. From the beginning, we must demonstrate our willingness to address racial issues.

When I talked to Mr. Blake I immediately validated his concerns about how he might be perceived by the police. I said, "I know that your fears about interacting with the police are warranted. Can you describe to me some of the things that they said or did that you found to be rude and offensive? I know that many Black organizations are now issuing national guidelines for African Americans when they are stopped by police officers. They are reminding us to keep our hands visible, stay calm, speak at a normal volume, cooperate, and not make any sudden moves. Is there anything that you are aware of that you said or did that made the officers treat you the way that they did?" I repeated these guidelines to Mr. Blake because I knew that he was due to see the police officers again, and I wanted to minimize any additional problems he might have.

It's also very important that we ask the client to tell us what resources and supports are available to assist with the current emergency. We need to develop an understanding of how much the client is capable of doing versus how much we'll need to do.

It was clear to me that Mr. Blake was in real danger of making a suicide attempt. He had a viable plan, guns at his disposal, and what he believed was strong motivation to end his life. In addition, we both knew that as a Black male, his fears of being found guilty, receiving a jail sentence, and losing his license were valid.

We knew that from his interactions with the police, they were likely to paint a very negative picture of Mr. Blake's behavior. His agitation, anxiety, and fear would be translated as resistance and lack of cooperation, and cast as further evidence that he was intoxicated and showing inappropriate behavior.

I tried to calm him down by diverting his attention from the immediate crisis. I wanted to know if there was anyone else I could call on that he would listen to, so I asked him if he lived with his girlfriend. I learned that he lived alone; he would not name anyone among his family or friends who could talk to him and dissuade him from his intent. He seemed to have no immediate resources.

As soon as the conversation began, I scribbled a note to a family member in my house to use my cellular phone and call the police department, have them to trace the call, and go to Mr. Blake's home. In bold letters I scribbled that we needed to get some African American police officers and mental health workers involved. I recognized that we had a very dangerous situation that could wind up harming not just Mr. Blake but others as well if there was an exchange of gunshots. I was worried that if more White police officers were involved and became more offensive, violence could result.

I continued to restrain my own anxiety. Keeping my voice even, I told Mr. Blake that I had requested that some Black police officers and Black counselors be sent to his home. I told him that because he was able to tell me how he had been treated by the police officers, I would be able to back up his story. I assured him that I would work with him to do all that I could to minimize any further racial bias in how he was being treated. I mentioned that we could talk about getting him some solid legal representation that would make sure that all the racial dynamics in his case were brought to light.

As I maintained phone contact with Mr. Blake, the call was traced and the back-up Black police officers and an African American crisis worker were sent to his home. Because he had been unwilling to give me his phone number and address and because I had maintained phone contact while I scribbled a note, Mr. Blake didn't really believe that I had asked for additional help for him. The police had requested that I ask him to come to the door and come outside with his hands visibly free of any weapons. I was also to tell him that armed police had surrounded his house but that the crisis worker wanted him to come out and talk to him.

When Mr. Blake said to me, "There's no one outside," I responded, "Mr. Blake, we've been on the phone for over two hours. If you look out your window, you'll see that I have been honest with you. Please, go outside with your hands up and turn yourself over to the crisis counselor."

I heard him fumble at the window; I heard a few choice curse words and then the receiver being slammed down. I ran to the cellular phone and then heard a police officer say to me, "It's all clear. It's over. He came out." I talked to the crisis worker after he had spoken to Mr. Blake. By this time he had been able to inform Mr. Blake that the driver in the other car was not seriously injured and had backed up Mr. Blake's report of what happened. Blood alcohol testing that was done after the accident failed to show any significant levels of alcohol in Mr. Blake's system. In part due to the intervention of the two Black officers that assisted, Mr. Blake was given a stern warning about combining alcohol with poor driving conditions, but he was not criminally charged.

DEVELOPMENT OF AN INTERVENTION PLAN

As was the case with Mr. Blake's acute emergency, we sometimes have to conduct our assessment at almost the same time we begin our intervention. When situations are not so acute, after we've completed our assessment we're in a position to collaboratively develop an intervention plan with the client. We want to make sure that we have our client's agreement with respect to

- What the major problem to be solved is

- What the client's preferences for a solution are

- What other priorities there might be with respect to solving related problems

- Who needs to be involved in the problem-solving process

After a discussion of possible actions and strategies to be used, it's useful for all involved to make a written contract of what is to be done, who is to do it, and when. This written contract can be helpful in empowering the client, providing a clear record of priorities and responsibilities, and facilitating an effective method of implementation. We also want to make sure our plans are specific, realistic, and concrete.

INTERVENTION STRATEGIES

The specific intervention plan that we develop with clients is based on each client's needs, resources, and current level of threat. For clients in acute emergencies, we may need to explain that we think hospitalization is necessary. At this point, if family members are not present we may need to ask the client's permission to contact relatives to facilitate the hospitalization. The following case involves a crisis requiring hospitalization despite the reluctance of the client's mother.

Mrs. Carroll escorted her nineteen-year-old daughter, Ms. Carroll, for an emergency evaluation. The mother reported that Ms. Carroll had

a long history of erratic behavior, but with careful support and structure from her family she had managed to graduate from school.
Clearly this family was trying its best to protect their child from having to deal with the mental health system. Mrs. Carroll told me that
she knew that patients in hospitals were often abused, raped, and
restrained. She felt that a petite Black female would be at great risk
for harm and abuse.

Recently, Ms. Carroll was emotionally labile, got into arguments
and physical fights with relatives, and complained that her head hurt
from a constant pounding. She also started telling all her family members that Denzel Washington, the famous actor, had been calling and
writing her. Because of this romance, Ms. Carroll took her mother's
credit card, made frequent calls around the country to get Denzel's
phone number, and went on a shopping spree. She also reported
that she could hear Denzel talking to her. Mrs. Carroll explained that
this romance developed right after a male high school friend, whom
Ms. Carroll had a crush on, told her he definitely was not interested
in her.

It seemed clear that Ms. Carroll was experiencing a psychotic
episode and needed to be evaluated for medication and hospitalization. I explained that I wanted her to see another doctor whom I
worked with at a nearby hospital. I told her that I thought this doctor would be able to give her some medication to help her feel better. I tried to reassure her that I knew this doctor, that he was Black,
and that both of us would do all we could to ensure her safety and
well-being.

I called the hospital, had my associate paged, and asked him to
be prepared to see my clients as soon as they arrived. I explained to
mother and daughter that they would be asked some additional
questions by the doctor that I was referring them to and that he
would decide whether or not medication or hospitalization were
warranted.

Mrs. Caroll seemed to be overwhelmed by all of these arrangements. She told me that she was afraid if she let her daughter see this doctor, her daughter would be locked up for years and she wouldn't be able to see her. I explained to Mrs. Carroll that the doctor would not hospitalize her daughter unless he felt it was absolutely necessary. I went on to say that it was likely that Ms. Carroll would be given medication. It also was possible that the doctor would suggest outpatient treatment or a day treatment program. I recognized that Mrs. Carroll had heard so many horror stories of Black clients being hospitalized and apparently forgotten that she feared a similar outcome for her daughter. By spending just a little time describing the possibilities and allaying her fears, I was able to help Mrs. Carroll feel more confident and comfortable about securing help for her daughter. The psychiatrist decided to hospitalize Ms. Carroll for two weeks, and then she joined a day treatment program.

In cases where we don't think hospitalization is necessary, we may be able to contract for safety with our clients. Here, clients sign a written form stating that they won't harm themselves. We make clear that, if they feel upset or at risk, they will call their therapist first; if the therapist is not immediately available, they'll contact an emergency service that is available on a twenty-four-hour basis. We also need to ask our clients to remove from their immediate environment any weapons, pills, or other devices that we consider sources of harm.

Sometimes we can do a lot to stabilize our African American clients by suggesting that we call them at prearranged times to check in on them and see how they're doing. We can let our clients know that if they're feeling panicky they can call or page us. We can return their call to see what is happening, and if we agree that an emergency session is warranted we can set one up. Throughout the process, we're open to any racial dynamics that may exacerbate their problems. By contracting with our clients along these lines, we're trying to meet them at their comfort and safety levels.

CRISES THAT AFRICAN AMERICANS EXPERIENCE

Black clients can be affected by a broad variety of crises that range from external events such as natural disasters to physical stressors such as AIDS, cancer, and psychotic illnesses, as well as interpersonal and individual situations such as divorces, deaths, suicides, and violence.

Some of the crisis situations that Blacks face are unrelated to racial or cultural factors, whereas other problems are exacerbated by racial status or gender. For example, we know that African Americans are one of the fastest-growing groups diagnosed as being HIV positive. We know that Blacks with cancer have a worse prognosis than Whites, even controlling for socioeconomic factors.

We also need to be aware that gender and race interact to put Black women at special risk with respect to health status. A recently released study by the American Medical Association confirmed what many African Americans already knew. The study found that Black women were treated less aggressively than White males, White females, and Black males with respect to heart disease. The fact that medical professionals don't take the health concerns of Black females as seriously as they do for other groups and that they perform less aggressive treatments sends a strong signal to Black women that their lives are not valued by society. Further, it reinforces a crisis mode of managing health issues for Black women.

We've mentioned earlier that, although African Americans only account for 12 percent of the population, they make up almost 50 percent of prison populations. As a result, many Black families must cope with the crises of arrests, court trials, and incarceration.

For a variety of racial, social, and economic factors, Blacks more frequently than Whites deal with homelessness, loss of employment, school problems, and interactions with social services that may involve removing their children from the home and seeking foster placements, sometimes in the homes of White families.

Likewise, we've discussed the complexities of intimate and social relationships in the African American community such as the challenges of finding compatible partners and maintaining healthy relationships. Blacks therefore may seek emergency services due to unwanted pregnancies (especially teenagers), infidelity in relationships, rape, abuse, neglect, and violence. In this section we will focus on some of the common crisis situations that lead African Americans to seek crisis services.

Health Issues

Mr. and Mrs. Thomas appeared for therapy three days after Mr. Thomas had been released from the hospital due to problems with angina and hypertension. Mrs. Thomas reported that she was both furious with her husband and frightened to death that he had just been hospitalized with two very serious illnesses that he hadn't told her about. She knew that her forty-two-year-old husband had a family history of hypertension, but after each checkup he always told her that his pressure was "a little high but the doctor and I are watching it."

What Mr. Thomas didn't reveal was that his pressure was dangerously high, and his doctor had prescribed diuretics and a prescription to lower his pressure. When the doctor explained that hypertension was a risk factor for a variety of other illnesses, Mr. Thomas became very nervous. The doctor explained that one of the side effects of the medication was reduced sexual desire and difficulty with sexual functioning. Because the doctor also indicated that diet and exercise could reduce his hypertension, Mr. Thomas decided not to worry his wife with the diagnosis. He further decided that he would try to modify his diet and not take the prescribed medication because he did not want to deal with the sexual side effects. Unfortunately, Mr. Thomas's plans to cut down on salt, eat less pork, and walk four times a week were never implemented. Instead, he was hospitalized after he was rushed to the hospital from work following his complaints of chest pains.

Mrs. Thomas was hurt and upset because her husband hid the seriousness of his health concerns. Mr. Thomas felt miserable due to his physical problems and was also sorry that he upset his wife. He explained to Mrs. Thomas and me that he really thought he could handle his physical condition on his own but found himself not fully understanding all of the information his doctor was relaying to him. He was also, like many other African American clients, afraid to ask any questions.

Traditionally, many Black clients view all physicians as authorities who shouldn't be questioned. Doctors are often given a kind of respect that conveys that patients can't raise concerns, questions, or dialogue about diagnosis and treatment options. The Thomas scenario is all too common for Black clients with respect to health issues. Many Blacks are not aware of the early signs of serious illnesses. When they become aware of potential problems, they often try self-medications or denial. For instance, when Mr. Thomas first started experiencing frequent headaches, he decided the problem was dehydration. So when he was out fishing on weekends, he treated himself with salt tablets, which of course only exacerbated his problems.

Another problem is that once African Americans seek assistance, they may not be compliant about taking medicine or following dietary and health recommendations. This lack of compliance is sometimes related to financial constraints, but incomplete explanations, fear of side effects, and the difficulty of changing eating and relaxation habits also contribute to this problem.

We know that many health professionals are not successful in conveying vital information to Black clients in a manner that is user friendly. As a result, when African American clients present in therapy with a health crisis, therapists need to help them interface with health personnel.

The first step in a health crisis is to get clients to tell us about their physical condition. We'll also need a signed release form to consult with medical personnel. Next, we want to find out if our clients have informed significant others about their health status. Our role as therapists may be to help our clients find ways to tell partners and family members about their health concerns in ways that are clear and informative without being frightening.

We also need to ask our clients what recommendations their doctor has made about treatment, prognoses, and ways to reduce risk factors. We can be helpful by asking our clients to tell us what fears and concerns they have about the course of their disease, as well as any risks or side effects of prescribed medications. It is often useful to help our clients develop a list of questions they can ask their health professionals. We can also have them role-play asking these questions.

As therapists we need to be aware of the fact that African American clients become wary of treatment regimens that they fear will have a negative impact on their job performance, that will adversely affect their ability to function in their intimate relationships, and that will affect their physical appearance. We need to raise these possible concerns with clients and work with them to develop solutions that work. For example, we can talk to our clients about when and how they may need to share health information with their supervisors at work. We need to be aware of the fact that because discrimination does exist in the workforce, Blacks may need to carefully review the health benefits they are eligible for in their positions. We may need to help them advocate for fair treatment.

Cancer and Potentially Disfiguring Illnesses

We may need to plan couple and family therapy sessions to help our clients explore any changes in their personal and intimate relationships due to their physical health. Black women are at high risk for breast cancer, and Black men are at high risk for prostate cancer. Black women who are dealing with breast and other types of cancer must cope with the challenges of radiation and chemotherapy, as well as changes in their physical appearance and body image.

We've already mentioned that hair, skin, and appearance issues are important to Black women because they are often compared to White beauty standards. We also know that Black men are very appearance-oriented. For many Black men and women, appearance is important because it can represent an aspect of their lives that they can control. As therapists, we need to actively help our Black clients address their feelings about their image and appearance along with physical challenges and mortality issues.

When it comes to appearance, we can now reassure our African American clients that they have opportunities to buy wigs that are flattering and realistic. Makeup shades are now available that match Black skin tones and can conceal scars and depigmentation. We also now have plastic surgery procedures that are more sensitive to Black skin.

For Black men, the detection and treatment of prostate cancer raises the real possibility of altered or reduced sexual functioning. It's vital to make sure that we help Black men explore their feelings of anger and helplessness as they deal with this disease. It's recommended that intimate partners be brought into discussions about changed appearance and functioning so that partners and families can be supportive and sensitive.

Many Black clients express difficulty in being cared for by others when they have previously seen themselves as caregivers. We need to deal with identity and esteem issues when Black clients must be driven to treatments or must receive assistance at home with basic activities such as mobility and self-care. I have been in the position of having to help Black clients accept the fact that they're no longer able to drive themselves and need to turn to others for their own safety, as well as to protect others from their possible unsafe driving.

AIDS and HIV Status

We know that the spread of the AIDS virus in African American communities is a serious concern. When a Black client learns that he or she is HIV positive or has been exposed to an individual with this status, we need to respond in very specific ways. First of all, we know that Black clients are going to be concerned about confidentiality. Legal guidelines around the confidentiality of HIV status and clients in therapy are still being decided. We can let our clients know that we can keep this information confidential if they are not jeopardizing others.

One of our first responsibilities is to make sure that our clients are tested for HIV if they suspect they have been exposed. We need to help our clients see that it is better to find out their status than ignore their potential danger. In situations where our clients are homosexuals, receiving a positive AIDS test almost inevitably leads to a revelation of their sexual orientation.

Some gay, lesbian, and bisexual African Americans are loved, accepted, and supported by their families and friends. However, Black clients who believe they will lose the support of their family and friends may be strongly tempted not to be tested so that they don't have to deal with the reactions of others. We need to be aware that many African Americans, including mental health and other health professionals, genuinely believe that homosexuality is a sin in the eyes of God. Although these professionals may try to relate to gay individuals in a respectful way, homosexual clients are accurate in their fears of being judged and found guilty in subtle and sometimes overt ways. Therefore, one of the issues that we need to immediately address is to help Black clients find resources and support that will not convey any message of condemnation. Many communities have crisis services for people who are HIV positive. We as therapists need to find those culturally sensitive services.

We also need to let our clients know how important it is to practice safe sex through a variety of practices, including condom use. Historically, many Black men have been uncomfortable with the use of condoms. These concerns relate to issues of not wanting to diminish sensation, wanting sex to be spontaneous, and believing that having a child is an affirmation even if these children were not planned.

Currently, many health professionals are concerned that younger Black males and females who once practiced safe sex are now less conscientious about being careful. These young people point to how well former basketball star Magic Johnson is doing and feel that the risks and seriousness of AIDS are exaggerated. They don't realize that Magic Johnson hasn't developed a full-blown syndrome of AIDS yet and can afford the best treatments and highest levels of medical expertise.

We need to ask our HIV-positive Black clients directly whether there are family members or close friends available to them for support. We can work with our clients to decide who should be told, and when and how that should happen. We can explore plans to have family sessions where we provide our clients with support. We also may need to help our clients decide if they want to share their health status with any of their religious or spiritual advisers. When clients feel that their ministers would not be receptive to hearing about their HIV-positive diagnosis, we need to talk to our clients about finding alternative ways to meet their spiritual needs.

Interactions with Law Enforcement Agencies

African Americans can come into contact with law enforcement agencies across socioeconomic status, gender, and age. Black men and women make up 12 percent of the general population, 47 percent of individuals facing trials or in local jails, 45 percent of inmates in state and federal prisons, and 40 percent of individuals sentenced to death.[1] As a result, we as therapists may interact with Black clients in crisis situations.

The media often focus on the high percentages of poor and young Black males involved in the law enforcement system. Black males from their early twenties until the age of thirty tend to make one-third less income than White males. They are at least double or triple the rates of unemployment.[2] As a result, some Black males decide to resort to illegal rather than legal means of obtaining an income. However, it's important for therapists to recognize the diversity of Black Americans involved in this system.

The first case involves the incarceration of a middle-class Black male for what is commonly referred to as a white-collar crime. In this case, his family and the Black community felt that his arrest and incarceration were politically motivated and represented the type of harassment that Black men may encounter in society.

Mrs. Spenser sought therapy following her husband's conviction on felony charges related to his improper administration of an antipoverty program. He was sentenced to seven years in prison, and she was left to figure out how to raise their three children under the age of twelve.

She and her husband had enjoyed a good marriage, were well educated, and came from healthy families. Nothing could have prepared her for the devastation of a public trial and the conviction and imprisonment of her husband. She felt that the charges against her husband were political in nature because he was an active critic of local politicians and had organized several successful rallies to challenge existing government policies and procedures. She wanted to know what she could tell her children about their father, given his jail sentence. How was she going to cope financially on her salary? How would she be able to provide the love and support that her husband could not give her children? What kind of moral support could her husband provide in a prison some four hundred miles away?

The case to follow represents the all-too-common situation of violence in the schools and involves a young Black male.

Mr. and Mrs. Jenkins were a working-class couple who sought therapy on an emergency basis following the arrest of their sixteen-year-old son Charles. Charles was charged with bringing a gun to school and attempting to shoot another male student who, Charles claimed, had beaten him up the week before. Charles was being held in jail.

His parents wanted to know what they could do to help their son and get him out of the serious trouble he was in.

The last case in this section describes a young Black female whose acting out behavior and subsequent arrest reflects a cry for help.

Anita and her mother, Ms. Porter, sought therapy following Anita's arrest. Anita was fourteen years old and the middle child in a family of seven children; all had a different father. The family had received public assistance since Ms. Porter had her first child. Anita was charged with shoplifting cosmetic items and hosiery at a local drugstore. The store had a "mandatory prosecution" policy for shoplifting, and Anita was charged with shoplifting about $30 worth of merchandise.

What these three vignettes illustrate is the range of motivations, circumstances, and challenges that African American clients and therapists must negotiate in crisis situations involving law enforcement agencies.

Justifiable Paranoia

When Black clients present in a crisis session regarding the criminal justice system they often feel angry, impotent, and fearful; they often believe they have been treated unfairly. We need to recognize that Black clients have good reason to be frightened about an arrest because research shows higher arrest rates and more severe sentencing for Blacks than other racial and ethnic groups.[3] We know that part of the reason for the disproportionate arrest rates for Blacks is that police are more likely to stop and question Blacks than Whites on a routine basis. Hence, Blacks talk about the apparent crime of DWB—driving while Black. Their only offense is the color of their skin.

"Black crime" also tends to be more visible and detectable, whereas "White crime" is more likely to be hidden behind respectable businesses and reputations. It's also useful for therapists to understand some of the cynicism that Blacks feel toward the law enforcement system. White crime tends to generate million-dollar sums but mild sentences of two to ten years, whereas Black crime is perceived to be more violent, although it usually involves lesser amounts of money and produces more severe jail penalties.[4]

The fact that Blacks tend to receive more severe sentencing for the same crimes that other individuals commit is related to the fact that higher socioeconomic status, better legal representation, and White skin are directly related to less severe consequences.

We need to be aware that African Americans as a group have received such disparate treatment by the law enforcement system that their views about guilt, conviction, and punishment may be very different from the perspectives of White individuals. This can be seen in high-profile cases such as the O. J. Simpson trial. Many Black individuals felt that had O. J. Simpson been charged with murdering a Black wife rather than a White wife, the case would not have generated such strong emotions. Blacks feel, and research supports the view, that in general Blacks receive more serious consequences when they commit a crime against a White person than a Black person.[5] This sends a clear message as to whose lives are most valued.

When appropriate, we must validate our client's feelings that they were treated unfairly or disrespectfully. After validating their feelings, we must then help them to move on to a place where they can actively minimize the potentially negative consequences that they may face.

Working with Families

As therapists, we need to begin by hearing from our clients what charges have been made and the status of bail options. Some Black clients are anxious to secure a release for their relatives. Other clients believe that they don't have the resources to post bond or may believe in the case of a chronic offender that they are unwilling to pursue bail.

Another pressing issue is to determine whether the family has secured legal representation or has to rely on public defenders. I encourage families to see whether they can manage to raise the funds for private representation rather than risk the variability of the public defense system. It's important to explain to Black clients that they deserve the best legal advice they can afford and that they're going to have to actively involve themselves in working with their lawyers.

We also must try to assess how well the family is currently functioning. Are they capable of making good decisions about legal representation or bail, or do they need assistance? Sometimes it's clear that our clients are too overwhelmed to make important decisions alone, and we may need to get involved with helping them understand, evaluate, and implement their options.

We also may need to inquire if additional family members, friends, or clergy can be of assistance. For many African American families, helping them gain spiritual counsel can be a significant resource as they deal with the legal system.

We also must recognize that many African American clients who are incarcerated or are chronically arrested are either illiterate or have limited reading ability; thus they have few marketable skills. For those who are acquitted of their crimes or eventually released from jail or prison, unless they get necessary assistance with finding a job that can allow them to be self-supporting, they're likely to become homeless, return to prison, or become a victim of violence. Because the rates of African American parents who are incarcerated are so large and continuing to grow, new programs have begun to develop that provide services to affected parents and children. These programs assist the parents in developing and maintaining a relationship with their children and help provide academic and emotional support to the family. We can investigate whether these services are available in our community and determine if our clients are interested and eligible for such assistance.

We also may have to help our clients and their families deal with a variety of emotions ranging from guilt and shame to indifference and callousness. In some situations, the actual alleged perpetrators may not show remorse, but their family members may be heartsick that they have raised a person capable of such brutality or lack of feeling. In these cases we may have to help family members recognize appropriate levels of responsibility for the actions of others.

As therapists, we also want to make some determination of the motivation behind the alleged crime. We need to assess if mental illness or competency is an issue and whether an intellectual or psychological evaluation is warranted.

We also need to be open to the possibility that political or racial factors may have played a role in the arrest of African Americans. For instance, in the case of Mr. Spencer, it was difficult for me to fully understand what he was actually guilty of. It appeared that he had not followed certain government procedures, but it was also clear that he was not charged with or guilty of diverting any funds to his personal use or in any way benefiting from noncompliance with regulations.

Mrs. Spenser also felt that the charges against her husband were nebulous, so we first spent time helping her vent her anger at the officials who were behind his arrest. Next, she got in touch with how angry she was with her husband for putting their family in their current position. What we worked on in that first session was how she could cope with the challenges of being a single parent for her children. As we discussed potential resources, she gradually came to the decision to relocate back to the neighborhood where she grew up so she would have the support of family and friends.

We also talked about how important it was to explain to her children what was happening in their lives at a level corresponding to their maturity. Although she was still upset and angry, we agreed that it was important to make sure that she and the children made regular visits to see her husband and to write letters to stay in touch.

In the situation with Charles and Mr. and Mrs. Jenkins, it was clear that Charles's motivation to strike out in violence was partly the need to protect himself but mainly his need not to be disrespected. It's hard to convey how seriously many Black males and some Black females feel about demanding a code of respect from others. For these individuals, this respect may be the major ingredient anchoring their identity and sense of self. So if another individual bumps into them by accident, says something negative about a family member or friend, or attacks them physically, these individuals feel that they'll lose face in their peer group if they don't retaliate.

Therapists will not usually be able to change the value system of their clients. In situations where clients have other sources of self-esteem or reinforcement, like a decent job and a positive relationship with a family that depends on them, we can make an argument for resisting impulses that can lead to losing their jobs or disrupting the family.

With young African Americans, our goal is often to buy enough time in treatment to help them develop a positive sense of identity beyond the peer group. This may happen when these youngsters are diverted to Wilderness Survival Programs or to a relative outside of the immediate area, or when they are able to develop a sense of success because of personal talent. I wasn't able to work with Charles because he was sent to a state facility following his trial.

When I met with Anita and Ms. Porter, it was clear to me after a short discussion that Anita's theft was essentially a cry for help from a young woman who felt ignored and passed over in her family. After interacting with Ms. Porter I recognized that she was too overwhelmed to be able to give Anita or her other children very much in the way of individual attention.

Ms. Porter was willing to work with community services to attend some parenting classes and to sign up Anita and several of her younger siblings for a Big Brother–Big Sister program. Because of the mother's active participation with therapy and community services, Anita was placed on probation.

How Police Are Viewed

Many children are taught in school, at home, and by the media that the police are their friends and that if they have a problem they can contact an officer for assistance. Although some Black children are exposed to part of this teaching, African American parents usually must also tell their children that the police may also be a source of harm.

Sometimes, African American clients present for a crisis session because of an interaction with a police officer when they failed to act in a deferential manner. As therapists, we may need to assist our clients, especially young Black males, to understand that if they're stopped by police or have to interact with individuals in the legal system, they can't joke, make light of the situation, or be sarcastic. African Americans need to make sure that they speak audibly but not too loud, and they must keep their hands visible to demonstrate that they don't have a weapon. They must move slowly, avoid any sudden movements, and use a respectful tone of voice.

The fact that Blacks are at higher risk for harm from Police than other racial and ethnic groups makes them more likely to believe that they have to evade, run from, or defend themselves when police officers stop them. As therapists we can acknowledge that Blacks are statistically at high risk for harassment from police, but unfortunately their immediate concern in an interaction with law enforcement is to not give the police an excuse to use undue force on them.

We know that in today's society more and more youngsters believe that it's necessary for them to carry weapons to protect themselves. Our young clients tell us that they feel safer, more adult, and more respected when they have a weapon. We have to let our clients know that when school officials or police detect their possession of a gun, they're likely to be expelled from school or arrested.

We have the hard job of validating our clients' feelings but letting them know that despite their perceptions, the reality is that they're at greater risk of harm with their weapons. For those of us who didn't grow up feeling the need to carry a gun or a knife for self-protection, we need to work hard to understand the changing environment that today's Black youngsters face.

Domestic Problems: Infidelity and Domestic Violence

Infidelity and domestic violence are two crises that can prompt African American clients to seek services. Where infidelity is concerned, as in the first case to follow, individuals can feel such a sense of shock, betrayal, and anger that they feel that they need outside help to sort through their emotions. The second case shows how the emotional and physical damage of violence and the fear of its repetition can motivate Black women to overcome their resistance and ask for help.

Mr. and Mrs. Ford were a Black couple in their mid-thirties who sought therapy following a traumatic event for Mrs. Ford. She had just received a call earlier in the week from another woman who informed her that her husband had been having an affair with her for the last three years and that they now had a two-month-old son. Mr. Ford had told his girlfriend that he had been married, but at the time he began seeing her he had just received his divorce.

Mrs. Ford stated that she and her husband had been through a lot of ups and downs in their seven-year marriage. She always thought that their major problems stemmed from the fact that they both had advanced degrees and spent a lot of time in their high-profile careers. Mrs. Ford confessed that there had been times when she wondered if her husband had been unfaithful but thought that if he had, it was better for her not to confront him lest the argument make their relationship worse.

She said that although she could have accepted his having an occasional affair, she was shocked to hear that he had basically developed a whole other existence with a new family while still married to her. She could not believe that he had been so deceitful, and she still couldn't understand how she was so unaware of what was happening in her husband's life.

Mr. Ford was understandably defensive. He explained to Mrs. Ford and me that he had begun the affair thinking it would be a brief relationship. He felt that his wife was not sensitive to his needs and devoted more time to her work than to him. Because he often traveled for business purposes, he had begun to see other women when he was away from home. He stated that he had not planned to get so involved with his new girlfriend, and her pregnancy was not planned. He told his wife that he still loved her but he had pretty much given up hope that they could fix all their problems with communication, values, and intimacy.

Mr. and Mrs. Ford's crisis related to their feelings of shock, anger, and betrayal over having to deal with being exposed about his other family. Neither of the Fords knew what the next step should be in handling their crisis. Mrs. Ford stated that she didn't think she could ever forgive her husband for all he had put her through. She told him that her family had always warned her that no Black woman could hold a Black man if she had too much education and seemed too uppity. Mrs. Ford felt that her husband had always given her mixed messages about her educational and occupational successes. Sometimes he told her how proud he was of her; other times he criticized her for not being attentive enough to his needs. It didn't help when she learned that Mr. Ford's girlfriend had considerably less education than she did.

Mrs. Ford was especially hurt to hear that her husband had a child with someone else. For years she had talked to him about how important it was to for her to have children, and he responded that he wasn't ready yet. Mrs. Ford said that their relationship was a constant battle of power and control. She felt that they didn't know how to effectively communicate their concerns or problem solve.

As we worked together in this crisis session, it was clear to me that although Mrs. Ford was extremely angry and hurt, she was still invested in the relationship. In contrast, Mr. Ford remained defensive and angry that Mrs. Ford had not met more of his needs and was basically noncommittal about his plans to work on the relationship. Both parties agreed to a follow-up session. Not surprisingly, in follow-up sessions, Mr. Ford announced his plans to leave the relationship permanently. I continued to see Mrs. Ford on a regular basis to work on esteem issues and on rebuilding her life.

As she loosened her scarf and took off her sunglasses, I could see her blackened eyes and the scratches and bruises along her face and neck. Mrs. Knott stated that she came from a low-income family. She obtained a clerical job right after her high school graduation where she met her husband. She explained that her husband-to-be seemed so attentive and loving to her that she was flattered by their whirlwind courtship, his intensity, and possessiveness. Although she knew that her husband had a bad temper before they were married, he did not begin to physically abuse her until a year after they were married when she was pregnant with their first child.

Mrs. Knott explained that she had stayed in her marriage despite the abuse for several reasons. First of all, she now had three children and was afraid she could not care for them well alone. Second, her husband had told her repeatedly that if she left he would kill her. Third, she explained somewhat matter of factly that she had endured the sexual abuse of her stepfather for four years during high school, so she thought that she could put up with her husband.

She knew that he, her husband, had a lot of pressure at work as a low-level manager and felt that it was to be expected that Black men sometimes took out their frustrations on females rather than on the White men who were in positions of authority; women couldn't retaliate the way these White men could. She told me that although she was still afraid of leaving her husband, he was becoming increasingly abusive to their children. In fact, her latest injuries were sustained when she tried to stop her husband from beating her eight-year-old son with a thick leather belt.

In the case of Mrs. Knott, she sought assistance because her husband's escalating violence no longer affected her only but also included her children. It's not unusual for Black women to tolerate abuse but become mobilized to leave their husbands when they feel their children are at risk.

Mrs. Knott was willing to go to a temporary shelter, but she wasn't willing to press charges against her husband. She felt that pressing charges would further enrage him, create grounds for his possible dismissal from work, and lead him to take out his feelings on her and the children. I asked her to seriously commit to ongoing therapy with another therapist or me. I explained that I knew it would be difficult to leave her husband and begin to care for her children alone. We discussed roles that her extended family could play; we talked about finances and what she could say to the children. We also talked about an alternative plan in case she was unable to implement her immediate plan to leave. Our focus was on how she could make an emergency escape from her husband with her children if the need arose.

Mrs. Knott had the insight to state that she knew her tolerance of her husband's abuse was related to her earlier abuse by her stepfather. She vowed that she would do all in her power not to let her children suffer the way she did as a child. I made sure that Mrs. Knott had a number to contact me on an emergency basis for any questions or concerns she had or for information. Although she didn't leave her husband after our first visit, she returned for therapy and did leave him for good a month later.

STABILIZING DOMESTIC CRISES

When a couple seeks assistance for a domestic crisis, they have strong feelings; therapists must proceed slowly in trying to understand client emotions. One of the issues that we need to be particularly sensitive to is making sure that African American male clients feel included and necessary to the process. In any initial contacts we have with potential clients, especially in a crisis situation, we want to use the crisis as an impetus for having all the relevant family members present.

Many Black males feel that their roles in the family have been ridiculed and scorned in the wider society. They are particularly reluctant to seek therapy when it involves airing family business or what they perceive to be dirty laundry. In addition, many Black males feel that therapy simply consists of talking, which they feel is more of a female thing. These men often don't understand how an outsider can help them problem solve in practical and concrete ways.

What I have found very consistently is that if Black men are willing to come in for therapy, they sometimes surprise themselves and their partners by being very participatory and sharing their thoughts and feelings. Sometimes this willingness to self-disclose scares Black men, and we need to reassure them that we appreciate their honesty and willingness to be part of the problem-solving process.

I have also found that Black women are often able to easily identify and vent their feelings in domestic crises. Even fairly mild-mannered women can let feelings of anger and hurt build to such a point that they raise their voices, point fingers, and in some cases leave their seats to "get in the face" of their partners.

We have the difficult job of helping our clients learn that, even though their feelings may be justified, verbal attacks, profanity, and insults will not help the couple resolve their difficulties. We often have to stop interchanges and have clients direct their comments to us instead of each other, practice stating their opinions in a less inflammatory manner, and role modeling examples of positive ways to have a difficult dialogue with their partners.

We want to make sure that in a domestic crisis we let our clients know that our role as a therapist is not to take sides, to keep them in a relationship, or to encourage them to terminate the relationship. What we want to do is help them sort through their thoughts and feelings and make plans as to how they would like to proceed. Because emotions are high and confusion a good possibility, it's important that we convey our concern, show that we understand clients' urgency, but proceed in a calm and flexible way that helps lend stability to our clients.

In situations where we feel that violence is a part of the crisis or a potential factor, we need to talk with our clients about a possible separation or cooling-off period; in cases of ongoing violence we need to seriously consider the use of a battered women's shelter. It's often not a good idea to recommend that Black clients use a family or friend's home as a shelter. Too often, crisis situations have spilled over to the homes of family and friends who were ill-equipped to handle escalating domestic violence and have led to more victims of violence.

Many domestic violence victims are advised to call the police and get a restraining order. African American women are sometimes reluctant to take these steps. They'll tell us that they want their partners to stop beating them, but they don't want to risk an altercation between the police and their abuser, knowing that any outcome will be negative. In addition, Black women know that calling the police, in a disproportionate number of times, results in arrest, court appearances, legal fees, and jail time for African American men. They also know that legal problems are likely to threaten if not eliminate their partner's ability to generate any income to support the family.

As a result, Black women do call the police, but they're most likely to do this when they're feeling most threatened and the violence has escalated and is repetitive. Unfortunately, African American women in the crisis of violence have to make some quick determination about the probability of their being seriously injured or killed versus trying to protect their partners from the almost certain abuse of the criminal justice system.

A major issue that we must confront is the feeling of shame and embarrassment and the perception (or reality) that many other people in a community know about the domestic problems. Sometimes Black females in particular feel that they can tell their sisters, mothers, or close friends anything about their personal relationships. This practice may really upset and enrage their partners, who may not understand why these women need to disclose and gain the support of others.

It's also true that sometimes hearing stories about one of the partners in a relationship causes negative attitudes. We may need to work with Black women to ask them to consider using therapy as a place to vent rather than doing it with relatives. Sometimes relationships take a real turn for the worse when relatives hear of poor treatment accorded to a husband or a wife. Offers to talk to the husband or wife who has "messed up" are usually not successful.

Crisis situations are difficult for all concerned. Because there's no way that we can prevent crises from occurring, we need to be aware of how we can help African American clients handle these situations. Although these interventions are challenging, they provide therapists with the opportunity to develop positive working relationships with Black clients. These relationships can lead the clients involved and other African Americans who learn of the effectiveness of our work to be more willing to be involved in the therapy process.

In Chapter Seven we'll explore the importance of understanding and managing our countertransference reactions.

7

Managing Countertransference Issues

The term *countertransference*, which generally refers to strong clinician reactions to clients, has been widely discussed in the psychotherapy field. These reactions traditionally were believed to be unconscious or subconscious. It has always been our responsibility as therapists to monitor our reactions so as to prevent or minimize communicating inappropriate reactions to clients.

We know that countertransference reactions can be stimulated by demographic and cultural variables between therapists and clients. Certain countertransference issues develop as a result of differences; others are the result of similarities. Because countertransference reactions are frequently viewed in a negative light, therapists are often reluctant or unwilling to look at these issues. Unfortunately, it sometimes takes a serious rupture in the therapy process before a therapist recognizes that a countertransference issue is involved and must be solved.

Interpersonal models of therapy have underscored that countertransference reactions can also have positive therapeutic value. If we are able to identify feelings and reactions that clients trigger in us, we can sometimes gain insight about their typical interpersonal dynamics. Whatever our therapeutic orientation, it's essential that we be active in identifying our reactions, thoughts, and feelings to our African American clients. Then we can move forward to decide if and how there is a way to use the information in therapy or at least to make sure that our issues are not damaging the therapy.

There are several important issues in our exploration of countertransference issues and African American clients. White and other non-Black therapists may feel uncomfortable about acknowledging their countertransference feelings toward African American clients. These therapists may feel that ambivalent or negative feelings are not "politically correct" because such feelings are incompatible with their image of being unbiased and culturally competent.

Equally important, African American therapists need to be aware of their own risk for countertransference reactions with Black clients. Overidentifying with some Black clients and feeling turned off and distant toward others are very disconcerting reactions for Black therapists. It is hard to acknowledge that they may have prejudices against members of their own race. Regardless of our race, countertransference reactions leave us unable to understand the verbalizations, attitudes, or actions of some of our clients.

In this chapter, we'll examine several topics related to countertransference issues. First, we'll talk about the stimuli for countertransference reactions, namely, our perceived areas of similarity and difference in relation to our African American clients. We'll discuss the inability to handle race and other complex cultural and demographic variables, and how we can be guilty of unintentional racism. Second, we'll examine some specific signs and examples of countertransference reactions. Finally, we'll highlight ethical concerns with respect to culturally competent practice, and we'll close with ideas about actions to take either to prevent countertransference reactions or to deal with them productively.

SIMILARITIES AND DIFFERENCES

Multicultural theorist Paul Pedersen has noted that if we're to be effective in working with clients, we must use both of our eyes but accord different functions to each eye. One eye must focus on similarities between our clients and us, while the other eye must record areas of difference. Only by using this combined approach can we recognize both the uniqueness of our clients and our areas of commonality.[1] Almost every countertransference reaction that we highlight in this chapter relates to an imbalance in our ability to see clearly and act appropriately on areas of similarity and difference between African American clients and ourselves.

Inability to Handle Race and Complexity

A fundamental countertransference issue is a counselor's inability to handle issues of race, culture, or demographic variability. Therapists may have a variety of reasons for ignoring issues of race, gender, class, religion, sexual orientation, ability status, geographic origin, and so on. The following are some of the rationales therapists often give for not discussing these vital issues:

> The presenting problem was unrelated to any of these issues.
>
> The client didn't raise these issues.
>
> We're limited in time and can't discuss everything.

The real reason that therapists typically don't discuss these issues is that they lack the skill, knowledge, and confidence in their abilities to adequately address them.

Just as we can't understand presenting problems without understanding related racial and cultural dynamics, we can't be effective if we're unable to explore the meaning of client-counselor similarity and difference across the aforementioned areas. Racial, cultural, and demographic variables all interact for both the client and the counselor to create unique worldviews and perspectives. Not being able to discuss areas of similarity and difference constricts and distorts the therapy process. If we acknowledge differences, we enhance our opportunities to reframe issues, expand perspectives, and share strategies. In contrast, if we are unable to process these issues, we can't tell how accurately we are hearing what the client is saying; we may distort the messages we receive because of our own issues or lack of awareness.

One of the major reasons that White therapists can't process race is because they've never thought about race or their "Whiteness." It's always the privilege of the dominant group not to have to think about issues that don't directly affect them. Hence, many White individuals have not thought about what Whiteness means to them, how Whiteness might be perceived by an African American client, or what the racial reality is of being an African American. But African Americans have to understand both what being Black means and what being White means in our society.

Further, some therapists may identify on the basis of shared gender without recognizing that race mediates different gender experiences. Or a therapist may note that an African American client started life in a low-income family; he or she may feel a sense of commonality and not recognize that White skin color offered privileges that the African American client could never receive.

To enable us as therapists to monitor possible countertransference issues, some theorists have suggested that we establish a personal psychohistory that increases our sensitivity to our racial and cultural values, experiences, and strategies.[2] In the area of race for example, we would do the following:

- Review understandings of and associations with race by examining self-definition and our views of our own and other races and our racial philosophies.

- Identify early and later developmental memories related to racial stereotypes and identifications.

- Analyze the overall tapestry of our racial experiences to understand areas of sensitivity or bias and potential blind spots.

Only by honestly investigating our personal psychohistories in racial, cultural, and demographic arenas can we learn about some of our hot buttons for countertransference issues.

Unintentional Racism

Charles Ridley has noted that although the majority of therapists are caring, compassionate, and ethical professionals, many are guilty of unintentional racism. Although these individuals may have the best intentions when it comes to working with African American clients, they can harm clients by being inadequately trained, ignoring the sociocultural complexity of the client's life, blaming the victim, and imposing White middle-class values and philosophies. Because unintentional racism is subtle and manifests as blind spots, therapists are unaware of this phenomenon and its potential for damage.[3]

Therapists who adopt a "color-blind" attitude are exhibiting unintentional racism. These therapists decide that race is irrelevant to their therapy with an African American client. It's a sign of both racism and countertransference for a therapist to eliminate race from consideration when treating African Americans. Doing so suggests that therapists are fearful of being seen as biased, uninformed, ethnocentric, and lacking in cultural competence.

Therapists also have frequently been trained to work with YAVIS—that is, young, attractive, verbal, intelligent, and successful—clients.[4] Although not stated, White is also implied. Many therapists want to be color-blind because they have no framework for knowing how to deal with clients who don't fit the YAVIS mold.

Therapists who overfocus on race or who show "color shock" are also showing racism and countertransference. In this case therapists are uncomfortable with race and are unsure of what to do, so they make race the central issue of the therapy, regardless of what the client has indicated as an area of concern. Some therapists overfocus on race because they want a simple rather than complex approach to African American clients. They have had enough training to know that African American clients are different from White clients. Rather than attempting to deal with all the possible dimensions of difficulty with which the client presents, these therapists simply select race and oppression as the central dynamic and view the client only from this one-dimensional perspective. This approach is a form of countertransference because these therapists are dealing with their own issue and not seeing the client clearly and accurately.

White shame and guilt is another source of unintentional racism. Some White therapists have thought about racial issues and learned the history of African Americans in this country. As a result of this learning, they develop feelings of shame and guilt about the discrimination and oppression that Blacks have endured at the hands of Whites. Clare Holzman has noted that feelings of shame and guilt can be helpful if used to change behaviors, attitudes, and policies.[5] However, some therapists are immobilized by these feelings of shame and guilt and can act countertherapeutically by

- Trying to gain the client's approval

- Attempting to show positive transference and a lack of bias

- Projecting their feelings onto the client and then blaming the client for his or her problems

- Ignoring the client's issues and problems

- Underpathologizing serious problems

- Compensating by taking responsibility for the client's difficulties and problem solving

Because unintentional racism by definition is something therapists are unaware of, the logical question has to be, What are some of the signs African American clients will exhibit that indicate this type of countertransference is occurring? Signs include the following:

- Anger

- Hostility

- Silence

- Superficiality

- Refusal to accept a second appointment or a referral

- Unwillingness to engage

If we see any of these reactions in our African American client, we need to take steps to find out what this client is experiencing. If the client confronts us with what he or she believes are biased or racist views, we must be able to listen nondefensively and accept responsibility for our actions. We need to apologize and decide whether we can get back on track with this client or whether we are truly unprepared to handle the case with cultural competence.

Although the forms of racism described here are unintentional, the potential for harm is so great that as therapists we must take steps to develop our personal psychohistories and learn about our areas of vulnerability and our blind spots. Just as in other areas of our lives, "not knowing or lack of intention" is not an adequate excuse for racism in therapy.

SIGNS OF COUNTERTRANSFERENCE

In discussing countertransference, we must acknowledge that some of our countertransference reactions occur with race playing little or no role. In other situations, racial or cultural factors are integral ingredients. We'll focus mainly on countertransference issues that are stimulated at least in part by race. The following are possible signs of countertransference:

- Strong or inappropriate reactions

- Forcing solutions

- Overinvolvement or underinvolvement

- Silence or overtalking

- Ignoring or minimizing client comments and responses

- Boundary violations

- Overidentification

- Viewing the client as exotic

- Inability to evaluate objectively

Strong or Inappropriate Cognitive or Emotional Reactions

Some situations prompt most therapists to react intensely. Situations that involve violence, sex, poverty, achievement, or interracial relationships trigger reactions deeply embedded in our value system. Typically, a strong or inappropriate response to our Black clients is an indicator of a countertransference reaction. These reactions can include feelings of anger, dislike, or blame toward Black clients for what we see as their problems.

Further, these reactions are also influenced by racial assumptions. For example, a White therapist might think that her Black client is in poverty because she doesn't work hard enough. Therefore, the therapist's intervention will focus on teaching the client new strategies to help her client work harder. Conversely, a Black therapist might assume his African American client is in poverty because of the learned helplessness caused by institutional racism. He then tries to develop solutions designed to increase the client's self-efficacy.

On the one hand, both assessments could be right. On the other hand, both could be wrong if the therapists were reacting out of their own biases rather than first listening carefully to the client's statement of the problem. We may feel these strong emotions when we feel that Black clients are not sharing or living up to our values and goals, and experience this as a personal affront to us.

Another major issue that may lead to strong reactions on the part of therapists is the whole area of interracial dating relationships. This issue cuts across race and ethnic background. When Black males talk about being involved in an interracial relationship, particularly with a White female, many therapists have an automatic negative response.

What's interesting is that therapists often disguise and rationalize their negative reactions when a client discusses an interracial relationship. These therapists may say things like "Why would you want to date outside your race when there are so many attractive single Black women?" or "It may be OK for you to decide to be in an interracial relationship, but have you seriously considered how hard it would be on your children?"

Sometimes therapists ask these questions even when the client has not asked for advice about the relationship. When therapists communicate these reactions to their Black clients, they bring into the therapy room the kind of discrimination these clients face in their daily lives.

It's important to note that African American therapists also can have strong countertransference reactions to interracial dating. In Black culture, Black men often view a Black woman's dating a White man as "siding with the oppressor," "selling out the race," and an insult to Black manhood. This reaction can be most intense for Black male therapists, who may feel hidden anger or resentment that a "dynamite sister" has hooked up with a "White dude."

However, a Black male dating or marrying a White female has a different valence in our society. Because U.S. society views White females as the epitome of femininity, beauty, and sexuality, society views Black men as competing successfully against White males when they're in a relationship with a White female. Some Black male therapists may feel a sense of pride that another Black male has attained "society's highest female prize"; others may feel envy, and still others react to these situations as affronts to Black pride. The point is that regardless of our race and gender, interracial dating is rarely a neutral event. It is therefore imperative that we monitor and reflect on our reactions to hearing about these situations.

For Black therapists, there's often a tendency to personalize a client's decision to date a White individual. The therapist may feel that dating outside the Black race is a rejection, put-down, or devaluation of the therapist's race, ethnicity, and culture. African American female therapists may have especially strong countertransference feelings when working with Black males in relationships with White females. They may feel that the Black male client sees them as less valuable, attractive, or worthwhile than White females.

In addition to feeling rejected or minimized, Black therapists sometimes feel more cautious about an individual who is dating outside the Black race. Questions arise in the therapist's mind as to whether the client has an impaired sense of racial identity or whether he or she is in denial or confusion about understanding what it means to be Black. At an unconscious or conscious level, Black therapists may provoke these Black clients into some type of test as to "how Black they are" or how committed they are to their race if they are dating interracially.

Forcing Solutions

When therapists allow countertransference reactions to prevail, they lose touch with what the client really needs and attempt to force solutions that are based on their own assumptions. These solutions won't fit.

I once supervised Candace, a White graduate student who was working with Mrs. Wilson, a mother of four children who was on welfare. Mr. Wilson suffered from chronic physical illness and had been hospitalized for the last three years. Mrs. Wilson was a wonderful mother who was adept at learning about services that could help her children. They participated in a variety of community activities. Mrs. Wilson sought therapy because of the stress of being a single parent with two of the children suffering from mild learning disabilities.

Candace told me that she was initially concerned about how effective she might be with Mrs. Wilson because of the difference in their backgrounds. Candace explained that she was from a White middle-class background and had virtually no knowledge of people on welfare. She was pleasantly surprised to find that Mrs. Wilson was very motivated to participate in therapy and had similar views to Candace with respect to child rearing. Although it appeared that the initial session was going smoothly, Candace reported a major problem. In an effort to understand what happened, I asked her when things became strained. Candace reported that Mrs. Wilson told her that she was worried about how to pay for all the costs associated with Easter preparations. In addition to new outfits, she had to pay for the substantial costs of hairdresser and barber fees for herself and the children.

Candace said to Mrs. Wilson, "No problem—I'm sure that you can pick up some really neat outfits at the thrift store, and you can do the kids' hair yourself. My friends and I always scout secondhand clothing stores."

Mrs. Wilson was deeply insulted and said, "I may be on welfare, but I'm not putting any used clothes on my children. When we go to church, we look just as good as everybody else in that church. We wear nice shoes and our hair looks good, not like someone experimented on us. I may be poor, but I have my pride!"

Candace was surprised by Mrs. Wilson's reaction and hurt that her suggestion was so thoroughly rejected. She replied, "Fine, whatever you want to do." During the rest of the session she listened to what Mrs. Wilson had to say with little comment.

Candace explained to me that she was simply astounded that Mrs. Wilson was willing to go into debt for clothes and hair-care fees.

Because she had already decided that Mrs. Wilson was a good mother and shared Candace's values, she automatically assumed that Mrs. Wilson would follow her suggestions.

We spent the supervisory session discussing Candace's feelings. She was hurt and angry, which was not only disproportionate but also disrespectful of the values that Mrs. Wilson held. I tried to help Candace see that wanting Mrs. Wilson to be different and acting as if Candace's values were better than Mrs. Wilson's could be perceived by this client as insensitivity at best and possibly racist. I pointed out that Candace missed understanding that going to church in new clothes with professionally created hairstyles was important to Mrs. Wilson's pride. Candace heard the concern about lack of money without also hearing how important looking good for church was.

"But how could making a suggestion about using the thrift store or doing the children's hair herself be seen as racist?" Candace asked. I pointed out that the problem was not in trying to brainstorm solutions but in the quick manner that she asserted that this would be a viable solution because she and her friends did it. I explained that deciding to shop at a thrift store when one has plenty of money is very different from having to shop there due to limited resources. In the latter case, people often feel embarrassment and shame at having to wear used clothes. Candace could see that because of her initial rapport with Mrs. Wilson, she had made several leaps in her assumptions about solutions. Finally Candace's worldview expanded, allowing her to see that Mrs. Wilson could be a good mother, even if she made decisions about money management with which Candace could not agree.

Overinvolvement or Underinvolvement

Many colleagues have told me that Black clients stir up countertransference feelings along the involvement continuum. In situations where Black clients are facing multiple stressors and chronic difficulties, therapists sometimes feel impotent, hopeless, and powerless to make significant progress. These therapists sometimes figuratively throw up their hands and adopt an attitude of "I give up. Nothing I can do will help. I can apply a few Band-Aids, but I refuse to try to help or start caring about this person: the challenges are too overwhelming."

Other therapists who feel overwhelmed by the presenting problems of Black clients may show a different countertransference reaction. Believing that their hard work can eliminate the clients' problems, these therapists may try to shoulder responsibility for them. This scenario of becoming overinvolved relates to possible issues of omnipotence, grandeur, or guilt about the plights of African Americans. Taking on too much responsibility is clearly just as problematic as giving up and not taking any responsibility.

Our African American clients can reinforce issues of overinvolvement. In some cases they want and expect therapists to take responsibility and solve problems for them. We need to be aware that taking too much responsibility deprives clients of the opportunity for them to grow and become more competent and empowered.

Silence or Overtalking

Because many Black clients will present for therapy with significant concerns about how the therapy process operates, it's important for us to demonstrate active involvement. We must be responsive to the verbalizations of clients. If a client brings up an issue that stirs up countertransference feelings, we may react with silence or overtalking to camouflage our discomfort. These reactions will usually be a clear signal to a Black client that something is wrong. I'm most familiar with this happening in situations where Black clients may recount or describe strong emotions of anger, aggression, or anti-White feelings.

I remember a countertransference reaction I experienced when working with Mark, a Black male in his junior year of college. He gave me some background information and explained that he grew up in a small southeastern town. He told me that the Black women in his family depended on Whites for domestic jobs and had to put up with sexual abuse and rape. He reported regular citings of the Ku Klux Klan and saw Black men beaten and tortured when they tried to protest the treatment of Black women.

Mark presented as very mellow and laid back. I knew that Mark was active in student government and seemed to get along easily with faculty, students, and staff. That's why I was so surprised when he concluded his recitation by saying, "That's why today, if I could kill a White person and know that I could get away with it, I'd do it in a heartbeat and not think twice about it."

Although I'm not usually at a loss for words, I could not come up with a ready response to Mark's statement. The countertransference issue for me dealt with the fact that I grew up understanding it was not OK for Black men to talk about expressing violence toward Whites, under any circumstances.

Although I knew that Mark was not in danger of harming anyone at that time, his repressed and quietly expressed anger and violence shocked me. His statement knocked me off balance, and I sat there trying to absorb what he had said and processing my own reaction. I was aware of Mark's steady gaze on me. I was so afraid of saying the wrong thing that I decided the best thing I could do was to be silent. I maintained eye contact and head nods as he recounted his feelings. After a short period of silence, I let him know that our time was up, and he agreed to return for a second session.

After that first session, I felt uncomfortable about my silence, and I wasn't sure how Mark interpreted my silence. I sought some supervision from colleagues. As I discussed the situation with them, they agreed with me that Mark's expression of such strong feelings in an initial session was somewhat unusual. We also wondered if Mark would have shared this comment with a White therapist or a therapist of another race, or if he shared only because I was Black. We thought that if Mark had made this comment to a White therapist, it would also have prompted some possible fear and anxiety about how to respond.

Some of my White colleagues mentioned that they thought they might have responded with overtalking. Barbara, a White colleague, said that once when she was working with a Black male with relationship problems, she asked the client what he was looking for in a woman, what her ideal characteristics would be. He looked at her slowly, smiled and said, "Actually, someone like you. Slender, blond, blue eyes, and smart as well." Barbara found this response so unexpected that she became flustered and started overtalking. She said, "OK, so you like blonds. Have you dated many blonds? Do you feel like your relationships are better with them? How are these relationships different than your other relationships?"

Barbara explained that in her discomfort, her first impulse was to move the focus away from the obvious seductiveness of the client's comment. By throwing out a barrage of comments, she tried, albeit unsuccessfully, to hide her discomfort. As she regrouped, she felt she was able to get the session back on track. She recognized that the client was being deliberately provocative, probably to gauge her reactions to him as a male and not just as a client. They refocused on problems the client was having and were not further sidetracked by his attempts to flirt.

My conversations with other therapists led us all to conclude that Mark's comment would be a challenge to therapists of any race. We felt that, like me, some therapists might have responded initially with silence while they did some processing and regrouping. Other therapists who are confronted with strong feelings expressed by a client may become agitated and react with overtalking. Either reaction signals to us as therapists that we're sorting through emotionally laden issues and that we need to calmly note our reaction and move on to a more even and balanced response to our clients.

Mark did return for his next session. By talking to colleagues, I now had a response. I felt it was important to explain my reaction of silence to Mark so that he was clear on what I was reacting to. I said to him, "Last week, your honesty about your feelings took me by surprise. I'm not used to Blacks being as straightforward about their feelings of anger and violence. It sounds as though your experiences have led you to have some very strong feelings."

It appeared that my comment, though delayed, gave Mark an acknowledgment of his feelings that he needed. He said that he didn't really talk much about his strong feelings to other people because he didn't think many people could understand or relate to his latent rage. He told me that he was unsure of what my silence in the last session meant. Mark told me he appreciated the fact that I clarified my reaction and validated his feelings.

Ignoring or Minimizing Client Comments and Responses

There are times when our countertransference reactions lead us to ignore or minimize client comments and responses. This is usually the case when our clients are talking about issues we're sensitive to. I've found that colleagues, students, and I have sometimes been reluctant to take on issues that our clients raise. Many therapists are nervous about raising issues of race regardless of whether or not there is a racial match between them and their client. We've mentioned that non-Black therapists fear that they'll be seen as racist or insensitive, and Black therapists know that some clients prefer to look at the world through "color-blind" lenses and are uncomfortable acknowledging racial dynamics.

We've mentioned earlier that issues about sexuality can fall into this category. Some therapists have heard so many stereotypes about Black sexuality that they feel uncomfortable or fail to ask necessary and appropriate questions about sexuality in the first session. If a couple is talking about relationship issues, we need to ask something about how satisfied each individual is with the frequency and nature of his or her sex life. Therapists I have supervised have told me that all the stereotypes they hear suggest how oversexed Black people are, and they sometimes feel intimidated about asking questions lest they give away any feelings of discomfort they have.

Another area that can pose countertransference reactions for therapists are issues of emotional responsivity for both male and female clients. In our society, when Black males express their strength, they're noticed and sometimes targeted. Many strong Black male leaders have been killed, others are the focus of smear campaigns and entrapment, and a significant number of Black men who have bucked the system are incarcerated or in the criminal justice system. As a result, Black men are often trained from an early age to restrain their emotions. Many Black males are better tolerated in the White culture if they're known for being mellow, laid back, and nonthreatening.

The countertransference issue here is that many White and non-Black therapists don't look at why these men are so unwilling or unable to share strong feelings or emotions. In some cases, we as therapists may need to have these Black men not show any of those threatening behaviors that we see and hear about so regularly in the media. So, when a client talks about strong feelings but wears a smile, our own need to keep the client calm may prompt us to ignore the mismatched affect that our client is displaying.

In the case of Black women, I also have seen and heard of therapists who ignore or minimize the anger that Black women express. I find this to be particularly true of White female therapists and other ethnic minority therapists who have been taught that it's not appropriate for women to directly express their anger. I've noticed that when many White females become very upset, it may be more culturally congruent for them to cry than to express their anger. Many Black women, in contrast, have been taught to "tell it like it is," and this includes feelings of rage. As a result of these different cultural styles, therapists can become frightened when Black women express their feelings, and to deal with discomfort they may ignore or minimize clients' reactions.

As the next case illustrates, in some situations non-Black therapists who can't deal with the strong affect try to shift the client to a more cognitive perspective.

I once worked with Ms. Greene, a Black female graduate student in her mid-fifties. She sought therapy to help her with the stress she felt in interacting with younger students and with White students.

Ms. Greene was working on a degree in counseling and stated that the specific precipitant for therapy was a comment that a White student made to her during a group dynamics class. As they were discussing an issue, a White female graduate student responded to what Ms. Greene had said by saying, "How could you know anything about how counseling could work with inner-city kids when you've spent your life down in the South?" Ms. Greene felt that this statement was racist and a put-down. She felt that the student was saying that Blacks in general and those in the South in particular were somehow not as knowledgeable as other people.

As Ms. Greene lashed out at the student and stated that this was a racist comment, the group leader, a White male, intervened and said, "Let's look at this rationally. Ms. Greene, there's no reason for you to get so upset. This comment is not really about race, it's about geographic origin and diverse experiences."

Ms. Greene felt ignored and unsupported by the group leader's comment. She felt that the group leader was unwilling to deal with her anger and wanted to deflect her emotion by interpreting the other student's comment on an intellectual rather than an emotional level. Although focusing on cognitive issues instead of emotional issues can be helpful, it is not appropriate when the primary motivation for doing so is to protect the therapist from the intensity of the client's feelings and ignores the needs of the client.

Boundary Violations

Some therapists are strongly attracted to their Black clients. The consequences of these strong reactions are varied. In some situations, therapists who have become too attached, attracted, or invested may overdisclose with their clients. They may fail to accurately hear what the client is saying because they're actually too caught up in their own issues. Some therapists may become over-protective; instead of helping Black clients establish appropriate short- and long-term goals, they see these clients as more in need of supportive approaches.

Therapists who become too attached to Black clients may wind up offering to see their clients socially as well as professionally. Obviously these confused boundaries make it harder for Black clients to understand the expected roles for clients and therapists, which leads to serious harm to the therapeutic process.

A boundary violation in therapy occurred with some friends of mine, the Pattersons, Black clients who sought treatment for marital problems in their one-year-old marriage when they relocated to a new area. The couple was referred to Dr. Hill, a Black female therapist in her mid-fifties. The Pattersons were both lawyers who worked long hours. The therapist shared with the couple that they reminded her of herself and her husband when they were first married. She told the Pattersons that they were very bright and motivated, and she felt sure that she could help them get their marriage back on track.

At the close of the session, problems arose when it became difficult to set the next appointment due to the demands of the Pattersons' schedules. At that point, Dr. Hill suggested that they meet the following week at a quiet restaurant that was closer to their offices. The Pattersons were surprised but agreed. Later, the couple felt uncomfortable with the "therapy lunch," canceled, and did not reschedule.

In this case, the first violation involved the attempt to bring therapy into a social situation. The second was that the therapist over-identified with the clients and tried to "take care" of them and solve a problem that was their responsibility, which was to make therapy a priority and to find a time for another session. Dr. Hill's accommodation actually had the unintended effect of pushing her clients away from, not toward, therapy and problem resolution.

One of the issues that can trigger boundary problems with Black clients is the fact that so many stereotypes exist about them. Because both Black males and females tend to be portrayed in the media as sexual symbols, therapists may find working with these clients to be different from their usual interactions with other clients and may develop sexual or romantic attachments.

These feelings are likely to be particularly problematic and threatening to non-Black therapists who may not have ever considered Blacks as a target for their romantic or sexual feelings. These feelings may be stimulated by the fact that many Blacks are more open, expressive, and direct about their emotional feelings and reactions. Therapists who are heterosexual are likely to be particularly uncomfortable when they have same-sex attractions to Black clients.

Overidentification

When countertransference involves areas of similarity, potential triggers can be issues of overidentification; unresolved personal issues; projection; and assumptions of shared feelings, values, and expectations.

Black therapists who work with clients who are similar with regard to race, gender, or socioeconomic status may find it hard to avoid overidentifying with clients who are struggling with some of the same issues they are. The fact that these Black clients can empathize and relate may cause therapists to go overboard. Therapists may become so caught up in relating to a shared issue that they lose objectivity and fail to explore additional components to the problem.

Therapists and clients can also engage in "ain't it awful" sessions in which they commiserate about shared experiences of racism, sexism, or other types of oppression. The problem is that it can be so reinforcing to vent that the therapist neglects to focus on problem solving and coping. Of course, if therapists have the same problem as their clients, one of the dangers is that they may be unable to help in resolving the issue.

That Black therapists are able to identify with issues can be positive. But it can also be problematic if therapists lose focus and respond more to their issues than to those of the client. If therapists overidentify with the client, they believe the client shares perspectives, views, and responses with them. Even if the client and therapist share some areas of similarity, such as race and culture, they can differ with respect to

- Generation

- Geographic origin

- Religion

- Politics

- Education

- Coping skills

- Racial attitudes

- Degree of comfort in identifying as African American

Some African American therapists will be insensitive to the fact that Black clients may be more White oriented or more Black oriented in their racial identity or worldview. These therapists may be unaware that they're trying to impose their racial views on their clients. This can be particularly problematic when the therapist is either very Afrocentric or very Eurocentric and these views don't match those of the client.

Black therapists can also bring their own countertransference issues with regard to skin color, hair texture, or other signs of privilege the client may have. If therapists have unresolved feelings about these issues, such as internalized racism, envy, or distrust, they can be communicated to clients and cause a rupture to rapport.

We know that the benefits of working with a Black therapist can be significant for Black clients. The client may engage more readily in the process of therapy, self-disclose more easily, and be more willing to remain in therapy. These benefits can accrue only when the therapist maintains appropriate boundaries and avoids over- or underidentifying with the client.

Viewing the Client as Exotic

Sometimes therapists find the lives of their Black clients exotic and therefore view a client's life as if it were a soap opera or great adventure. The problem here is that therapists fail to understand the ways in which Black clients have similarities to other people. Therapists may feel that the skills and talents they have honed in other clinical experience can't work with Black clients. This attitude is an overreaction.

Although I advocate culturally competent practice, it's important not to exaggerate the differences of Black clients or to lose track of the ways in which people across race and culture also have similarities.

Inability to Evaluate Objectively

When therapists are deficient in their knowledge, skills, and experience with Black clients, they may make such errors as seeing Black clients as more disturbed than they really are or failing to appropriately identify serious problems when they exist. Understanding Black culture allows us as therapists to understand a broader context so that some behaviors, such as strong religiosity or strongly tied families, may be seen as strengths, not weaknesses.

In other situations, a fear of not understanding or fear of contributing to an individual's problems makes some therapists afraid to let the client know the seriousness of his or her problems. We can only be accurate and confident in our analysis of Black clients when we have a strong foundation of knowledge and experience.

Many non-Black therapists have had limited contacts with African Americans. I've had colleagues and students tell me they have never been close friends with an African American, never been in their homes; the closest connection they may have had is with someone who worked for their parents in the home doing domestic, garden, or repair work.

As a result, some therapists have difficulty understanding the lives of average Blacks, and the problems experienced by wealthy Blacks and very poor Blacks may be out of their realm of training or experience. Therapists may find themselves listening with interest and fascination rather than focusing on understanding how to empathize and help.

It's important to note that upper-income Blacks seem to pose as much of a challenge as lower-income Blacks. Countertransference issues can be triggered when therapists recognize that some of their Black clients come from families with several generations of higher income, education level, and socioeconomic status than their own families had. It also can be difficult for therapists to resolve their feelings about Black individuals who were able to work up from a lower-income status to a position of status and income that is higher than theirs.

A few years ago, I supervised Michelle, a twenty-five-year-old White female who developed a countertransference reaction to Loretta, a Black female undergraduate. Loretta was nineteen, attractive, bright, and from a very wealthy family. She was not very academically motivated in her second semester of college and had been referred for therapy after being placed on academic probation for her first-semester grades. Her parents were hoping that Loretta would go into law or business as her siblings had, but Loretta wasn't interested in these career paths and was unsure of her academic major.

Loretta readily confessed that she was not motivated to do well and knew that if she wanted to leave school, her parents would allow her to spend a year in Europe on her own at their expense.

When Michelle discussed Loretta with me in supervision, she described Loretta as "immature, self-centered, a typical rich brat." I asked Michelle how she felt during the session. She said that she felt irritated and angry with Loretta. I pointed out how strong and unusual her reaction was to this client. As we processed Michelle's feelings, she was able to get in touch with the fact that whereas she, Michelle, was struggling desperately to pay for her graduate education, this Black female was blowing her parents' money by partying and getting poor grades. She felt that Loretta was capable of doing better academically, and Michelle personally resented that Loretta didn't have to worry about money and was free to leave school and travel if that was what she wanted.

Michelle was from a working-class family and had been taught that the way to succeed was to work hard. She had paid for her undergraduate education through scholarships and loans. She said, "Loretta probably was admitted based on some affirmative action program. It's not fair that Blacks like her have all these special programs at college, and people like me don't."

During our supervision session, we worked through Michelle's anger at what she felt were all the entitlement programs Blacks had that were unfair to people like her who didn't have a lot of financial resources and had to struggle for an education. I asked Michelle if she would be as upset if Loretta had been White. She admitted that she didn't think so because she had always known many White students who were wealthier than she.

Michelle was able to get in touch with the fact that deep inside she still held on to what her parents had always taught: that Blacks were poor, on welfare, used drugs, and were always looking for someone else to help them, usually the government. We processed the fact that her strong reactions to Loretta were based on Loretta's being Black and wealthy, not just wealthy. I asked Michelle if it was fair to judge Loretta negatively simply because she had some options that Michelle didn't. As we talked, I pointed out that it was unlikely that Loretta was receiving the many race-related benefits and resources that Michelle thought. We talked some about affirmative action programs, but we focused on helping Michelle see Loretta's humanity, not just her wealth. Loretta was immature, unsure of herself, and afraid to commit to college because she didn't know what she wanted. Michelle suggested that she work with Loretta on some values clarification and would also recommend vocational counseling sessions offered by the university career center. Although Michelle retained her negative evaluation of affirmative action programs, I think she was able to understand and work through her countertransference issues and be effective with Loretta.

PROFESSIONAL AND ETHICAL GUIDELINES

Many therapists who are working with Black clients should not be doing so. Although the therapy literature describes a broad variety of standards for the provision of culturally competent services, the majority of therapists have minimal academic training in cultural competence and little or no supervision with working with African American clients.

As a result of academic and supervisory experiences that minimize exposure to African American clients, many therapists don't get the opportunity to discuss and explore the countertransference issues discussed in this chapter. Usually culturally competent guidelines are discussed only after damage has occurred. In order to minimize and prevent negative countertransference issues and thereby to protect African American clients, we as therapists need higher levels of training and vigilance about attending to racial, cultural, demographic, and ability issues.

To accomplish this formidable task we'll need to eliminate the practice of using our African American clients as a continuing education experience to teach us cultural competence. Second, we must carefully screen our prospective clients to ensure that we are competent and prepared to meet their professional needs.

As we meet with Black clients and listen to their presenting concerns, we need to be prepared to refer clients if we find ourselves in the following situations:

- We don't have supervised experience with the presenting problem.

- We have unresolved issues that are similar to those of the client.

- We're uncomfortable about addressing or are unable to address the full complexity of the client's difficulties.

- We're uncomfortable raising issues of race, gender, religion, sexual orientation, and culture.

- We note that we're not connecting with an African American client, and we're unable to figure out why and resolve the problem.

- We violate therapeutic boundaries by doing more or less for the client.

- We're unaware of areas of difference and commonality between the client and ourselves.

- We experience strong emotional or cognitive reactions.

- We impose our values and philosophies.

- We lack objectivity.

- We're unable to be responsive and spontaneous.

- We behave voyeuristically.

- We get stuck in the client's descriptions of problems without moving to the client's solutions.

We need to be mindful that practicing outside our areas of competence is unethical. We are doing a disservice to clients and to our profession when our countertransference issues waste the time, money, energy, and emotional resources of African American clients. There have been too many times in the past that this group has been exploited by the mental health field for us to prolong this abuse.

If we determine that we're not equipped to work with Black clients, we need to make an appropriate referral. As we make this referral, we should ensure that the client understands that the problem is with us and not with some deficiency of theirs. For those of us who have had training in working with Black clients, we need to continue to take coursework and seminars and to seek consultation and supervision when we become aware of any possible countertransference issues. Only by practicing the highest levels of ethics and vigilance can we protect Black clients from the problems and distortions of countertransference reactions.

8

Self-Awareness and Cultural Competence

In this chapter we'll explore a variety of issues that will increase your cultural competence in your work with African American clients. We'll focus specifically on how to combine principles of cultural competence with self-understanding and important issues in the lives of African American clients. First, we'll discuss self-awareness as it relates to privilege, power, status, and therapist use of self and of interpersonal styles. Second, we'll look at positive ways to have difficult dialogues about such issues as racial and ethnic identity, race, financial status and class, gender, sexuality, and religion.

SELF-AWARENESS

A vital component of being a successful therapist is for you to understand yourself so that you can be an effective therapeutic instrument. When it comes to working with African American clients, you must reflect on what you know about Blacks from both academic and clinical perspectives. You must ask yourself:

What have I learned about this group in classes, seminars, and supervision?

Do I have a solid knowledge base about the history, culture, and current issues that African Americans face?

Have I had enough supervised experience with Black clients to know that I am effective?

Why do I think that I am competent to work with this group?

Second, you must examine your readiness to be effective by examining your subjective experiences and feelings with respect to African Americans.

How much personal experience have I had with African Americans professionally or socially?

To what extent are my attitudes toward Blacks based on personal experiences versus what I have heard or read from others or the media?

What are my areas of uncertainty, discomfort, anxiety, or bias?

What cultural baggage or blind spots might I have in working with Black clients?

After you do some personal work by asking yourself these questions, you need to continue your self-analysis by examining your personal levels of privilege, intercultural sensitivity, and therapist use of self and interpersonal styles.

Privilege

Therapists need to be familiar with the idea of *privilege*. The term as we use it here was coined by Peggy McIntosh and refers to a package of unearned assets that some people can claim in our society while others can't. In our society, privilege is highest for those individuals who are White, male, heterosexual, Protestant, financially secure, young, and able bodied.[1]

When individuals are privileged, they have very little motivation to analyze why they are in a desirable category relative to others. Likewise, they have no motivation to understand the lives of individuals who are not so advantaged. These individuals take their privilege for granted. In contrast, people who are not privileged are constantly confronted with their lack of status and can't avoid the impact this has on their lives.

Most Whites don't spend much time thinking about what it means to be White. Consequently, they often have not thought through the meaning of race, class, and gender as it relates to different races. But African Americans and other groups without White privilege don't have this luxury. They can't ignore the forms of oppression they must constantly face.

The notion of privilege is important because many Whites are complacent, and although they'll acknowledge that prejudice exists for some people, they're not comfortable with accepting the idea of White privilege. It therefore can be difficult for individuals with privilege to understand what it feels like to be, for example,

- Followed around stores

- Harassed by police

- Asked additional questions when using a check

- Stared at when with a partner of the same sex or of a different race

Therapists need to understand that it's much easier for White individuals to believe that we live in a fair and just society. Because privilege exists for White individuals, they're more likely to be opposed to affirmative action programs and to believe in the values of hard work being rewarded. If therapists don't understand where they're located on the privilege spectrum, they won't comprehend how different their experiences, attitudes, and perspectives are from those of African American clients.

We also must note that the privilege of education, status, and power that characterizes therapists can be intimidating to Black clients. As we mentioned earlier, just as some African Americans are reluctant to question their physicians, they may feel reluctant to raise concerns, ask questions, or disagree with us. Blacks have learned to "go along to get along" when they interact with privileged people.

As therapists, we have an obligation to recognize that our clients may see us as unapproachable. Consequently we'll need to take the initiative to minimize the hierarchical relationship of therapy in order to promote a free and open exchange of thoughts and emotions.

One of the ways we can do this is by stating our ideas as only a theory, by asking clients for their opinions, and by encouraging their input and by being comfortable when they disagree with us. We can also show our humanness with appropriate self-disclosure, such as, "Yes, I've also forgotten where I parked my car in the parking lot," or "It's so frustrating when you can't remember a name," or "I know it's dumb, but I hate to stop and ask for directions even when I'm lost."

Intercultural Sensitivity

Along with recognizing the impact of privilege, we also need to understand where we fall with respect to intercultural sensitivity. Many individuals, including some ethnic minority therapists, believe that it's ideal to be "color-blind." This term refers to the idea that we should not notice color and that as a result we'll magically treat everyone the same, and prejudice, racism, and other ills will disappear.

As I state to my supervisees and students, we live in a very color-conscious society, and for therapists to claim they don't notice color makes me concerned about their ability to accurately perceive reality!

Work by Milton Bennett and Barbara Deane suggests that therapists fall somewhere along a continuum of five levels with respect to their intercultural sensitivity to clients.[2] The five levels are as follows:

1. At the lowest level of intercultural sensitivity, the Contact stage, therapists tend to universalize the norms of White culture, are limited in their knowledge of diversity, and believe

that all clients should be treated in the same ways despite their differences. These therapists are usually unaware of and uncomfortable with racial differences, and practice denial of racial themes.

2. At the second stage of sensitivity, Disintegration, therapists become aware of situations that emphasize different cultural experiences. Therapists begin to recognize that they can't use a "one size fits all" approach. At this stage, therapists are likely to be defensive about their lack of skills and insights with Black clients but are unsure how to implement culturally competent practice.

3. In the third stage, Reintegration, therapists explore racial and cultural differences and finally begin to get in touch with feelings of bias and confusion with respect to Black clients. Therapists understand that these negative feelings are inappropriate and may try to hide or minimize their feelings of discomfort. They may be patronizing or overly solicitous, or they may adopt a facade of understanding the complexities of Black culture.

4. In the fourth stage, Pseudo-Independence, therapists gain some factual understanding of racial issues but still lack the affective capacity to empathize with Black clients. Racial issues are still uncomfortable for these therapists.

5. In the final stage of development, Autonomy, therapists are comfortable initiating conversations about race and cultural differences. Therapists can understand and relate to the affective as well as the cognitive concerns of African American clients. They have also learned how to respond with culturally competent approaches to treatment.

Let's use an illustration to demonstrate how therapists with different levels of intercultural sensitivity may respond in myriad ways to the same client.

Ms. Roberts presents for a first session of therapy. She explains that she is a registered nurse but is having trouble on the job. She works in the critical care unit and faces a lot of stress. Ms. Roberts has been written up twice for minor infractions at work with respect to not following the proper protocol. Although Ms. Roberts acknowledges that it's true that her work performance has slacked off a bit, she resents younger White nurse supervisors reprimanding her. She feels that they have criticized her without hearing her side of the story and that they lack respect and are condescending in their treatment of her. Ms. Roberts feels she has had more nursing experience than they have had, but because they have college degrees and she has a nursing degree from a nursing school, they feel superior to her.

A therapist at stage one (Contact) would ignore all the possible racial issues in this case. The therapist might immediately move to the work issue and ask Ms. Roberts, "What are the specific work problems that you're having? If you can share with me what your supervisors are concerned about, we can talk about how to meet their work expectations."

This approach acknowledges the presenting problem of work that Ms. Roberts has discussed. It's premature, however, to jump immediately to the conclusion that work is the primary issue for Ms. Roberts. It's also important to find out what racial dynamics may be important in this work situation. Therapists can't automatically side with Ms. Roberts's supervisors without hearing more from Ms. Roberts. We need to be aware that bias does exist in the workplace and look to see if it's significant in this case.

A therapist in stage two (Disintegration) may recognize that there are possible racial and cultural dynamics in the presenting concerns and background provided by Ms. Roberts but not know what to do. The therapist might say something like, "It sounds like a personality conflict to me. Sometimes Blacks and Whites do things differently on the job. Do you think you should inquire about a transfer?" This response is an improvement over a stage one response, which ignores race and culture. But due to discomfort or to lack of skill or confidence, the therapist is unable to develop a way to talk to the client and assess and help alleviate the specific racial and cultural factors.

In stage three (Reintegration), if the therapist has some baggage around issues of race and discrimination, he or she may raise the issue of race but in a nonproductive and defensive way. The therapist might say to Ms. Roberts, "Why do you feel that it's a problem to have a supervisor who is younger than you even if she's White? What's important is that this person has been trained for her leadership role on the staff." More than likely, if Ms. Roberts has a therapist who is at any of these three levels, she is not going to feel that the therapist is fully hearing and responding to her concerns.

In stage four (Pseudo-Independence), the therapist is aware of and can raise racial issues but doesn't really empathize with how Black clients feel; he or she is just going through the motions. A typical phrase might be, "Well, it sounds like you think that there's more to this situation than your actual performance. You think that because of your race and degree status you're not being treated with the respect that you deserve."

In the fifth stage (Autonomy), the therapist feels comfortable about speaking up about racial issues and understands the perspectives of African American clients. In the case of Ms. Roberts a therapist might say, "Well, we both know that racism at work is a day-to-day reality for many Black individuals. What are some of the behaviors and comments the supervisors have used that offended you? Let's talk about how you can sit down with your supervisors and have a productive discussion about how their comments make you feel. You can then suggest some other ways that they could communicate more effectively."

Successful therapy interactions with Black clients depend on the therapists' responding appropriately to what clients say. We'll talk later in this chapter about how therapists must adjust their comments to be in tune with the racial identity stage of their particular client.

Therapist Use of Self and of Interpersonal Styles

Fortunately, more and more theorists have highlighted the importance of understanding how therapists can best use ourselves as a therapeutic tool. This process is particularly important when working with African American clients, because so many of these individuals have very strongly honed skills in understanding the interpersonal strengths and weaknesses of therapists. We know that many children in confusing and conflictual families can develop exquisitely sensitive abilities to read and respond to family members. Similarly, for basic survival reasons and to protect themselves from harm, African Americans have learned to quickly assess the personality dynamics of individuals with whom they must interact. As a result, as we go through our assessment process in therapy, we can expect to be thoroughly evaluated by our Black clients.

Use of Self

To use ourselves effectively in therapy, our first step is to reflect on and understand our strengths and weaknesses, our family-of-origin issues, and our ongoing or periodic areas of vulnerability. As we inventory our traits, we will see that some of our issues are more serious than others. The following are some examples of areas of vulnerability reported by my students and colleagues:

- Major problems with sibling rivalry

- Strong paternalistic feelings for male clients due to a positive relationship with their father

- Feelings of competition with men or women

- Enmeshed boundaries

- Problems with being able to be in touch with their emotions

- Going through a relationship breakup or divorce

- The recent death of a loved one

- Sexual or physical abuse

Cultural and Political Beliefs

In addition to understanding our personal family-of-origin issues, we need to explore our own cultural and political beliefs. Usually this is challenging to White therapists. Because U.S. culture is normed on White values, many majority members are unaware of their ethnicity, culture, political beliefs, and values.

Unless we are able to get in touch with what we believe in and what we value, we risk showing bias in ways that are invisible to us and therefore harmful in our work with African American clients. We gave the example earlier of the different perspectives that Whites and sometimes other ethnic minority groups have with respect to affirmative action as compared to African Americans. Black clients may have strong convictions that are different from White majority views with respect to the following:

- Stereotypes about racial and ethnic groups

- Delaying marriage

- Having children rather than abortions

- Accepting public assistance

- Risking prosecution to make money illegally

- Male and female roles

- The authority given to extended family members

- Credibility of the media and officials

- The importance of material goods such as clothing, cars, and maintaining a polished appearance

- Black history, culture, and pride

- Feminism

- Prioritizing race over class and gender issues

I have found that many White therapists are particularly clue-less about the ways Blacks may view them. Somehow these White individuals don't connect with the idea that they could be the vic-tims of bias, caricature, and prejudice by African Americans.

For example, one of my White female colleagues was shocked to hear her Black female client make fun of White females in movies and belittle the therapist's attempts to help the client as well. The client was discussing how tired she was of being compared to White females as though they were so much better than other women. The client pointed out that in most movies that she had seen, as soon as danger looms, White females promptly sprain an ankle, swoon, or stand screaming, making no attempt to get out of danger. The client wanted to know how women who always seem to get themselves in trouble, make the situation worse, and then wait to be rescued became the models for female behavior? Why should anyone see these White females as competent and worthy of respect?

Interpersonal Style

If we haven't noted and explored our values, we risk problems in therapy if we subtly or overtly convey that we're right and our clients are wrong. Our challenge is to learn how to know ourselves, be genuine, integrate who we are with professional interventions and guidelines, and help and not harm our African American clients.

With respect to interpersonal style, Black clients expect us to be professional, genuine, and accessible. We need to demonstrate our knowledge and skill to reassure our Black clients that we are credible professionals and that they can relax in the therapy process because we know what we're doing.

I sometimes had experiences with my Black clients, particularly when I was younger, where they felt responsible for the progress of the therapy session. It was disconcerting for some of these clients to trust that someone the age of their children could really help them solve their complex problems. They sometimes had difficulty relaxing their tight reins of control and direction and engaging in a process of collaboration.

In fact, many Black clients tend to be pretty up-front about asking therapists about their education, age, marital status, and whether they have children, to get a sense of the therapists' competence. It's important that we answer these questions while keeping the focus on our clients. We need to be prepared for our Black clients who are direct and confrontational as well as those who are more indirect and less forthcoming in expressing their questions or concerns.

I think that many Black clients are unimpressed with therapists who have a lot of "book knowledge" but are lacking in interpersonal skill and practical strategies. Black clients are often quick to ask us if we think we can help them and how.

With respect to the area of accepting and confronting, some therapists are so afraid of alienating African American clients that they tiptoe around sensitive issues and are afraid to appropriately confront clients. I have found that Black clients often expect to be confronted when necessary and don't think highly of therapists who let them off the hook.

It's actually somewhat scary for Black clients to feel that they have fooled the therapist or that they as clients have so much power that the therapist fears being up-front and honest with them. Firm and appropriate confrontation can actually build rapport and allow for effective problem solving with Black clients, because it is a sign to these clients that their therapist is perceptive and knows what he or she is doing.

POSITIVE WAYS TO HAVE DIFFICULT DIALOGUES

We can have difficult dialogues with our clients in ways that facilitate the goals of therapy. One of the first areas we need to understand is racial identity. We must also know how to sensitively discuss race, financial status and class, gender, sex and sexual orientation, religion, and any other relevant areas of difference between the African American client and us.

Racial Identity Theory

One of the questions we need to ask our Black clients in the beginning of the first session is, "Could you tell me about your racial background?" This general question allows clients to choose the words that they prefer in describing their racial lineage. It also opens the door for clients to tell us something about the diversity of race, culture, and ethnicity in their families.

I listen for any significant issues with respect to facial features, hair texture, or skin color or tone. If these issues seem germane to the presenting problem, I decide whether to ask more questions at this point or later, depending on how comfortable the client seems to be with this subject.

I once worked with a fifteen-year-old teenager named Anna. Her parents were concerned that she wasn't interested in school and that all she was interested in was cutting classes, spending the night with her girlfriends, and talking about hairstyles, clothes, and boys. In our first session, she commented to me, "Your hair is pretty long. Why don't you wear it like that lady on television who does the news? I think it would look good on you."

In this situation I wanted to keep the focus on Anna, so I thanked her for the suggestion (without promising to make any changes) and asked her what she thought about her hair and hairstyle. "Oh, I like the way I look. I have a friend who fixes my hair in a different style every week. She's going to go to beauty school when she's eighteen. I know I look good; you should see all the guys who look at me." From this interchange and other comments, I felt reassured that hair and skin color were not an issue for Anna.

On another occasion I was working with Kelly, a college freshman. When I asked her to describe herself as others saw her she said, "Medium build, average height, really nice straight hair, and kinda pretty for a dark-skinned girl." With Kelly, we did some work on how she had learned to evaluate her darker skin color as a handicap that had to be overcome by her hair and overall attractiveness. We then moved to talking about how she could see herself as pretty and dark skinned.

In addition to learning how clients self-identify, we also need to understand how comfortable they are with the issue of racial identity. Thomas Parham, Robert Carter, Janet Helms, William Cross, and others have devoted a great deal of attention to outlining the stages of racial identity through which African Americans progress.[3] These theories of racial resocialization, or *Nigrescence*, explain how African Americans develop a Black identity. It is important for us as therapists to understand what stage or stages of racial identity we are in, as well as the stage of our client, so that we can tailor our comments in accord with our combined perspectives and worldviews. The following are the five stages of racial identity, including one category of combined stages:

1. In stage one, Pre-encounter, African Americans vary from not actively thinking about their race to having anti-Black feelings. Individuals at this stage may readily understand that

their race is associated with stigma and oppression, but in general these individuals subscribe to and accept White cultural values and interpretations.

2. In the second stage, Encounter, some dramatic event or a series of events has a personal and profound impact that leads individuals to reevaluate their views about race. The events can be negative, as they would be in the case of enduring racist treatment, such as being mistreated at work or hassled by the police. The precipitant can also be positive if it involves getting in touch with the beauty and splendor of African American art and culture. This is a stage of confusion, disorientation, shame about their past ignorance of race, and upheaval as individuals experience a major shift in the way that they view the world.

3. In the combined stages of three and four, Immersion-Emersion, individuals commit to a radically new way of thinking and embrace Black culture and identity. Here we see signs of the new identity in African-inspired hairstyles, such as braids, dreadlocks, or Afros; African garments; and Afrocentric ideologies and analyses.

   Whereas in the past, individuals in this stage had idealized White middle-class values, they now reject and repudiate White culture and demonstrate a "Blacker than thou" orientation and attitudes of Black superiority. Blacks go through a cycle of anger toward Whites and White culture, guilt at having embraced the White ideals in the past, and pride in Blackness and African ancestry.

   Some African Americans become active in cultural celebrations, such as Kwaanza and rites-of-passage programs, become jazz enthusiasts or collectors of African American art, or join book clubs to read and discuss Black literature.

4. The third and fourth stages involve both immersion and emersion. The immersion phase reflects interest in overcom-

pensatory activities, whereas the emersion stage shows a transition from a romantic and simplified ideology of Black superiority to a more complex and balanced worldview.

5. In the fifth and final stage, Internalization, individuals have worked through identity issues and adopt a perspective on racial identity that can range from a more nationalistic or Afrocentric orientation to a perspective that is bicultural or multicultural. Individuals feel a sense of peace and pride about themselves and their ancestry and culture.

Some theorists assert that individuals who sustain the gains of the internalization phase show "internalization-commitment."[4] According to Thomas Parham, it is also possible that African Americans may repeat their cycle through these phases at different points in their lives, such as adolescence and middle and late adulthood, as different external events may stimulate a return to a particular stage of identity development.[5]

These ideas about racial identity are important because we can use this schema to understand something about how our African American clients feel about themselves and their history and culture and how they view other ethnic minority groups and the White mainstream culture.

For example, if we were working with Mr. Lambert, a Black male in his late fifties in the Pre-encounter stage, he would perhaps be somewhat uncomfortable about direct discussions of race and racial difference. He may believe that if Black folks work hard, they will be accepted and not discriminated against. He might be opposed to affirmative action programs and not trust a therapist whom he perceived to be too liberal about racial issues.

Beginning in the Encounter stage, individuals may voice a preference for an African American therapist and may express some discomfort with a White or non-Black therapist as they get in touch with their sense of racial identity and pride. As individuals move into Immersion and Emersion, they will be more receptive to Black frameworks of analysis and will expect that an effective therapist will understand and respect the legitimacy of African American perspectives, viewpoints, and culture.

Individuals who have achieved the Internalization stage of Black identity vary with respect to how much of a separatist versus an integrationist perspective they take on racial issues. Clients who embrace a Black nationalist or Afrocentric perspective may be unwilling to work with therapists (of any race) who don't share their views. Black clients with a bicultural or multicultural perspective may be more accepting of the idea that there are good, competent therapists of all races and may be more comfortable in working with therapists who have a worldview different from theirs.

Talking About Race

Race continues to be a taboo subject both in and out of the therapy room. As I listen to my students and supervisees describe their clinical work, few of them feel comfortable initially in even identifying the race of their client. I find myself asking, "How are you going to discuss race with a client you don't know when you're uncomfortable talking about race with someone you already know and with whom you have a relationship?"

Reluctance to talk about race appears to be a deep-seated phenomenon. Therapists have often not been trained with respect to what to say about racial topics and so fear that they will say the wrong thing and offend clients. Consequently, they take the path of saying nothing. Because we know that our society regularly works on a system of granting or withholding privilege based on race and culture, as therapists we have to know how to comfortably and confidently discuss race with our African American clients.

Unfortunately, many texts on interviewing and therapy don't address the issue of race, or they give conflicting advice about how and when to address this issue. In a situation in which a Black client is working with a non-Black therapist, I think that the therapist should initiate the issue of race before the session is over to learn how the client feels about the racial difference between them.

If the client makes a direct or indirect reference to race, culture, gender, or class issues, it makes sense to me to use that opportunity to say to the client, "How do you feel about working with a White [or Asian or Native American or Hispanic] therapist?"

As we ask this question, we need to note both what clients say and their nonverbal responses. Clients who are more assertive and are in a racial identity stage that leads them to want a Black therapist may respond with "Well, to tell you the truth, I would prefer to have a Black therapist."

In this case we would need to address this request directly by letting our clients know that we respect and understand their request and that we'll arrange for a referral to an African American therapist. In some situations, however, we may have to acknowledge that although the request is certainly a legitimate one, in our clinic or practice, we don't have a Black therapist available. We then need to process with our clients whether or not it's possible for us to be culturally competent enough to meet their needs.

Here we need to be able to say something about our training and experience with African American clients that reassures clients that we're proficient. We can say, for example, "I understand that your first choice is to have an African American therapist. Since we don't have a Black therapist available to work with you, I'd like to propose that we continue to work together if you would be comfortable with that idea. I have worked with more than fifty Black clients over the last three years that I've been working in this city. I completed internship and practicum work where I worked with a number of Black clients and received supervision from African American therapists. From our work together today, I think that I understand your concerns and that we can work effectively together. Are you willing to consider our working together on a trial basis of, say, four sessions to see how well our work together is proceeding?"

If the client agrees to proceed with us we can add, "It's my inten-tion to understand what you tell me. As we go along, if you feel that I'm off base or not being sensitive to what you're communicating, please let me know."

I don't feel the same urgency to ask about race in the first ses-sion when both client and therapist are African American. In some cases, however, it may become clear that because of the client's racial identity stage, pre-encounter feelings may lead the client to be uncomfortable with the idea of an African American therapist. Such a client may have feelings of internalized racism and feel offended about being placed with a Black therapist.

I've had clients raise this concern by asking me, "How come they assigned me to you? Are people in this clinic hung up about racial issues? I don't think that race stuff matters. I just want a well-qualified therapist. I don't care about race." In this situation I can honestly admit that assignments to therapists are not done on a racial basis. I ask these individuals directly if they're comfortable continuing to meet with me, an African American female.

If my sense is that their verbal and nonverbal responses seem positive, we can proceed. If I gain a sense that the client is still uncomfortable, we talk about making a referral. We need to recog-nize that some Black clients fear that Black therapists may raise racial and cultural issues that these clients don't want to deal with given their stage of racial identity. These cues are usually pretty evi-dent. Often these clients profess to being "color-blind"; have a high sense of internal control; and are disdainful of minorities who are on welfare or are unwilling to work hard, or who blame racism for all their problems.

When I work with a client who is resistant to dealing with racial and cultural issues, I respect those feelings. It's not wise to push ideas or perspectives with which a client is uncomfortable.

We also need to take the initiative at any point in our session to ask if what our clients are saying relates to race and culture. When we can be forthright and comfortable talking about racial issues, clients usually relax and feel more confidence in the therapy process and us.

I'm not suggesting that we raise the issue of race in a forced manner. I'm proposing that we talk about race when it seems appropriate. It sends a negative message to Black clients when we ignore and minimize racial dynamics that relate to their concerns.

Talking About Financial and Class Issues

Some therapists and clients show considerable discomfort in talking about financial and socioeconomic issues. Usually class issues become salient when there appears to be a considerable discrepancy between the client and therapist. We typically think of therapists as middle class, if not because of the status of their family of origin then at least by virtue of their having received advanced educational degrees and professional status.

I think that for some therapists the first step is to recognize that even though they may work with low-income individuals, these clients are not "lower-class" individuals. This distinction is important mentally and in how we treat our clients. How much income a person has doesn't determine how much class he or she has.

I don't think it's necessary for therapists to overtly raise differences in socioeconomic status. It's important for us to be alert to these differences and to assess our client's level of comfort or discomfort.

We also need to be alert to some of the cultural experiences that lower-income individuals may have had that cause problems in therapy. For instance, in my work at a community mental health clinic, some Black clients thought that an appointment time of two in the afternoon meant that they had either to come earlier to see me on a first-come basis or to come later and be prepared for a long wait. These clients were used to waiting for hours to see a physician in another department. It was important for me to clarify that an appointment time with me meant that I would be ready to see them at that time.

We also have to be prepared to be sensitive and responsive to issues of discrimination and oppression that Black clients face when they are poor and have limited resources. We need to acknowledge the poor treatment they often receive, and work with clients to help them maintain a positive identity in a society that devalues people lacking in financial resources. Those of us who have reliable cars and a stable source of income may not realize that transportation and finances can pose significant barriers to therapy.

Some clients have to rely on public transportation or rides from family members or friends in order to come for therapy. We also need to be able to have frank conversations about our fees for therapy and recognize that even with sliding-scale options, clients may have difficulty keeping up with the costs of therapy unless we make some adjustments in our fees.

Even when we are working with working-class and middle-income Black clients, we need to check in the first session to make sure they feel comfortable with the financial arrangements we have made with them, whether it includes public assistance or private insurance. We also have to be sensitive to the fact that because our Black clients may have discomfort about talking about financial arrangements, we must be alert to possible problems and try to avoid losing clients because they were afraid to admit to their financial pressures.

Talking About Gender Issues

We need to understand that the intersection of race, gender, class, sexual orientation, and other status issues can create complex feelings and dynamics for Black clients. When we meet with Black males, we need to make sure that we consult, include, and directly address them as a significant member of the family or couple. We want to make sure that we speak with respect in terms of forms of address, tone, and body posture. Some Black men are sensitive to sharing their deeper feelings with others and may have difficulty in revealing areas of anxiety or insecurity, especially in front of a male therapist.

When we want to create a safe climate for Black men to share feelings, we can use direct eye gaze, head nodding, and verbal encouragers to reinforce self-disclosure.

I recently worked with Mr. and Mrs. Phillpotts. Mr. Phillpotts was in his mid-fifties and worked for a security firm as a night watchman. He had worked briefly as a supervisor but quit due to political pressures and tensions from another individual, who wanted the permanent position of supervisor. Recently, there was again a job opening for the supervisor position. Mr. Phillpotts stated to me and his wife that he wasn't interested in this position. He said, "I don't want all those problems, given the money they pay supervisors." It seemed obvious to Mrs. Phillpotts and me that Mr. Phillpotts was clearly interested in the position but was afraid to risk applying for the position and not be successful. As Mr. Phillpotts described the job opening, I decided to challenge his facade of indifference by saying, "It seems to me that you're really interested in this job."

Mr. Phillpotts said, "Well, I'm slightly interested because I know that I would do a good job. But in three years I can retire. I don't know if I want that stress at this point in my life."

I asked Mr. Phillpotts to verbalize the advantages and disadvantages of the job. As he talked about the advantages, he became more animated and excited. When I pointed out his affect to him, he was finally able to laugh and say, "OK, I am interested. But I don't know if I'm ready to put myself out there for this job." With his last comment, we were then in a place to talk about what he wanted to do about his interest and what the risks were.

I have found that some African American women may be willing to open up quicker in a first session than Black men, but they may still keep their guard up with respect to whether they can trust the therapist. Black women also expect to be treated with respect and courtesy, because others do not always accord these everyday behaviors to them.

African American women may be suspicious of the intentions of therapists across race and gender. Black women have endured a history of oppression from White males and females and from Black men. They have learned to be careful about whom they trust.

Although many Black women feel they can turn only to other Black women for support and understanding, society often places Black women in competition with each other for the scarce resources of attention in intimate relationships and in the workplace. As a result, I have found that a Black woman will go through a process of "checking out" a Black female therapist to make sure that she will not feel put down by the professional status of the therapist or by how the therapist speaks, dresses, or acts.

As therapists we need to be particularly sensitive to not engendering feelings of jealousy, suspicion, or resentment when we work with Black families and couples. In our attempt to be supportive and to help clients express their feelings, clients may question our motives or intentions. Nancy Boyd-Franklin has commented that in working with families and couples, therapists may need to monitor their behaviors and the reactions of clients to make sure that communication is clear and appropriate.[6]

For example, Mr. and Mrs. Andrews sought therapy because Mr. Andrews had recently been severely ill with a heart condition. Because he thought he was near death, Mr. Andrews decided to get his relationship right with his wife. He felt compelled to tell his wife about a brief affair that he had about three years into their thirty-three-year marriage when he was on sea duty during his navy career.

Mrs. Andrews felt very hurt and betrayed, and she wondered if she could trust her husband again and keep their marriage together. Not surprisingly, Mrs. Andrews had mixed feelings about working with a Black female therapist. On the one hand, she felt some relief in getting her feelings out in the open and receiving support for her feelings from the therapist and her husband.

On the other hand, she became upset to hear her husband disclose some of his thoughts and feelings in front of the therapist when he had not shared them previously with her. As the "victim" of her husband's infidelity, Mrs. Andrews also felt that I should chastise him more in the session and praise her for being such a supportive wife.

At the beginning of any couple therapy, I explain that my goal is not to keep clients together or break them up. I am simply interested in facilitating a dialogue that will enable the couple to understand their thoughts and feelings and then establish their goals. I alert clients to the fact that although I'll do my best to be objective when a couple is in the midst of a disagreement, whenever I offer any validation to one person, the other may feel unsupported and feel that I'm siding with the other.

In the case of Mr. and Mrs. Andrews, after we talked about her feelings and she asserted that she wanted the marriage to continue, we started talking about some of the weak areas of the marriage that would need shoring up.

As Mr. and Mrs. Andrews talked about their difficulty in communicating, I asked them some general questions about their communication style and what worked and what caused problems. Each time Mr. Andrews shared his thoughts and feelings, Mrs. Andrews became angry that he was so comfortable in sharing with the therapist, a stranger, when he seemed to find it so hard to talk to her.

It was clear that I had to help Mrs. Andrews see me as an ally and not a threat if our work was going to be successful. I told Mrs. Andrews that I could understand her suspicions of me. I knew that she expected me to berate her husband for his behavior and not accord him the same respect that I was giving her. She agreed that these were her feelings.

I proceeded to explain that because the two of them had decided that they wanted to continue their relationship, if she or I pursued a cycle of chastising and berating her husband, I wasn't sure how the two of them would be able to heal the relationship. I asked Mrs. Andrews if she believed in the sincerity of his apology and his vow not to be unfaithful to her again. She told me that her head believed him but her heart didn't. I agreed with her that it would be a long and challenging battle for her to learn to trust her husband again.

I also told Mrs. Andrews that I could understand why she felt upset and threatened that he was more willing to speak openly to me in the therapy session than he was at home. I pointed out that this was a typical pattern for many people because therapy sessions offered possibilities for dealing with issues in new ways.

I reinforced the fact that my job was to encourage both of them to improve in their communication with each other, not with me. I explained that the two of them were the experts on their relationship, as they had been involved with each other for more than thirty-three years. I also asked Mrs. Andrews to stop me at any point if she felt that I was treating her unfairly or showing bias toward her husband. I underscored that I was very appreciative of her ability to share her concerns with me.

I feel that my comments with Mrs. Andrews had a positive effect. This couple chose to engage in follow-up therapy with me, and they made good progress in rebuilding their marriage.

Talking About Sex and Sexual Orientation

We also have to demonstrate tact and sensitivity when we suspect or learn that our Black clients are gay, lesbian, or bisexual. In general, I try to let my clients set the pace for deciding when they feel it's appropriate to share sexual orientation or sexual aspects of the relationship. However, in the case of a couple seeking therapy because of a relationship difficulty, I first try to establish a comfort level, but if the clients don't volunteer the information, I ask them what is happening in their sexual relationship. I'm always interested in asking the couple to elaborate when they offer two radically different reports of the adequacy, frequency, and satisfaction of their sexual relationship.

I have found that I need to proceed slowly in discussing sexual issues with Black individuals. Some of my clients have been raised with the view that sex is something you do and you may joke about, but you don't talk about it. Many African Americans learned basic sex dynamics from talking to friends and have a great deal of misinformation about contraception, fertility, sexually transmitted diseases, and what is considered "normal" sex.

I have found that I need to use equal parts calmness and a sense of humor to get couples to talk frankly about their sexual concerns. Some of my Black clients complain that they must just be "boring" because they don't understand or practice many of the sexual behaviors that they hear about or read about in popular culture. I have to encourage them to tell me what they're referring to.

Several years ago I worked with a Black woman, Mrs. Watkins, who felt overwhelmed in caring for two sick relatives. After we had finished talking about some of her feelings for a while, she asked me if she could briefly change the subject. I assured her that we could do so. Mrs. Watkins said that she needed my advice. She lived in a small home with five of her children. Mrs. Watkins came home earlier than she had been expected and thought she was home alone.

When she heard sounds from her twenty-year-old daughter's room, she instinctively pushed the door open to see who was in there. She saw her daughter performing a sexual act on her boyfriend. Mrs. Watkins said that she didn't think that the couple noticed her, but she was upset by what she saw. Having sex in the way that she witnessed had always been deemed inappropriate. She asked me if I thought there was something wrong with her daughter.

I said that based on this example I didn't think that something was wrong with her daughter. We talked about how different people have different styles of making love and that if this worked for her daughter and her boyfriend, she shouldn't worry about it.

Overall, talking about sex, sexual orientation, separations and divorces, infidelity, children born outside of marriage, and general relationship issues can be very sensitive and volatile topics for Black clients. We have to be able to evaluate if one of these sensitive topics is critically involved in first-session issues and therefore must be addressed. We also must create a climate of safety that allows clients to feel comfortable discussing these issues with us.

Talking About Religion

Mr. and Mrs. Fields sought therapy due to communication problems and the stress of Mrs. Fields's multiple sclerosis. As we went through introductions and beginning questions, Mr. Fields said, "Wait, I have some questions for you. I'm a deacon in my church. I'm not sure about this counseling business, but if we're going to work with you, we need you to tell us something about yourself and your beliefs. Are you a Christian? Have you accepted Jesus as your Lord and Savior? Would you be willing to pray before we get any further involved in this therapy process?"

I answered Mr. and Mrs. Fields by saying that I was a Christian. (Obviously, if you are not a Christian, you can say no.) I added that I would not be willing to pray because as their therapist, I had an obligation not to impose my religious views on them. I thought that it would be fine if they wanted to pray. Mr. Fields indicated that my plan was acceptable. He gave a comprehensive prayer that invoked a blessing for our work together, and when he finished I joined him and his wife in saying "Amen."

I think that in therapy with Black clients we want to focus as little as possible on what our beliefs are. Sometimes Black clients want to hear that a therapist has a belief in something bigger. Believing in a higher power may be more important than a specific faith.

If a client pins you down and you share that you don't have any particular religious beliefs, you can tell the client that you still think that you can be effective as a therapist but that the final decision will be with the client.

It seemed clear to me that Mr. and Mrs. Fields needed the blessing of their religion to enter into therapy. I have had several Black clients who have asked me the kinds of questions that the Fields did. If we can respond honestly and comfortably, we can enhance rapport even if our beliefs are different than our clients'. I think that we can acknowledge and support our clients' faith while being responsible and not imposing our views on them.

As previously mentioned, I often raise the issue of religion in a first session by asking if the client has a church or spiritual home. I explain that the support of a minister and other church members and resources can be helpful to a client in need. I also try to assess whether religion or religious advisers are a source of help or harm for Black clients. In situations where a clergy member is encouraging a wife to stay in an abusive relationship and submit to her husband, we need to tread carefully. But we also have an obligation to help our clients gain the support they need not to follow the advice of their religion if this information is dangerous to them.

We must deal carefully with the issue of spanking in the Black community. Many individuals believe very literally that they're not practicing their religion if they don't spank their children. We have to point out that as therapists we know that the consequences of misbehavior in our society for Black children tend to be worse than they are for White children. Therefore both for religious reasons and from a pragmatic desire to keep their children out of trouble, spanking is a common discipline strategy for Black parents.

We understand that Black parents take discipline seriously for religious reasons and to teach kids societal rules. But many times our decision to spank is based more on the mood we're in and what our day was like than on the specific misbehavior of our children. I try to have parents self-assess how much they're in control when they're disciplining their children. I also have found it helpful to reinforce the idea that because children are different and respond to different approaches, it's useful for Black parents to learn a variety of discipline techniques in addition to spanking.

At this point we've covered a broad variety of skills and cultural competencies necessary to have effective first sessions with Black clients. In the final chapter, we'll discuss a lengthy case example in which we integrate the skills and perspectives we've developed so far.

9

Managing Racial Concerns in Therapy: Mrs. Lucas

In this chapter we'll examine how to put together all the material we have discussed so far to create a successful first session with African American clients.

CASE STUDY OF MRS. LUCAS

An employee assistance program (EAP) referred Mrs. Lucas, a thirty-five-year-old Black female, to therapy after she agreed that she needed longer-term therapy. In our first session, I invited Mrs. Lucas to accompany me to my office. When she entered my office, she stopped and said, "Where should I sit?" I told her that she could sit anywhere she wanted, and gestured toward two chairs and a couch. Mrs. Lucas paused for several seconds, then perched on the edge of the couch, where she appeared tense and ill at ease.

Right away I noticed that Mrs. Lucas was attractive, heavyset, and brown skinned. She was "dressed down," wearing no makeup and casually attired in a drab T-shirt and a long skirt. Her hair was neat and short; she wore it in cornrows. She had on a plain watch, a wedding band, and no other jewelry or adornments. I was intrigued by her casual appearance because so many of my African American clients seem to take an extra effort with their appearance when meeting authority figures for the first time.

I sat in a chair adjoining the couch. I asked Mrs. Lucas if she had any questions about the process of therapy or any of the financial arrangements. She said, "No. I've just gone through the EAP process, so I know all that stuff about confidentiality." Given her reserved demeanor, I decided to bring up directly the topics that led Mrs. Lucas to get help. Mrs. Lucas didn't seem interested in any small talk as we walked to my office or after we sat down. She maintained a very passive and bland affect.

I asked Mrs. Lucas if she could tell me why she was seeking therapy at that time. She told me she was a computer operator working twelve-hour shifts in order to have more days at home with her husband and three children—two sons aged ten and eight and a twelve-year-old daughter. As a result of these long workdays, she was feeling tired and stressed both at home and at work.

Although she thought that working four days instead of five would give her more time with her children and husband, her family complained that she actually was spending less time with them. They were upset that Mrs. Lucas was withdrawn and that she slept most of the time and did virtually no cooking, cleaning, or socializing with them.

Knowing that Mrs. Lucas had been referred by the EAP, I asked her if there were any other sources of stress in her work. Mrs. Lucas paused before she answered that her work performance had also deteriorated since she changed her working hours. I asked her if she could explain how her work performance had changed.

Mrs. Lucas asked, "Why do I have to answer so many of the same questions with you that I've already answered for the EAP counselor? Haven't you talked to that other lady? Where are you from, anyway? Your accent doesn't sound like you're from around here."

I responded to her second question by telling her that she was correct that I had lived up north for most of my adult life before moving to the South for schooling and work opportunities. I then answered her first question by explaining that I had received a call from the EAP counselor but thought it was important for me to hear directly from her what her concerns were.

I told Mrs. Lucas that I could understand her frustration in having to repeat material that she had already shared with someone else. I noticed that talking to Mrs. Lucas was like pulling teeth, as she tended to give minimal answers to my questions. Her affect was restrained, she rarely gave me any eye contact, and I realized that she had not smiled once in our interaction so far.

Mrs. Lucas gave a deep sigh, then answered my question. She said she had been warned by her supervisor that she had made several minor errors over the last few weeks and that she was on the verge of being given a letter of reprimand if her work accuracy and productivity didn't improve. She said that she didn't know why they were so hard on her. Mrs. Lucas said she had a very strong work record and was one of the top employees. She had worked hard all during her training to show people that Blacks could be just as smart and successful as Whites. It was humiliating to her to be having work problems, because this was an area in her life in which she felt great pride. Because there was no reason to suspect that racial issues were significant at this point, I didn't challenge Mrs. Lucas's statement.

I asked Mrs. Lucas if the change in her schedule was causing her performance problems. She said that part of the problem was the schedule change and part of the problem was worrying about the well-being of her children, especially her daughter, when they were home from school and unsupervised. As she made this last comment, she looked at me defiantly and sat up straighter on the couch. I sensed there was more to what was going on with her daughter, but Mrs. Lucas's nonverbal behavior suggested that she wasn't ready to share very much more on this subject at this time.

I decided to try another avenue of discussion, as it seemed that Mrs. Lucas was uncomfortable sharing more information about her daughter. I said, "I want to come back and talk more about your stress at work and at home a bit later in our session. I'm wondering if you have any other stressors in your life, such as financial prob-

lems, health concerns, or problems in any of your important relationships with your immediate family or extended circle of family
and friends."

Mrs. Lucas stated that she was on heart medication but only
took the medication when she felt palpitations or was dizzy. I asked
her when she had last had her heart checked by a physician; she
shrugged her shoulders and stated that she was unsure but that she
thought about six months ago.

I asked her if she would be willing to visit her doctor and have
a complete physical. I urged her to consider the fact that all the
stress she was under could have a major impact on her health. I told
her she would feel better and be more able to cope if she took her
medicine regularly and stayed in frequent contact with her doctor
so that she would have a clear idea of any health risks. She told me
that she was willing to make an appointment with her doctor and
get back on her heart medication.

At this point in the session I sometimes ask for a family history
of physical or emotional problems. I didn't do this with Mrs. Lucas
because she seemed so guarded with me. I didn't feel that we had
established a strong enough rapport to talk about possible family
issues of alcoholism, abuse, or emotional problems.

Given the restrained affect that Mrs. Lucas was exhibiting, I felt
that depression might be one of her problems. I asked her if her
sleeping or eating schedule had changed lately. She reported that it
seemed to her that all she did when she was not at work was to eat
and sleep. I asked if she ever woke up after she fell asleep. She indicated that she would sometimes wake up in the middle of the night
and toss and turn without being able to fall asleep until she was due
to wake up. She said that she didn't have any energy for anything
else but work because she always felt so tired.

I asked Mrs. Lucas directly if she felt depressed. She said yes, but
she felt that being depressed was normal for her. She really couldn't
remember when she hadn't felt the way she did now. She didn't cry
or get upset; she just never was one of those "isn't life great" people.

I knew that I'd need to refer Mrs. Lucas for a psychiatric evaluation, but because I had just pushed the issue of getting a checkup with her physician, I decided to bring up this referral later.

I next asked Mrs. Lucas if she could tell me about her husband and their marriage. How long had they been married? Where did they meet? What was their relationship like? I noted that Mrs. Lucas still showed little affect as she spoke about her husband.

She told me that they had been married for fifteen years and had grown up in a small community in a rural part of the Midwest. Mrs. Lucas said that she had always known her husband's family because they lived in a small town where you regularly saw people in stores, churches, and at school. She said that she got to know him better in high school when they found themselves in the same social group. Although he was one year older, Mrs. Lucas had started hanging out with older students. She stated that she was on the brink of getting involved with sex and drugs when she met her husband. She was impressed with how mature, solid, and capable he seemed to her.

Mrs. Lucas said that her husband was one of those people who liked to interact with people who were complex and hard to understand, and she thought that he had correctly picked up on the fact that she would be a challenge to figure out. Mrs. Lucas also said her husband wanted to "fix" her. I asked why her husband would want to fix her. She again remained silent for about thirty seconds and said, "I don't think I can make you understand. What do you know about people making fun of you because you're too dark, too heavy, have short hair, and you're poor?"

I responded by saying, "I certainly can't say that I know what you've experienced, but I know that we live in a society that gives Black people a hard time and often rewards and punishes Black women based on the degree to which they meet White beauty standards. I think that I can understand and relate to your experiences, even if some of them are different from my experiences. Have you tried before to get other Black women to understand what you've gone through and found them insensitive?"

"Yes I have," she retorted. "That's why I sometimes talk more to Whites and men at work than to other Black females. At least I know where they're coming from. If they want to be friends, I can trust them. All the Black women I know try to use their looks to get ahead of other women. The only person who never tried to put me down was my cousin Nicole. Even though she looked half White herself, she and her family were always there for me."

It was clear to me that Mrs. Lucas had some deep-seated feelings about color, hair, and attractiveness that I was not going to be able to turn around in a single session. Having stated that I thought I could relate to her, I felt it was important that I not be drawn into trying to defend or explain any similarities or differences I shared with Mrs. Lucas in appearance or financial status. I simply noted to myself that these were sensitive issues of which I would have to be aware.

I continued the discussion by saying, "It sounds like you have had at least one experience with a Black woman who accepted you for who you are. I'd like you to continue to share your concerns with me and decide by the end of our session if you feel that I'm able to understand and appropriately relate to the issues you raise. If you feel uncomfortable with me, I'll be happy to try to find someone else to work with you."

I continued by asking Mrs. Lucas if she could tell me more about her husband, her cousin Nicole, and what it was like growing up for her. In a somewhat belligerent tone she explained that she was the eldest of five children who were raised in poverty. Her mother had married Mrs. Lucas's father after she told him that she was three months pregnant.

Mrs. Lucas's father was of Caribbean descent and determined to be successful. He met Mrs. Lucas's mother while visiting from Boston. Mrs. Lucas said that her mother was fair skinned, had long hair, was slender, and was always able to manipulate men. The marriage between her parents lasted less than two years. Mrs. Lucas believed that her father left when he realized that his wife shared none of his dreams to work hard, buy a home, and have a stable and respectable home life. Mrs. Lucas believed that her father couldn't tolerate the fact that his wife seemed disinterested in family life and wanted to continue an active social life of card playing, partying, and drinking. He left town and reestablished himself in the Northeast.

I asked Mrs. Lucas if she maintained any ties with her father or her father's family after he left. She replied that for many years her father was busy trying to make money and support the new family that he had after he left her mother. Mrs. Lucas didn't identify with any of her Caribbean heritage, and she never established any close ties with her father's relatives up north or on the islands.

Mrs. Lucas stated that her father had died one year ago and had spent the last few years of his life trying to reconcile with her. She said that she couldn't forgive him for being a wonderful father to his four children in his second marriage when he hadn't been available to her financially and emotionally when she needed him as she grew up. Mrs. Lucas said that she knew that her mother played a big role in alienating her father and making it hard for him to stay connected with her, but she still blamed her father for his unavailability.

As angry as Mrs. Lucas was with her father, she was even more enraged by her mother. Mrs. Lucas said that her mother was promiscuous; she had three additional children with different fathers and always had boyfriends in the home. It was clear that Mrs. Lucas saw her mother as "fitting all those terrible stereotypes about poor Black women, who just sit around and don't work, have babies and survive on welfare." She described her mother as needy, dependent, shallow, and unable to meet her children's basic needs.

It was Mrs. Lucas's maternal aunt, who lived close by, who was responsible for making sure that Mrs. Lucas and her siblings were clothed, cleaned, fed, and baby-sat. Mrs. Lucas said that although this aunt was not very affectionate, she provided the family with the only warmth and stability they knew in their home.

As I listened to Mrs. Lucas describe her family life, it was clear to me that she was angry with her parents for not being responsive to her needs. She seemed to understand very clearly what parents should do and recognized that her parents were far from ideal. Overall, Mrs. Lucas seemed intelligent and perceptive about many of her family dynamics. Although she seemed able to analyze her family very accurately, I was unsure of how much self-insight she had about how her experiences had shaped how she related to others. I also was curious about the nature of her interpersonal relationships in general and especially with her husband, children, siblings, and close friends.

I asked Mrs. Lucas what her relationship with her mother was like at this time. She told me that she tried to have as little to do with her mother as possible. Mrs. Lucas said that her mother and siblings only called her when they needed something from her, usually financial assistance. She said that sometimes she returned to her hometown but stayed with her cousin Nicole, who still lived in the area. She explained that Nicole and Nicole's parents had always treated her like a family member and continued to welcome her into their homes. Mrs. Lucas said that she saw Nicole about three times a year and that every now and then they talked on the phone. Mrs. Lucas visited her aunt but typically didn't even go to her mother's house despite her aunt's urging her to do so.

I asked her if she was close to any of her brothers and sisters. Mrs. Lucas said that she felt she had a decent relationship with one of her sisters, who was trying to attend a community college and make something of herself, unlike her other siblings, who were as "bad as our mother." Mrs. Lucas emphasized that she wanted her children to have as little as possible to do with her mother and her family except for her aunt and the one sister. When I asked her why she felt this way, she said, "I don't trust them to know how to take care of children. None of them seem able to be decent parents or show any responsibility."

I was clearly hearing a theme that Mrs. Lucas felt very protective toward her daughter and sons and alienated from her family. I asked her if we could spend some time talking about her husband.

She said, "What's there to know? We've been married for fifteen years, we have a daughter and two sons, he has a stable job, and we own our home." I stated that I wanted to know if she was happy in her marriage. She had mentioned that she and her husband got together because he liked to figure out and help other people, so how did their relationship work now?

Again, Mrs. Lucas seemed somewhat uncomfortable. She said, "We're still pretty different. He likes to go out with his friends from work and with people in the neighborhood, and I don't feel like being bothered." I asked if she and her husband always differed in this way or if there had been a change.

Mrs. Lucas said that in the early years of the marriage, her husband had been in a sales job that required frequent moves, and they met new people every few years. She liked moving like this because then she didn't have to deal with any social group for very long. Once Mr. Lucas left this job and settled locally, he wanted to develop stable friendships.

Mrs. Lucas explained that she was not comfortable interacting with the wives and girlfriends of her husband's friends. She felt that some of them were too flirtatious and friendly with her husband. I asked her if her husband flirted with these other women. She explained that he didn't do anything wrong. It just seemed that his basic personality was warm and open, and just as she felt comfortable with him, other women did as well.

I still couldn't get a handle on how Mrs. Lucas felt about her husband, so I tried a different tack. "I know that most marriages go through ups and downs. What were some of the highs and lows in your marriage?" Mrs. Lucas said she was happiest when they first got married and just spent time alone together. She explained that they were happy when each of their children were born, but Mrs. Lucas suffered from postpartum depression for almost a year after her daughter's birth.

I asked Mrs. Lucas what was happening in her relationship with her husband now. She said, "Well, he complains that I don't do anything. He thinks he's doing all the cooking and cleaning and taking care of the children." She said that her husband was upset that he had to help out around the house so much because he felt that these were jobs for which she should be responsible. He felt that his friends would tease him if they knew how much he did and how little she did. (Mr. Lucas showed a phenomenon that I often see. Many Black men do show flexible gender roles and may help out with "women's work," but they're not happy about it and don't want their peers to know.)

I asked Mrs. Lucas if her husband was doing more of this work than she was. After a short silence she acknowledged that he was doing more now. She quickly added that there were times in the past when "I did most of the work at home, but he never sees it that way." I asked her if work at home had caused arguments in the past, and she said that they didn't argue. They simply disagreed.

I asked what their communication was like. Mrs. Lucas gave a short laugh without smiling and said, "We don't have any." I asked her what their sexual relationship was like, and she said, very quickly, "It's fine. Why are you asking?" I explained to Mrs. Lucas that I had asked this question because sometimes when couples were having trouble talking to one another, it could be reflected in their sex life. She said, "OK, so it's not good. I don't know how you can expect me to have a good sex life given all my experiences. I didn't get affection from my parents. My mother has sex with anybody. People thought that I would wind up being just like my mother, but I have gone out of my way to let people know that I'm nothing like her. So yes, we have some problems with sex." I wondered to myself if Mrs. Lucas's issues with sex were tied in with her rejection of her mother and cultural stereotypes of Black women and promiscuity.

I gently raised the issue of whether the stress in her relationship with her husband was something she might want to address in therapy. She paused and said, "Maybe. I don't know anymore which bullet to dodge. It feels like I have problems coming at me from all directions." I told Mrs. Lucas that before we ended we would talk about some possible goals for our work together and some priorities.

At this point I thought that it was important for me to return to the issue of her daughter. "Mrs. Lucas, you've mentioned on a couple of occasions that you're concerned about the well-being of your children and being available to spend more time in particular with your daughter Rosa. Can you tell me if you have any specific concerns about her right now?"

To my surprise, Mrs. Lucas sat back on the couch and started crying softly. It appeared that she had held herself tightly in check the whole session until we got to this issue. All her rigidity and defensiveness decreased, and Mrs. Lucas said, "I'm afraid for her."

I asked, "Mrs. Lucas what are you afraid of with Rosa?"

"I'm afraid that I'll be a lousy mother like my mother was. I'm afraid that I won't keep her safe the way no one protected me. I don't know how to be affectionate to her, and I don't want her to turn to sex and boys to make herself feel good."

I asked Mrs. Lucas what was happening now that made her so worried about Rosa. She said that she could see how much Rosa was maturing physically. She was getting more attention from males at school and when they were out shopping, and she noticed that boys were starting to call the house. She said that Rosa and the two boys had always been easy children who seemed to have inherited their father's disposition. At this point I saw Mrs. Lucas smile for the first time. She reported that Rosa, like her younger brothers, had always been an excellent student, and Mrs. Lucas didn't want any of the children to become distracted from their goals to attend college and have rewarding careers. I asked her if she was concerned about all of her children. She clarified that she thought that her sons were doing OK but she was very worried about her daughter. I then focused our attention on Rosa.

Although Rosa wasn't overweight, Mrs. Lucas was afraid that because her daughter looked like her and had a similar build, Rosa would also start doubting her attractiveness because she definitely had more African than European features. She feared that Rosa would repeat her own history and suffer from low self-esteem or start hanging out with the wrong crowd. I asked her what Rosa's self-esteem was like now. Again I saw a smile as she said, "Right now, she's full of herself!" I told Mrs. Lucas that it seemed that she and her husband must have done many of the right things if they had a twelve-year-old daughter who got good grades, had high self-esteem, and felt good about her sense of identity as a Black female.

Mrs. Lucas seemed to visibly relax with that statement. I said I thought we could talk about how she could continue to give Rosa the type of strong parenting that could help Rosa continue to develop in positive ways. With respect to Mrs. Lucas's work schedule, I wondered if the four-day schedule was really helping her spend more time with her husband and children. Mrs. Lucas said her work schedule wasn't working, and she was going to change it.

As we talked, she decided to request working only a thirty-hour workweek. She realized that she and her husband could afford for her to work less, and with this change she would be more available to her family and not feel as exhausted as she was currently.

At this point I asked Mrs. Lucas if she had any support system besides her aunt and her cousin Nicole. She stated that she was trying to develop a few friendships at work with some White females and Black females but that the relationships were moving slowly. Mrs. Lucas acknowledged that it was hard for her to trust other people, and her work schedule left her little time to socialize. She didn't have much time for her husband and children. I asked her if she had a church home, and she responded that she took her children to a neighborhood church, but she didn't feel that the service did anything for her.

Given the high level of guardedness Mrs. Lucas showed in this first session, it was clear to me that I needed to focus more on trying to build a positive working relationship than on getting a lot of background history. My assessment attempts had to be as subtle and unobtrusive as possible because she was fairly suspicious and paranoid. I tried to develop our relationship by following up on the topics about which she seemed to be most concerned and by helping her clarify her presenting concerns and issues. I felt it was important that we accomplish something concrete in that first session to help Mrs. Lucas believe therapy would be worthwhile; otherwise, I was afraid she would not return. That's why I focused on discussing her work schedule to see if we could provide her with some immediate relief of her stress.

I let Mrs. Lucas know that we needed to figure out our next steps before our session ended. I first asked her if she felt that I had understood her and if she would feel comfortable continuing to work with me. She calmly said that I had "done OK, I guess, the best you could," and said that she was comfortable in continuing our work.

I asked her what she saw as the issues she wanted to work on. She surprised me by saying, "I know I came in here because of work problems, but I have a lot of issues that I haven't talked to other people about. I want to work on some of this stuff, but I'm going to have to get to know you first and see if I can trust you enough to talk to you about these issues. In the meantime, I guess I need to work on what's happening at home. I wish that my husband and I could talk more and have fun. My number one issue is that I want to be a better mother. I want to make sure my daughter and sons turn out OK, and I don't know how to do it given my mother as a role model."

I told Mrs. Lucas I thought that her goals seemed reasonable and that I could be of help to her. I mentioned that at some point down the road, if it was agreeable to her, we could have her husband and children join us for some sessions. She indicated that she found this acceptable.

I added that I wasn't sure yet how long we might need to work together to accomplish her goals but that as our work proceeded I would try to give her some estimates. We reviewed her commitment to schedule appointments with her family doctor. At this point I told her that I also thought she should see a psychiatrist for a possible prescription for an antidepressant.

Mrs. Lucas asked me if I thought she was crazy and whether that was the reason I had referred her to the psychiatrist. I told her, "No, I don't think you're crazy. I do think you're depressed and over-whelmed by the stress you have in your life now and maybe also by some of the stress that you endured growing up." Mrs. Lucas said that she would think about going to see the psychiatrist but wouldn't call for an appointment at that time.

I thanked her for her honesty in sharing concerns and asking me questions, and I asked her to continue. I reminded her to please let me know if I said something with which she disagreed or was uncomfortable. I checked to see if she had any questions about the office procedures or financial arrangements that she had discussed with my receptionist. We agreed on a date and time for the next session, and I escorted her to the waiting room. I often shake hands with a client after the first session, but Mrs. Lucas's reserve made me decide not to do this, as I sensed that she would find the gesture intrusive.

IMPRESSIONS AND FOLLOW-UP

I used this case example for several reasons. First, it was easy to recount because it is based on elements from real cases. Second, this client was actually more guarded, defensive, and hostile than most clients whom I meet in a first session. I've tried to give you some ideas of how to handle a more challenging case with the expectation that most clients would be easier.

This client did become a long-term therapy client. Although work issues precipitated her entrance to therapy, the bulk of our sub-sequent work dealt with relationship issues and self-esteem. This was a client who posed challenges in establishing rapport and who stirred up some immediate transference and countertransference issues. Mrs. Lucas didn't seem responsive to my attempts to make her feel comfortable, and she let me know right away that she had some issues with me or, more accurately, with people in her past who looked like me or who I reminded her of.

I felt somewhat defensive initially but knew that all I could do was to keep the focus on Mrs. Lucas's reactions and experiences. I also knew that she had established a positive relationship with her cousin Nicole and her aunt, so I was hopeful that Mrs. Lucas had enough positive transference from these women to engage in therapy with a Black woman.

I realized that Mrs. Lucas's major issues were tied to feelings of loss, rejection, and abandonment related to her parents. It seemed clear that she very much needed me to be supportive and consistent but that she expected me to disappoint her, as did so many other significant people in her life. It seemed that she had learned to be withdrawn, reserved, and pulled back in her interpersonal interactions, and she was wary of investing in or showing emotions to others.

I sensed that many of Mrs. Lucas's issues of racial identity and attractiveness were related to her poor relationship with her mother. She saw her mother as being very attractive but also very manipulative, seductive, and promiscuous. It appeared that Mrs. Lucas made a determined effort to minimize her attractiveness in an attempt to avoid looking like and then acting like her mother. As we talked about how she associated looking nice with her negative feelings toward her mother, Mrs. Lucas was able to see that she could be attractive without adopting her mother's behaviors.

We gradually were able to talk more easily about race, issues of attractiveness, and her feelings of trust with Black women. We were able to talk about the fact that her aunt, her cousin Nicole and Nicole's mother, and some of the Black women she had known had been supportive of her. We worked to point out that she did have positive experiences with Black women, that she was attractive, and that she no longer needed to buy into ideas of White superiority. We talked about the fact that Whites were just as likely as Blacks to accept her or reject her as a friend or colleague.

I helped her consolidate a sense of herself as smart and as an excellent worker and that she didn't need to constantly push herself to prove she was just as good as Whites. Instead she needed to focus on self-care and doing her job.

Over time, Mrs. Lucas started to take more of an interest in her appearance by wearing brighter clothing, and she let loose sometimes and wore earrings and lipstick. For her, these changes were a sign of self-acceptance of her attractiveness as a Black woman and reflected a desire to look her best. Mrs. Lucas had asked me if I was married and if I had children. I answered yes to both of her questions. I hoped that as a Black female professional, I could also serve as a role model to Mrs. Lucas, showing her that although combining careers, mothering, and partnering was challenging, it was possible. I also tried at a subtle level to demonstrate that I could work in a profession in which I interacted with Whites but also felt positively about my identity as a Black female.

I found myself adopting a unique way of responding to Mrs. Lucas. I felt that I needed to be somewhat more restrained than is normal for me in order not to present such a glaring contrast to her affective level. What was interesting is that Mrs. Lucas at one level seemed to very much want warmth and support from other people, but in her interactions she used her body language and speech to push people away and keep them at a distance.

In fact, on one occasion she talked about how nice, sweet, and kind her psychiatrist was to her. I asked her how often she saw this psychiatrist and what her behavior was like with the psychiatrist. She saw where I was heading and smiled. Mrs. Lucas understood that I was reminding her of how withdrawn and emotionally restrained she usually was with me. She acknowledged that she saw her psychiatrist only every three months and made a point to be cheerful and upbeat to convince the psychiatrist that she was getting better, as she hoped to be allowed to stop taking her antidepressant medication.

I pointed out to Mrs. Lucas that she was able to open up and be warm to people on a short-term basis, especially if they were White. But when I as a Black woman attempted to be supportive to her, or if she felt at all attached or dependent toward me, she reacted by canceling sessions or saying that she wanted to come less frequently. Mrs. Lucas was able to hear and use this interpretation. She admitted that she still struggled with issues of trust and vulnerability with Black women. She pointed out and I agreed with her that her ability to stay in therapy with me was a sign of growth for her.

It may not surprise some readers to hear that about four months into therapy Mrs. Lucas shared with me that she had been sexually assaulted by one of her mother's boyfriends at about the same age that her daughter was currently.

Much of her anger toward her mother stemmed from her mother's failing to protect her from advances and harm from this man and then not really comforting and supporting her after she told her mother what had happened. As we processed these long-term feelings of anger, hurt, and low self-worth, Mrs. Lucas accepted my recommendation that she participate in an Adults Molested as Children group, which she found to be very helpful.

Mrs. Lucas's problems with self-care and trust manifested in her resistance to therapy and to taking her antidepressant and heart medications. When the work was difficult, she talked about stopping therapy, but I encouraged, supported, and pushed her to continue. Gradually she expanded her circle of friends to include two Black women who were very supportive.

We also had family and couple sessions in which I was able to gain a clearer sense of her relationships with her children and husband. In talking to her husband in particular I learned more about how ashamed Mrs. Lucas felt about growing up poor and coming from such a dysfunctional family.

Overall, therapy was successful in helping Mrs. Lucas resolve some of her childhood issues that contributed to her difficulties in her interpersonal relationships. She accomplished a great deal of healing related to her early experiences with abuse, and she developed some ability to nurture herself and gain support from friends and family to compensate for what she never received from her mother and would not accept from her father.

CONCLUSIONS

The first session of therapy is critical for all clients. But African American clients are at high risk for not resolving problems, not accepting referrals, and not returning for additional sessions when they have therapists who are unable to provide culturally sensitive and appropriate interventions. As I have noted throughout this book, there are several key components to successful first sessions with African American clients:

- Understanding of African American culture and history in all its diversity

- Recognition of the specific demographic, cultural, and experiential forces that have shaped the worldview and perspectives of the individual client

- Ability to relate presenting problems to possible racial and cultural mediators

- Skill and confidence in establishing a healthy rapport and positive working alliance

- Ability to help the client articulate presenting problems and goals

- Strategies to promote culturally sensitive assessment, evaluation, and diagnoses

- Facility with culturally competent interviewing skills

- Ability to recognize and manage countertransference issues and knowledge of when to refer clients

- Sensitivity in handling crisis situations

- Expertise in integrating self-awareness with culturally competent practice

As we demonstrate the aforementioned skills in our work with African American clients, we must be mindful of time and financial restraints and the need to promote and deliver on the expectancy that we can provide concrete assistance for clients' problems. As our society becomes more multicultural, we must be prepared to provide African Americans and all clients with the highest possible levels of respect and competence.

If the profession of therapy is to prosper in the twenty-first century, culturally competent practice is no longer an option—it's a necessity. I hope this book helps you meet the challenge.

Notes

Foreword

1. Kleinke, 1994, p. 176.
2. Heaton, 1998, p. 69.

Introduction

1. Kleinke, 1994, p. 176.
2. Sue, Zane, & Young, 1994, p. 787.

Chapter One

1. Aponte & Crouch, 1995.
2. Baker & Bell, 1999.
3. See note 1, p. 4.
4. Herskovitz, 1970.
5. King, 1976; Sudarkasa, 1997.
6. Hill, 1972.
7. Jones, 1997, pp. 483–493.
8. See note 7, pp. 488–490; Boyd-Franklin, 1989.
9. Majors & Billson, 1992.
10. Cheung & Snowden, 1990; Snowden & Cheung, 1990; Sue, Zane, & Young, 1994.

11. Magoon, 1987/1988; Neighbors, 1985.

12. Sue, Zane, & Young, 1994.

13. Beutler, Machado, & Neufeldt, 1994.

14. Wohlford, 1991.

Chapter Two

1. Williams & Fenton, 1994.

2. Neighbors, 1991.

3. Parham & McDavis, 1993.

4. Aponte & Crouch, 1995.

5. See note 3, pp. 93–94.

6. O. Espin (personal communication, March 23, 1996).

7. Sanchez-Hucles, 1997.

8. Rivers, 1995.

9. Rouse, 1998.

10. Fabrega, Mezzich, & Ulrich, 1988; Williams & Fenton, 1994.

11. Anderson, 1990.

12. See note 1, p. 257.

13. Baker & Bell, 1999.

14. Franklin, July/August 1993.

15. Pike & Walsh, 1996.

16. Neal & Turner, 1991.

17. See note 3, p. 91.

18. Commission on Violence and Youth, 1993, p. 45.

19. Ropp, Visintainer, Uman, & Treloar, 1992.

20. Aponte & Morrow, 1995.

21. Hampton & Yung, 1996.

22. Hammond & Yung, 1994.

23. Scott, Lefley, & Hicks, 1993.

24. Hampton, Gelles, & Harrop, 1989.

25. See note 21, p. 107.

26. See note 21, p. 111.

27. Thurman, Swaim, & Plested, 1995.

28. Rouse, 1995, p. 63.

29. Groves & Amuleru-Marshall, 1994.

30. See note 26, p. 218.

31. Obot, 1996.

32. Grier & Cobbs, 1968.

Chapter Six

1. Hacker, 1992.

2. McAdoo & McAdoo, 1994

3. Mauer, 1994

4. See note 1.

5. See note 3.

Chapter Seven

1. Pedersen, 1997.

2. See note 1; Tyler, Biome, & Williams, 1991; Ridley, 1995.

3. Ridley, 1995.

4. Schofield, 1964.

5. Holzman, 1995.

Chapter Eight

1. McIntosh, 1988.

2. Bennett & Deane, 1994.

3. Carter & Helms, 1987; Parham & Helms, 1981; Cross, 1991.

4. Cross, 1991.

5. See note 4.

6. Boyd-Franklin, 1989.

References

Anderson, E. (1990). *Streetwise: Race, class and change in an urban community.* Chicago: University of Chicago Press.

Aponte, J. F., & Crouch, R. T. (1995). The changing ethnic profile of the United States. In J. F. Aponte, R. Y. Rivers, & J. Wohl (Eds.), *Psychological interventions and cultural diversity* (pp. 1–18). Needham Heights, MA: Allyn & Bacon.

Aponte, J. F., & Morrow, C. A. (1995). Community approaches with ethnic groups. In J. F. Aponte, R. Y. Rivers, & J. Wohl (Eds.), *Psychological interventions and cultural diversity* (pp. 128–144). Needham Heights, MA: Allyn & Bacon.

Baker, F. M., & Bell, C. C. (1999). Issues in the psychiatric treatment of African Americans. *Psychiatric Services, 50,* 362–368.

Bennett, M. J., & Deane, B. R. (1994). A model for personal change: Developing intercultural sensitivity. In E. Y. Cross, J. H. Katz, F. A. Miller, & E. W. Seashore (Eds.), *The promise of diversity* (pp. 286–293). Burr Ridge, IL: Irwin.

Beutler, L., Machado, P., & Neufeldt, S. (1994). Therapist variables. In A. Bergin & S. L. Garfield (Eds.), *Handbook of psychotherapy and behavior change* (4th ed., pp. 229–269). New York: Wiley.

Boyd-Franklin, N. J. (1989). *Black families in therapy: A multisystems approach.* New York: Guilford Press.

Carter, R., & Helms, J. E. (1987). The relationship between Black value orientations to racial identities. *Measurement and evaluation in counseling and development, 19,* 185–195.

Cheung, F. K., & Snowden, L. R. (1990). Community mental health and ethnic minority populations. *Community Mental Health Journal, 26,* 277–291.

Commission on Violence and Youth. (1993). *Violence and youth: Psychology's response*. Washington, DC: American Psychological Association.

Cross, W. E. (1991). *Shades of Black: Diversity in African American identity*. Philadelphia: Temple University Press.

Fabrega, H., Mezzich, J., & Ulrich, R. F. (1988). Black-White differences in psychopathology in an urban psychiatric population. *Comprehensive Psychiatry, 29*, 285–297.

Franklin, A. J. (1993, July/August). The invisibility syndrome. *Family Therapy Networker*, 33–39.

Grier, W., & Cobbs, P. (1968). *Black rage*. New York: Basic Books.

Groves, G., & Amuleru-Marshall, O. (1994). Chemical use and dependency among African Americans. In I. L. Livingston (Ed.), *Handbook of Black American health: The mosaic of conditions, issues, policies and prospects* (pp. 205–215). Westport, CT: Greenwood Press.

Hacker, A. (1992). *Two nations, Black and White, separate, hostile and unequal*. New York: Scribner.

Hammond, W. R., & Yung, B. R. (1994). African Americans. In D. Eron, J. H. Gentry, & P. Schlegel (Eds.), *A reason to hope: A psychosocial perspective on violence and youth* (pp. 105–118). Washington, DC: American Psychological Association.

Hampton, R. L., Gelles, R. J., & Harrop, J. W. (1989). Is violence in Black families increasing? A comparison of 1975 and 1985 national survey rates. *Journal of Marriage and Family, 51*, 969–980.

Hampton, R. L., & Yung, B. R. (1996). Violence in communities of color: Where we were, where we are, and where we need to be. In R. L. Hampton, P. Jenkins, & T. P. Gullotta (Eds.), *Preventing violence in America* (pp. 53–86). Thousand Oaks, CA: Sage.

Heaton, J. A. (1998) Building basic therapeutic skills (p. 69). San Francisco: Jossey-Bass.

Herskovitz, M. J. (1970). *The myth of the negro past*. Boston: Beacon Press.

Hill, R. (1972). *The strengths of Black families*. New York: Emerson Hall.

Holzman, C. (1995). Rethinking the role of guilt and shame in White women's antiracism work. In J. Adelman & G. Enguidanos (Eds.), *Racism in the lives of women: Testimony, theory and guides to practice* (pp. 325–332). New York: Harrington Park Press.

Jones, J. M. (1997). *Prejudice and racism* (2nd ed., pp. 483–493). New York: McGraw-Hill.

King, J. R. (1976). African survivals in the Black American family: Key factors in stability. *Journal of Afro-American Studies, 4*, 153–167.

Kleinke, C. L. (1994). *Common principles of psychotherapy*. Pacific Grove, CA: Brooks/Cole.

Magoon, T. M. (1987/1988). *College and university counseling center data bank*. College Park: University of Maryland Counseling Center.

Majors, R., & Billson, J. (1992). *Cool pose: The dilemmas of Black manhood in America*. San Francisco: New Lexington Press.

Mauer, M. (1994). A generation behind bars: Black males and the criminal justice system. In R. G. Majors & J. V. Gordon (Eds) *The American black male: His present status and his future* (pp. 81–94). Chicago: Nelson-Hall.

McAdoo, J. L., & McAdoo, J. B. (1994). The African American father's role within the family. In R. G. Majors & J. V. Gordon (Eds.), *The American black male: His present status and his future* (pp. 285–297). Chicago: Nelson-Hall.

McIntosh, P. (1988). *Understanding correspondence between White privilege and men's privilege through women's study work* (Working Paper No. 189). Wellesley, MA: Wellesley College, Center for Research on Women.

Neal, A. M., & Turner, S. M. Anxiety disorders research with African Americans: Current status. *Psychological Bulletin, 109*, 400–410.

Neighbors, H. W. (1985). Seeking professional help for personal problems: Black Americans' use of health and mental health services. *Community Mental Health Journal, 21*, 156–166.

Neighbors, H. W. (1991). Mental health. In J. S. Jackson (Ed.), *Life in Black America* (pp. 221–237). Thousand Oaks, CA: Sage.

Obot, I. S. (1996). Problem drinking, chronic disease, and recent life events. In H. W. Neighbors & J. S. Jackson (Eds.), *Mental health in Black America* (pp. 45–61). Thousand Oaks, CA: Sage.

Parham, T. A., & Helms, J. E. (1981). Influence of a Black student's racial identity attitudes on preference for counselor race. *Journal of Counseling Psychology, 28*, 250–257.

Parham, T. A., & McDavis, R. C. (1993). Black men, an endangered species: Who's really pulling the trigger? In D. R. Atkinson, G. Morten, & D. W. Sue (Eds.), *Counseling American minorities: A cross-cultural perspective* (4th ed., pp. 89–99). Madison, WI: Brown and Benchmark.

Pedersen, P. B. (1997). *Culture centered counseling interventions: Striving for accuracy*. Thousand Oaks, CA: Sage.

Pike, K. M., & Walsh, T. (1996). Ethnicity and eating disorders: Implications for incidence and treatment. *Psychopharmacology Bulletin, 32*, 265–274.

Ridley, C. R. (1995). *Overcoming unintentional racism in counseling and therapy: A practitioner's guide to intentional intervention*. Thousand Oaks, CA: Sage.

Rivers, R. Y. (1995). Clinical issues and interventions with ethnic minority women. In J. F. Aponte, R. Y. Rivers, & J. Wohl (Eds.), *Psychological interventions and cultural diversity* (pp. 181–198). Needham Heights, MA: Allyn & Bacon.

Ropp, L., Visintainer, P., Uman, J., & Treloar, D. (1992). Death in the city: An American childhood tragedy. *Journal of the American Medical Association, 267,* 2905–2910.

Rouse, B. A. (1995). *Substance abuse and mental health statistics sourcebook.* Rockville, MD: Department of Health and Human Services.

Rouse, B. A. (1998). *Substance abuse and mental health statistics sourcebook.* Rockville, MD: Department of Health and Human Services.

Sanchez-Hucles, J. V. (1997). Jeopardy not bonus status for African American women in the workforce. *Journal of Community Psychology, 25,* 565–580.

Schofield, W. (1964). *Psychotherapy: The purchase of friendship.* Englewood Cliffs, NJ: Prentice Hall.

Scott, C., Lefley, H., & Hicks, D. (1993). Potential risk factors for rape in three ethnic minority groups. *Community Mental Health Journal, 29,* 133–141.

Snowden, L. R., & Cheung, F. K. (1990). Use of inpatient mental health services by members of ethnic minority groups. *American Psychologist, 45,* 347–355.

Sudarkasa, N. (1997). African Americans and family values. In H. P. McAdoo (Ed.), *Black families* (3rd ed., pp. 9–40). Thousand Oaks, CA: Sage.

Sue, S., Zane, N., & Young, K. (1994). Research on psychotherapy with culturally diverse populations. In A. Bergin & S. L. Garfield (Eds.), *Handbook of psychotherapy and behavior change* (4th ed., pp. 783–817). New York: Wiley.

Thurman, P. T., Swaim, R., & Plested, B. (1995). Intervention and treatment of ethnic minority substance abusers. In J. F. Aponte, R. Y. Rivers, & J. Wohl (Eds.), *Psychological interventions and cultural diversity* (pp. 215–223). Needham Heights, MA: Allyn & Bacon.

Tyler, F. B., Brome, D. R., & Williams, J. E. (1991). *Ethnic validity, ecology and psychotherapy: A psychosocial competence model.* New York: Plenum Press.

Williams, D. R., & Fenton, B. (1994). The mental health of African Americans: Findings, questions and directions. In I. L. Livingston (Ed.), *Handbook of Black American health: The mosaic of conditions, issues, policies and prospects* (pp. 253–268). Westport, CT: Greenwood Press.

Wohlford, P. (1991). Trends in NIMH support for clinical training for ethnic minorities. In H. F. Myers, P. Wohlford, L. P. Guzman, & E. R. Echemendia (Eds.), *Ethnic minority perspectives on clinical training and services in psychology* (pp. 13–22). Washington, DC: American Psychological Association.

The Author

Janis Sanchez-Hucles is a professor of psychology at Old Dominion University, a faculty member for the Virginia Consortium for Clinical Psychology, and a community faculty member at Eastern Virginia Medical School in Norfolk, Virginia. She works part-time as a clinical psychologist in private practice and has worked at the Old Dominion University Counseling Center.

Sanchez-Hucles's clinical work, research, and training have focused on clinical training, women of color and families, diversity, feminism, and issues pertaining to urbanicity and violence. She has become a national speaker and trainer in the areas of diversity, clinical training, violence, ethnic minority issues, and the psychology of women.

At Old Dominion University, Sanchez-Hucles has been the director of undergraduate practicum training since 1979. She supervises interns as well as undergraduate and graduate students. Sanchez-Hucles served for seven years as the director of clinical training and as the graduate program director for the Virginia Consortium for Professional Psychology.

In addition to teaching basic courses in life-span development, personality, and psychopathology, Sanchez-Hucles has taught courses in the psychology of women and a doctoral course on psychodynamic therapy, and she has developed a course on African American psychology.

Sanchez-Hucles is a fellow of the American Psychological Association (APA) in the Psychology of Women division, and she has served on an APA Presidential Task Force on Violence and the Family and on the APA council of representatives representing the Psychology of Women division. She is past chair of the APA's Committee on Urban Initiatives.

Sanchez-Hucles was a founding member of the Virginia and North Carolina chapters of the Association of Black Psychologists. She has spent over twenty years as a researcher, teacher, clinician, supervisor, and trainer who is committed to inclusiveness and multicultural ideals.

Index

instant solutions, 170–172; negative, 168; positive, 167–168
Externalization of problems, 147–149
Externally mandated therapy. *See* Involuntary or pressured clients
Eye contact, note taking and, 94–95

F

Family: in African American culture, 8–10; extended, 9, 45, 75–76, 100; fictive kin and, 9, 100; involvement of, in client hospitalization, 179–181; strengths of African American, 9; as support system, 9, 45; tradition of caring for, 152, 155; tradition of sharing resources with, 9, 103; working with, of individual involved in criminal justice system, 191–195
Family of origin: assessment of relationships and dynamics in, 101, 102, 264–266; clients' self-comparison with, 104; history taking about, 99–102; history taking about, in case study, 264–266; mental illness in, 102; socioeconomic status of, 102–105; therapist's, 238–239
Family secrets: about mental illness in family, 102; sensitivity about, 101, 262
Family tree, 100
Fees, 250. *See also* Financial transactions
Female work, 10, 268
Feminist therapy, 72–73
Fictive kin: assessment of, 100; defined, 9
Fifty-minute session, explaining, 69
Financial transactions and issues, handling, with sensitivity, 62–64, 79–80, 249–250
First contact: in crisis situations, 174; office personnel and policies and, 62–64
First names, 82
First session: assessment in, 91–131; case study of, 259–276; components

of successful, listed, 276; crisis intervention in, 173–202; interviewing strategies for, 133–172; objective of, 135; rapport building in, 61–89; special challenges in, 164–172; things to convey in, 61; time and financial constraints and, 277. *See also* Assessment; Interviewing; Rapport and working alliance
Foster placement, 182
Franklin, A. J., 46
French Canadian Blacks, 5

G

Gangs, 41, 52
Gangsta rap slang, 12
Gays, lesbians, and bisexuals: church attitudes and, 33, 112, 113; HIV-positive status and, 187; issues of, 33–34, 110; talking about sexual orientation and, 254–256; violence and, 52. *See also* Sexual orientation
Gender issues: racial dynamics and, 206, 250–254; talking about, 250–254
Gender roles, 9–10, 39–40, 268; violence and, 53
Generalized anxiety, 45
Genuineness, 81–82
Geographic origin, 2, 4–5; assessment of, 97–98, 100; immigrant versus nonimmigrant status and, 5–6
Glaucoma, 111
Global assessment, 106, 129–131
Godparents, 100
God's Will, 15
Grandparents, clients raised by, 100–101
Grief issues: in case study, 143–144; and depression in the elderly, 43–44; prevalence of, as presenting problem, 27; support groups for, 161–162
Grier, 59
Grooming, 122
Guilt, White, 208

tion, 179; for safety from self-harm, 181

Y

Young African American males: "cool pose" behaviors of, 11–14, 48; involved in criminal justice system, 188, 189–190; police interactions with, 195–196; teachers' misunder-

standing of, 34–35. *See also* African American men; Masculine identity

YAVIS (young, attractive, verbal, intelligent, and successful) clients, therapist training for, 207

Young African Americans: alcohol and substance abuse in, 55; high-risk activities and suicidality of, 45; risky sex among, 188

DATE DUE